Positions and Interpretations

Trends in Linguistics
Studies and Monographs 245

Editor
Volker Gast

Founding Editor
Werner Winter

Editorial Board
Walter Bisang
Hans Henrich Hock
Heiko Narrog
Natalia Levshina
Matthias Schlesewsky
Niina Ning Zhang

Editor responsible for this volume
Volker Gast

De Gruyter Mouton

Positions and Interpretations

German Adverbial Adjectives at the Syntax-Semantics Interface

by

Martin Schäfer

De Gruyter Mouton

ISBN 978-3-11-048536-3
e-ISBN 978-3-11-027828-6
ISSN 1861-4302

Library of Congress Cataloging-in-Publication Data

A CIP catalog record for this book has been applied for at the Library of Congress.

Bibliographic information published by the Deutsche Nationalbibliothek

The Deutsche Nationalbibliothek lists this publication in the Deutsche Nationalbibliografie; detailed bibliographic data are available in the Internet at http://dnb.dnb.de.

© 2013 Walter de Gruyter GmbH, Berlin/Boston

Printing: Hubert & Co. GmbH & Co. KG, Göttingen
∞ Printed on acid-free paper

Printed in Germany

www.degruyter.com

For my parents, Kord-Hinrich and Sabine Schäfer

Contents

1   Introduction
1   Scope and aim   1
2   On adverbials and adjectives   3
2.1   Defining adverbials   4
2.1.1   Adverbial vs. subject   5
2.1.2   Adverbial vs. object   6
2.1.3   Adverbial vs. predicative   12
2.1.4   Adverbial vs. particle   14
2.1.5   Summary   16
2.2   Adverbial adjectives   17
2.2.1   Adjectives   17
2.2.2   Adverbs   19
2.2.3   Adjective or adverb?   21
2.3   Summary   23
3   Basic distinctions   24
3.1   Class properties of adverbial adjectives   25
3.2   Set-theoretic classifications of adjectives   25
3.3   Sentence and non-sentence adverbials   28
3.4   Other important semantic properties   29
3.4.1   Opacity   29
3.4.2   Veridicality   30
4   Structure of the book   30

2   The readings of sentence adverbials
1   Introduction   33
2   Subject-oriented adverbials   34
2.1   Adverbial adjectives as subject-oriented adverbials   36
3   Speaker-oriented adverbials   37
3.1   Speech-act adverbials   38
3.2   Epistemic adverbials   39
3.3   Evaluative adverbials   42
4   Domain adverbials   45
5   Semantic constraints on possible sentence adverbials   47
6   Conclusion   48

3   **The readings of verb-related adverbials**

1   Introduction 49
2   Manner adverbials 51
2.1   Introduction 51
2.2   Pure manner adverbials 56
2.3   Agent-oriented manner adverbials 58
2.4   Further orientations 62
3   Degree adverbials 63
3.1   Contexts and constraints for degree modification 65
3.2   Degree-manner ambiguities 66
4   Method-oriented adverbials 67
5   Verb-related adverbials and secondary predication 69
5.1   Resultatives 69
5.2   Ambiguities and blends 71
5.3   Depictives 75
6   Adverbial adjectives and the verb-adverbial combinatorics . . 78
6.1   Statives that allow manner modification 79
6.2   Mannerless statives 83
7   Verb-related adverbials and negation 85
7.1   Negation, adverbials, and the sentential base 86
7.2   Verb-related adverbials with scope over negation 89
8   Conclusion 94

4   **Event-related adverbials**

1   Mental-attitude adverbials 97
1.1   Mental-attitude adverbials and opacity 99
1.2   Mental-attitude adverbials vs. secondary predication 100
1.3   Transparent adverbials 101
1.4   Transparent adverbials, depictives and negation 103
2   Event-external adverbials 104
2.1   Inchoative readings of *schnell* and *langsam* 105
2.2   Holistic usages 106
2.2.1   Holistic usages and the internal structure of the event 106
2.2.2   Quantified direct objects 110
2.2.3   Modifiers of complex events 115
3   The *wobei*-paraphrase 117
3.1   *Wobei* vs. *während* 118
3.2   Event-related adverbials and the *wobei*-paraphrase 120

3.2.1 Mental-attitude adverbials and the *wobei*-paraphrase 120
3.2.2 The *wobei*-paraphrase and event-external modification 121
3.2.3 The *wobei*-paraphrase and associated readings 123
4   Summary 125

5   The syntactic position of manner adverbials
1   Introduction 127
2   Establishing syntactic positions 129
3   Adverbial modification and information structure 130
3.1   Focus projection 130
3.2   Adverbials and normal word order 134
4   Eckardt's account: Scrambled indefinite direct objects 135
4.1   Restricted combinations:
       Implicit resultatives and verbs of creation 136
4.2   The readings of indefinites and topicality 138
4.3   In-group readings 138
4.4   Problems for Eckardt's account 140
4.4.1 Frey vs Eckardt: The strong reading of indefinites 140
4.4.2 Manner adverbials and verbs of creation 141
5   Frey and Pittner: Object integration 141
5.1   Resultatives and integration 144
6   An alternative account:
       It's the adverbial's reading that is decisive 145
6.1   Adverbials out of the blue 145
6.1.1 Thetic sentences 148
6.2   Re-interpreting the controversial examples 152
6.2.1 Existentially interpreted w-phrases 152
6.2.2 W-phrases: Re-interpreting the data 154
6.3   Theme-rheme condition 157
7   More evidence and some subtleties 160
7.1   Clear minimal pairs 160
7.2   Lexical semantics and verb-adverbial combinatorics 163
7.3   Scrambling 164
8   Summary 165

6   **Adverbials in formal semantics: The classical analyses**

1   The operator approach 167
1.1   Thomason and Stalnaker 169
1.2   The operator approach and scope 170
1.3   The operator approach as a general analysis
         of modification structures 172
1.4   Criticism of the operator approach 173
1.4.1   The cognitive inappropriateness of the intensional solution . . 173
1.4.2   Entailments in the operator approach 175
2   The argument approach: McConnell-Ginet 176
2.1   Entailments in McConnell-Ginet's approach 178
3   The predicate approach: Event-based semantics 178
3.1   Event-based semantics and intuitive plausibility 181
3.2   The scope of the event-based approach 182
3.3   Neo-Davidsonian approaches 182
4   Possible combinations:
         Events and the predicate-modifier approach 183
4.1   Adding events 183
4.2   Event-based semantics as a refinement 184
5   Conclusion 185

7   **The semantic analysis of verb-related adverbials**

1   Manners in the ontology 188
1.1   The history of the idea 188
1.2   The cognitive status of manners 190
2   Manners in the representation 191
2.1   The technical aspects:
         Getting manners into the representation and specifying them . 192
3   Benefits of the analysis 194
3.1   Differentiating the readings and the link to syntax 194
3.2   The syntax-semantics interface 195
3.3   Event-related modification: The difficult cases 198
4   Summary 201

8   **Summary and outlook**

1   Results 203
2   Outlook 208

Notes   211

References   223

Index   232

Preface and acknowledgements

The starting point for this book was my dissertation, finished in the summer of 2005. Although both works tackle the same subject matter, the current book is a different work altogether, from its overall organization down to the individual chapters. The introduction has been rearranged and rewritten so that the discussion of the classical formal analyses of adverbials now forms the new chapter 6, while parts of the completely scrapped final chapters 6 and 7 of my dissertation now occur in changed form in the introduction and in chapters 2 through 5. The chapters on the different usages have been extended and heavily rewritten. In particular, this book includes a separate chapter for sentence adverbials and a much more detailed description of the adverbial usages below the sentence level, which are now divided into event- and verb-related adverbials, each presented in their own chapter. While my dissertation contains two chapters on the syntactic positioning of adverbials, I took the opportunity to rearrange and largely rewrite the material to form a single, more focussed chapter on the syntactic position of manner adverbials. And finally, the semantic analysis presented in chapter 7 is completely new.

Not suprisingly, this book has benefited from input by quite a number of people over quite a number of years.

The feedback and encouragement from Claudia Maienborn has been particularly valuable, as has our work on our joint HSK-entry *Adverbs and Adverbials*. Many thanks go to her.

Of almost equal importance was the possiblity to present an early form of my new analysis at the 2007 CSSP conference in Paris, and to publish that analysis later in the conference proceedings. During this process, I received extremely helpful comments from Christopher Piñón and Olivier Bonami.

A continous source of input and feedback for the development of the ideas presented in this book were the event semantics workshops that originated in Leipzig and later took place in Wuppertal, Tübingen, Berlin, Mannheim, Flensburg, and Kassel. These almost annual meetings allowed me to present various new aspects and developments of my work that in one way or another all made their way into this book, and I profited a lot from the feedback, discussion and support of its core group of participants, not only at the workshops themselves: Johannes Dölling, Markus Egg, Stefan Engelberg, Wilhelm Geuder, Holden Härtl, Daniel Hole, Claudia Maienborn, Irene Rapp, Britta Stolterfoht, and Tanja Zybatow.

We are now getting closer to the actual mechanics of writing, and here I would first like to thank the three native speakers here in Jena that served as my ad-hoc language advisory panel, Erica Haas, Allan Turner, and my assistant by special appointment, Chunky Liston.

In addition, my thanks go to the one anonymous reviewer and to Niina Zhang for their comments on the manuscript.

Finally, I would like to thank Volker Gast. Without his seemingly boundless enthusiasm, I would probably not have tried to publish this work. While already supporting this enterprise when he was not officially associated with my current publisher, he also later proofread and commented on the final version of the whole manuscript and suggested many improvements and clarifications.

This book was typeset with LaTeX on computers running Linux.

Abbreviations and notational conventions

Notational conventions:

1. Morphological marking for case, number and gender is only included in the glosses when this information is relevant for the discussion at hand.
2. Ungrammatical sentences are glossed but not translated.
3. Unless stated otherwise, references to other sections refer to sections of the current chapter.

Abbreviations:

NOM = nominative case
GEN = genitive case
ACC = accusative case
DAT = dative case
EFF = effective case

DEM = demonstrative pronoun
PASSP = passive participle

PL = plural
SG = singular
FEM = feminine
MASC = masculine

Chapter 1
Introduction

This chapter has three aims: In section 1, I set out the main ideas behind this book. In section 2, I explain in detail my usage of the term 'adverbial adjective', the term that describes the set of adverbials whose different usages stand at the center of this investigation. In section 3, I introduce the semantic notions that are needed in order to get the most out of the following chapters. Finally, I lay out the structure of the book in section 4.

1. Scope and aim

The topic of this work is German adverbial adjectives. The starting point for this investigation is the question of what these adverbials contribute to sentence meaning and the extent to which this contribution depends on their syntactic position within a sentence. Special attention is given to those adverbial usages that are traditionally understood as manner modification.

German adverbial adjectives are adjectives that are used as adverbials. Examples of typical occurrences of the adverbials of interest are given in (1), where the adverbials are printed in boldface.

(1)   a.   *Sie hat **laut** gesungen.*
                she has loud sung
                'She sang loudly.'
        b.   *Der Zug fuhr **schnell**.*
                 the train drove fast
                'The train drove fast.'
        c.   *Er löste die Aufgabe **intelligent**.*
                 he solved the problem intelligent
                'He solved the problem intelligently.'

The contribution of adverbial adjectives to the sentence meaning cannot be subsumed under a single cover term. Different usages must be distinguished. In (1), for example, the adjectives are used as manner adverbials. Their contribution to the sentence meaning consists in specifying the manner in which the events referred to by the verbal predicate are carried out. Examples of other usages include adjectives serving as mental attitude adverbials, cf. (2a), or adjectives serving as frame adverbials, cf. (2b).

(2)   a.   *Martha geht **widerwillig** zur Schule.*
            Martha goes reluctant   to   school
            'Martha goes to school reluctantly.'

      b.   *Wir wissen, dass **wirtschaftlich** die USA den Krieg gewonnen*
            we   know,   that economical   the USA the war   won
            haben.
            has
            'Economically, the United States have won the war.'

Roughly, mental attitude adverbials characterize the attitude of the agent of
a sentence towards carrying out the activity described by the rest of the sentence. In contrast, frame adverbials limit the domain in which the proposition
expressed by the rest of the sentence holds.

A single adjective may have different adverbial usages or different adverbial readings. An example is provided by the adjective *wirtschaftlich* 'eco-
nomical', which functions in (2b) as a frame adverbial, but may also serve as
a method-oriented adverbial, cf. (3).

(3)   *Dieses Problem ist nur **wirtschaftlich** zu lösen.*
       this   problem is only economically to solve
       'This problem can only be solved economically.'

Wirtschaftlich 'economically' in (3) specifies a set of methods, namely economic methods, which present the only way to solve the problem referred to
by the subject noun phrase.

These different adverbial usages of adjectives interact with the syntactic
position of the adjectives, cf. e.g. (4).

(4)   a.   *Wir wissen, dass **wirtschaftlich** die USA den Krieg gewonnen*
            we   know,   that economical   the USA the war   won
            haben.
            has
            'Economically, the United States won the war.'

      b.   **Wir hörten, dass **laut** die Leute   gesungen haben.*
            we   heard,   that loud die people sung   have

The position before the subject is possible for the frame adverbial *wirtschaftlich* 'economically', but not for the manner adverbial *laut* 'loudly'. In contrast, *laut* 'loudly' is unproblematic in positions adjacent to the finite verb,

whereas for *wirtschaftlich* 'economically' the reading as a method-oriented adverbial is preferred, cf. (5).

(5)   a.   *Wir wissen, dass die USA den Krieg* **wirtschaftlich** *gewonnen*
          we know, that the USA the war   economical   won
          haben.
          has
          'Economically, the United States won the war.'
      b.   *Wir hörten, dass die Leute* **laut** *gerufen   haben.*
          we heard, that the people loud screamed have
          'We heard that the people screamed loudly.'

That is, (5a) is preferably interpreted to mean that the USA used economic means in winning the war.

These characteristics of adverbial adjectives lead to the main questions to be dealt with in this work:
(a) Which different adverbial usages of adjectives need to be distinguished?
(b) Which usages are tied to which syntactic positions?
(c) How can different usages of adverbial adjectives be formally analyzed?
(d) How can the derivation of the formalizations be linked to the different syntactic positions?
In seeking answers to these questions, the focus will be on the usages of adjectives as non-sentential adverbials. There are two reasons for this decision: On the one hand, these usages, among them the large class of manner adverbials, represent the core usage for adverbial adjectives. On the other hand, they yield a bewildering number of further usages that is traditionally underdescribed in the literature. One important aim of this book is therefore to give an adequate descriptive overview of these usages, which will be divided into two larger classes: verb-related adverbials and event-related adverbials. As I will show, these two classes are bound to distinct syntactic positions. Based on the descriptive differentiation, I propose a new semantic analysis for the verb-related adverbials that allows a formal semantic distinction between the two groups. Finally, it is shown how the two distinct syntactic positions can be used in order to derive the correct formal representation for the two usages.

2.   On adverbials and adjectives

This section (a) explains my usage of the terms *adverbial, adjective* and *adverb* and (b) argues for the classification of the word forms of interest in this work as *adverbial adjectives* as opposed to the alternative classification as *adjectival adverbs*.

2.1.   Defining adverbials

The term *adverbial* is used in this work to refer to a specific syntactic function, on par with other syntactic functions such as subject, object, particle, predicative and verb, cf. the labeled examples in (6) and (7) for illustration.[1]

(6)   *[Im   Wald]*_{adverbial} *findet*_{verb} *Peter*_{subject} *auch*_{particle} *Pilze*_{object}.
      in.the wood   found   Peter   also   mushrooms
      'In the wood, Peter found even mushrooms.'

(7)   *Peter*_{subject} *ist*_{verb} *klug*_{predicative}.
      Peter   is   intelligent
      'Peter is intelligent.'

Informally, adverbials are those elements that serve to specify further the circumstances of the verbal or sentential referent. They are restricted to a set of semantically limited usages, prototypically specifying time, place, or manner, and they are typically optional, cf. (8).

(8)   a.   *Roland tanzte   den ganzen Abend.*
           Roland danced the whole evening
           'Roland danced the whole evening.'
      b.   *Frieda arbeit an einem Gymnasium.*
           Frieda works at a   grammar.school
           'Frieda works at a grammar school.'
      c.   *Roland und Frieda tanzten wunderschön.*
           Roland and Frieda danced beautiful
           'Roland and Frieda danced beautifully.'

As shown by (8), adverbials can be realized by a variety of phrasal types: a noun phrase in (8a), a prepositional phrase in (8b), and an adverbial phrase in (8c). Formally, German adverbials can be identified with the help of the four criteria given in (9). Optionality, though a prototypical feature of adverbials, cannot be used here, as some adverbials are obligatory.

(9)   (i)   Adverbials can serve as a *Satzglied* (see definition in (10)).
       (ii)   The form of the adverbial is not determined by the verb.
       (iii) There are no agreement relations between adverbial and verb.
       (iv)   Adverbials are restricted to a set of semantically limited us-
              ages.

The term 'satzglied' is used in German linguistics to refer to clause-level constituents which conform to the following three criteria (cf. e.g. Pittner 1999:47), corresponding to constituent tests at the sentence level:

(10)   (i)   A satzglied can be positioned relatively freely in a sentence.
              More specifically, a satzglied can appear as the sole constituent
              before the finite verb in verb-second sentences in German. In
              terms of traditional German topological theory, the adverbial
              can constitute the *Vorfeld* 'prefield' of verb-second sentences
              on its own.[2]
       (ii)   A satzglied can be elicited by questions.
       (iii) A satzglied can be pronominalized.

These properties of adverbials can be used to distinguish adverbials from other clause-level constituents.[3] Below I will demonstrate this, focusing on the adverbial usage of adjectives.

2.1.1.   Adverbial vs. subject

Subjects are prototypically realized by noun phrases, adverbials by prepositional phrases or adverbs. As adverbs and prepositional phrases cannot serve as subjects, this leaves noun phrases and clauses. In German, noun phrases serving as subjects have to agree with the verb in number. Adverbials do not enter into any agreement relationships, and consequently do not agree with any other clause-level constituents.

    In contrast to noun phrases, clauses cannot be marked for agreement. In order to identify clauses as subjects, the theta-criterion can be used. Clausal subjects always carry the specific thematic role assigned by the verb to its subject argument. Furthermore, just like noun phrase subjects, clausal subjects are obligatory in the active voice (cf. the next section for more on thematic roles). Adverbials, in contrast, are never assigned a subject-theta role, and their status does not change with a change from active to passive sentence. And finally, subjects can always be elicited by using the question words *wer/was* 'who/what', whereas adverbials can never be elicited by these questions words.

2.1.2.   Adverbial vs. object

The difference between adverbials and objects is most obvious when comparing objects with the prototypical case of an optional adverbial, but becomes harder to establish for those cases where the adverbial is non-optional. I therefore discuss the differentiation between adverbials and objects in two steps. First, I address the cases of free adverbials vs. objects. Secondly, I cover instances where the adverbial is subcategorized for by the verb.

Free adverbials vs. objects

The differentiation between free adverbials and objects revolves around the second point in the list of criteria in (9): the form of the adverbial is not determined by the verb. German transitive verbs, for example, select an object either in the accusative or in the dative case, cf. (11) and (12).

(11)   *Fritz hat **den**   **Kuchen** gegessen.*
         Fritz has the.ACC cake   eaten
         'Fritz ate the cake.'

(12)   *Das   Spiel gefällt **dem**   **Jungen.***
         the.NOM game pleases the.DAT boy.DAT
         'The game pleases the boy.'

In contrast, if a noun phrase serves as an adverbial, its case marking is independent of the verb. For example, noun phrases in the accusative case can serve as temporal adverbials, specifying a time span. Their case marking is not affected by the choice of verb, cf. (13) and (14).

(13)   *Fritz hat **den**   **ganzen**   **Tag** den   Kuchen   gegessen.*
         Fritz has the.ACC whole.ACC day the.ACC cake.ACC eaten
         'Fritz ate the cake for the whole day.'

(14)   *Das   Spiel   gefällt dem   Jungen **den***
         the.NOM game.NOM pleases the.DAT boy.DAT the.ACC
         ganzen   Winter.
         whole.ACC winter.ACC
         'The game pleases the boy for the whole winter.'

This criterion already suffices to distinguish optional adverbials from objects. However, the relationship between object and verb is not limited to form, but also concerns other factors. To explicate this, I follow Jacobs (1994) and assume a multi-dimensional conception of valency, which differentiates between four conditions for complements X of Y:

(15) (i)   X is obligatory for Y, i.e. it must be realized.
      (ii) X is specific for Y with respect to its form (e.g. X is case marked).
      (iii) X is specific for Y with respect to its content (e.g. X must be [+volitional] etc.).
      (iv) X is an argument, filling an open position in the meaning of Y.

Free adverbials do not fulfill any of the conditions in (15). Objects may optionally conform to (15i), but, as we have seen, must conform to (15ii). In addition, they also conform to (15iii) and (15iv). Thus, some verbs require their object to be sentient, e.g. *quälen* 'torment', cf. (16).

(16) a. *Peter quälte*   **den Mann.**
          Peter tormented the man.
          'Peter tormented the man.'
      b. **Peter quälte*   **den Stein.**
          Peter tormented the stone.

The argumenthood of objects can be established with the help of (a) thematic roles and (b) tests for argumenthood, which I will discuss in turn. Thematic roles are semantic relations that a noun phrase may carry based on the involvement of the entity denoted by the noun phrase in the action denoted by the verb. Classic thematic roles are agent, patient, beneficiary etc. A German verb can select for up to three thematic roles, one for the subject, one for the direct object and one for the indirect object.[4] This also accounts for the limitation of the numbers of objects in a clause to two. The relation between an object and its thematic role is always stable; that is, if the thematic role *patient* is assigned to the direct object of a verb, then this thematic role (a) remains unexpressed if the direct object is not realized and (b) cannot be realized by the indirect object. In German, the *geschehen/tun*-test is often used to establish argumenthood (cf. Engelberg 2000:88-89). Thus, the impossibility to paraphrase (17a) by (17b) is argued to establish the direct object *der Mann* 'the man' as an argument of the verb *töten* 'kill'.

(17) a. *Fritz tötet **den Mann**.*
          Fritz kills the man
          'Fritz kills the man.'
      b. **Fritz tötet, und das geschieht/tut er den Mann.*
          Fritz kills, and that happens/does he the man

In contrast, the very same test shows that the instrumental adverbial *mit dem Gewehr* 'with a gun' is not an argument of the verb *töten* 'to kill'.

(18) a. *Fritz tötet **mit   dem Gewehr**.*
          Fritz kills with the   gun
          'Fritz kills with the gun.'
      b. *Fritz tötet, und das geschieht/tut   er mit   dem Gewehr.*
          Fritz kills, and that happens/does he with the   gun
          'Fritz kills, and that happens/does he with the gun.'

To conclude, objects, in contrast to free adverbials, usually fulfill at least three of the conditions given in (15).

Subcategorized adverbials vs. objects

Some verbs subcategorize for adverbials. The verb *wohnen* 'live',[5] for example, subcategorizes for either a location (answering the question *Where do you live?*) or a certain mode of living (answering the question *How do you live?*), cf. (19) and (20), respectively.

(19) *Fritz wohnt **in Landau/in der Parkallee**.*
      Fritz lives   in Landau/in the Parkallee
      'Fritz lives in Landau/in the Parkallee.'

(20) a. *Fritz wohnt **schön/mit allem Komfort**.*
          Fritz lives   nice/with all comfort
          'Fritz lives nicely/with all comfort.'
      b. *Fritz wohnt **zur Miete/billig**.*
          Fritz lives   for rent/cheap
          'Fritz lives for rent/for little rent.'

A sentence without either of the two adverbial modifiers is felt to be infelicitous, cf. (21).

(21)   *Fritz wohnt.*
        Fritz lives

As *schön* 'nice' and *billig* 'cheap' in (20) show, adverbial adjectives can be used to fulfill subcategorization requirements. Sometimes, verbs exclusively subcategorize for adverbial adjectives, cf. (22).

(22)   a.   *Er benimmt sich   **gut/schlecht**.*
              he behaves himself good/bad
              'He behaves well/badly.'

        b.   *Er riecht **gut**.*
              he smells good
              'He smells good.'

        c.   *Er gebärdet sich   **merkwürdig**.*
              he acts   himself strange
              'He acts strangely.'

These adverbials can in some cases be dropped. For the three verbs in (22), this seems possible for *sich benehmen* 'behave oneself' and *riechen* 'smell', but not for *sich gebärden* 'act', cf. (23a) and (23b) vs. (23c).

(23)   a.   *Fritz benimmt sich   (gut).*
              he   behaves himself (well)
              'He behaves himself.'
        b.   *Jürgen riecht (schlecht).*
              he   smells (bad)
              'He smells.'
        c.   **Er gebärdet sich.*
              he acts   himself

However, both (23a) and (23b) have to be interpreted in the same way as the sentences with the adverbial given in parentheses added. This makes the relationship between the verbs in (23) differ from e.g. the relationship between the verb *essen* 'to eat' and its optional object, cf. (24).

(24)   *Fritz isst.*
        Fritz eats
        'Fritz is eating.'

In (24), although Fritz is certainly eating something, this 'something' is not explicitly specified.

If we resort to the criterion of form specificity, we could still argue that case marking distinguishes between objects and adverbials, but this hardly seems an adequate criterion, as the adverbials discussed do not allow any case marking, since they are not realized as noun phrases. The criteria for complementhood given in (15) and repeated in (25) are again a better guide, and it is useful to go through them step by step.

(25)   (i)   X is obligatory for Y, i.e. it must be realized.
       (ii)   X is specific for Y with respect to its form (e.g. X is case marked).
       (iii) X is specific for Y with respect to its content (e.g. X must be [+volitional] etc.).
       (iv)   X is an argument, filling an open position in the meaning of Y.

Similar to objects, subcategorized adverbials may or may not be obligatory, that is, (25i) may or may not hold. As already said, (25ii) does not hold, but this is due to the phrasal categories of the adverbials under discussion. The third criterion, (25iii), is fulfilled by the adverbials. Thus, the subcategorization for e.g. *sich benehmen* 'behave oneself' in (22a) cannot be fulfilled by just any adverbial: local or temporal adverbials cannot be used for this purpose. This leaves us with (25iv).

If we use the the *geschehen/tun*-test introduced in example (17), we arrive at the conclusion that these adverbials are arguments, cf. (26) for *riechen* 'smell' and (27) for 'behave oneself'.

(26)   *Fritz riecht, und das tut er/geschieht   schlecht/gut/unerträglich.*[6]
       Fritz smells, and that he does/happens bad/good/unbearable

(27)   *Doris benimmt sich,   und das tut   sie/geschieht*
       Doris behaves herself, and that does she/happens
       gut/schlecht/unmöglich.
       good/bad/impossible

A further argument for argumenthood is that the thematic role that an argument bears must be determined by the verb. For the adverbials under investigation this point is problematic. Standard accounts of thematic role systems assume that thematic roles allow the differentiation of entities, cf. the following quote from Dowty (1989):

> When I say that a thematic roles system distinguishes one argument from an-
> other semantically, I mean that it permits (real-world, non-linguistic) objects
> to be distinguished from one another by virtue of the distinctive properties
> they have as they participate in an event named by a verb, properties that can
> be identified ("in the real world") independently of a language or its "seman-
> tic representations." (Dowty 1989:73)

Clearly, this view of thematic roles excludes adverbials from being assigned
one, since they do not denote objects. To include adverbials, the term *object*
would have to be extended to also encompass directions, manners etc.

However, just as the assignment of thematic roles to objects results in
a stable semantic contribution of the objects to the sentence, the semantic
contributions of subcategorized adverbials are semantically stable. Thus, although adverbials subcategorized for by *sich benehmen* 'behave oneself' can
be realized as adjectives, cf. (28), or comparison clauses, cf. (29), the semantic contribution is stable: it always specifies the manner of the agent's
behavior, and consequently answers the question *How . . . ?*

(28) *Doris benimmt sich **gut/schlecht/unerträglich/unmöglich**.*
      Doris behaves herself good/bad/unsustainable/impossible
      'Doris behaves well/badly/unsustainalbly/impossibly.'

(29) a. *Doris benimmt sich **wie ein Trottel**.*
          Doris behaves herself like an idiot
          'Doris behaves like an idiot.'

      b. *Doris benimmt sich, **als ob es hier einen Preis zu***
          Doris behaves herself, as if it here a price to
          ***gewinnen gibt/als ob sie der Chef wäre**.'*
          win gives/as if she the boss were
          'Doris behaves as if there were a price to win/as if she were the
          boss.'

The phenomenon of verbs subcategorizing for adverbials is not limited to
German. In English, often cited examples include *word, phrase, treat* and
behave, cf. e.g. the remarks in Huddleston and Pullum (2002:574) and the
minimal pair in (30), (65) in Goldberg and Ackerman (2001).

(30) a. *Pat behaved to Chris.
      b. Pat behaved **badly** to Chris.

Parallel to its German counterpart, *behave*, if it occurs without subcategorized
adverbial, is reinterpreted as *behave well*.

2.1.3.   *Adverbial vs. predicative*

In German, the difference between adverbials and predicatives is extremely difficult to establish. Predicatives, just as adverbials, can be either obligatory, cf. (31), or optional, cf. (32).

(31)　　a.　*Hunde sind **dumm**.*
　　　　　dogs　are　stupid
　　　　　'Dogs are stupid.'
　　　　b.　**Hunde sind.*
　　　　　dogs　are

(32)　　a.　*Fritz wurde **jung** Vater.*
　　　　　Fritz became young father
　　　　　'Fritz became a father at an early age.'
　　　　b.　*Fritz wurde　Vater.*
　　　　　Fritz became father
　　　　　'Fritz became a father.'

As the examples show, both types of predicatives can be realized by adjectives. The construction with *dumm* 'stupid' in (31) is parallel to constructions where the copula combines with noun phrases in the nominative case, cf. (33).

(33)　　*Hunde sind **Tiere**.*
　　　　dogs　are　animals
　　　　'Dogs are animals.'

In grammars of German, both *dumm* 'stupid' in (31) and *Tiere* 'animals' in (33) are standardly called *Prädikatsnomen* 'predicative noun' (cf. e.g. Eisenberg 1999:85).

Syntactically and morphologically, there is no reason to consider *dumm* 'stupid' in this usage as a predicative and not an adverbial.[7] As shown in section 2.1.2 of this chapter, adverbials are also sometimes obligatory and can also be realized by noun phrases, cf. the repeated examples in (34) and (35), corresponding to (22c), (23c), and (13), respectively.

(34)　　a.　*Er gebärdet sich　　**merkwürdig**.*
　　　　　he acts　　himself strange
　　　　　'He acts strangely.'
　　　　b.　**Er gebärdet sich.*
　　　　　he acts　　himself

(35)   *Fritz hat **den   ganzen   Tag** den   Kuchen gegessen.*
       Fritz has the.ACC whole.ACC day the.ACC cake   eaten
       'Fritz ate the cake for the whole day'

However, there is a clear semantic difference between adverbials and obligatory predicatives. The fourth criterion for German adverbials, (9iv) on page 5, states that adverbials are restricted to a set of limited usages. In the discussion of adverbials vs. subjects, I pointed out that adverbials never answer the question *Who/What … ?* Obligatory predicatives, on the other hand, answer exactly these questions, cf. (36).

(36)   *Was sind Hunde?*
       what are dogs
       'What are dogs?'

   a.   *Hunde sind **Tiere**.*
        dogs   are animals
        'Dogs are animals.'
   b.   *Hunde sind **dumm**.*
        dogs   are stupid
        'Dogs are stupid.'

This behavior with regard to questions reflects the fact that the copula *sein* 'be' makes no semantic contribution in either sentence. This can also be seen when comparing the sentences in (36) with sentences that seem at first glance similar, cf. (37a) and (37b).

(37)   a.   *Fritz ist **hier**.*
            Fritz is here
            'Fritz is here.'
       b.   *Die Wahl   ist **morgen**.*
            the election is tomorrow
            'The election is tomorrow.'

The adverbs *hier* 'here' or *morgen* 'tomorrow' (for more on the lexical category *adverb*, cf. section 2.2.2) in (37) both fulfill typical adverbial functions, specifying the place and the time, respectively. However, in contrast to the usage of *sein* 'be' in (36), it is plausible to argue that *sein* 'be' makes a distinct meaning contribution in each case, in (37a) *sich befinden* 'located at' and in (37b) *stattfinden* 'take place'. In the case of locatives, this difference is in some languages morphosyntactically reflected: different copulas are employed, one for locative adverbials and one for the adjectival and nominal predicates, cf. Dryer (2007:238-240).

In the case of free predicatives, the so-called *depictives*, a syntactic distinction between them and adverbials is also impossible.[8] Even when turning to question tests, the distinction is very difficult. To see this, consider (38a) vs. (38b).

(38)   a.   *Fritz starb **langsam/enthusiastisch**.*
             Fritz died   slow/enthusiastical
             'Fritz died slowly/enthusiastically.'
        b.   *Fritz starb **jung/krank**.*
             Fritz died young/sick
             'Fritz died young/sick.'

Traditionally, *langsam* 'slowly' and *enthusiastisch* 'enthusiastically' in (38a) are considered to be adverbials, while *jung* 'young' and *krank* 'sick' in (38b) are considered to be depictives. The adverbials in (38a) answer the question in (39a), those in (38b) the questions in (39bi) and (39bii), respectively.

(39)   a.   How did Fritz die?
        b.   (i)   When did Fritz die?
             (ii)   Under what circumstances did Fritz die?

Neither question in (39b) indicates that the element in question does not serve as an adverbial. The problem of distinguishing between free predicatives and adverbials will be discussed in more detail in chapter 3 and 4.

2.1.4.   *Adverbial vs. particle*

The first criterion for adverbials given in (9) allows them to be differentiated from particles, which cannot function as a satzglied. I will show this by comparing the behavior of the modal particle *halt* 'just so' and the focus particle *sogar* 'even' to the adverbial adjective *laut* 'loudly'. Beginning with the first condition for satzglied status from the list in (10), it turns out that adverbials as well as particles can be positioned quite freely in a sentence, cf. (40a) for adverbials, (40b) for modal particles and (40c) for focus particles. For adverbials as well as particles only the position between subject and auxiliary and the sentence-final position are impossible.[9] The former constraint follows from the fact that German is a verb-second language; the positioning of the subject at the beginning of a sentence thus excludes the positioning of additional material before the finite verb.

(40) a. *Peter (*laut) hat (laut) das Lied (laut) gesungen (*laut).*
          Peter (loud) has (loud) the song (loud) sung   (loud)
          'Peter sang the song loudly.'
      b. *Peter (*halt) hat (halt) das Lied (halt) gesungen*
          Peter (just.so) has (just.so) the song (just.so) sung
          (*halt).
          (just.so)
          'Just so, Peter sang the song.'
      c. *Peter (*sogar) hat (sogar) das Lied (sogar) gesungen*
          Peter (even)   has (even) the song (even) sung
          (*sogar).
          (even)
          'Peter even sang the song.'

However, the critical condition, namely the possibility to constitute the Vorfeld of a verb-second sentence, is prototypically only fulfilled by adverbials, not by particles, cf. (41a) vs. (41b) and (41c).[10]

(41) a. **Laut** *hat Peter das Lied gesungen.*
          loud has Peter the song sung
          'Loudly, Peter sang the song.'
      b. *****Halt**   *hat Peter das Lied gesungen.*
          just.so has Peter the song sung
      c. *****Sogar** *hat Peter das Lied gesungen.*
          even   has Peter the song sung

The second condition from the list in (10), the possibility of elicitation by questions, is again fulfilled only by *laut* 'loud', not by *halt* 'just so' and *sogar* 'even'. The question-answer pair in (42) illustrates the elicitation of *laut* 'loudly' with the help of the question *Wie ... ?* 'How ... ?'.

(42) a. *Wie hat Peter das Lied gesungen?*
          how has Peter the song sung
          'How did Peter sing the song?'
      b. **Laut.**
          loud
          'Loudly.'

In contrast, particles cannot be elicited with the help of questions. Note, though, that the possibility to be elicited is a property of the prototypical time, place, and manner adverbials, and does not hold for all adverbs, cf. especially the discussion of sentence adverbials in chapter 2.

The third condition, pronominalization, cannot be directly applied to the adverbials under investigation, since they are not nominals nor do they contain nominals. However, the adverbial can be expressed by a deictic adverbial, for example *so* 'in this manner', cf. (43).

(43)   *Peter hat den Feind so   abgewehrt.*
        Peter has the enemy in.this.way warded.off
        'Peter warded off the enemy in this way.'

To interpret (43), the utterance of *so* 'in this way' must be accompanied by some gesture specifying the manner of Peter's action. A deictic reference to a particle is not possible.

Of the three conditions for satzglied status, the first and the second are clearly met by adverbials, and the last at least partly. By contrast, particles do not meet any of the three conditions.

2.1.5.   Summary

The aims of this section on adverbials were twofold: First, I have explained my usage of the term *adverbial* as referring to a particular syntactic function. Second, I have shown how this syntactic function can be differentiated from the other syntactic functions.

The decisive characteristic that distinguishes adverbials from particles is the fact that only the former, but not the latter, can serve as satzglied.

Subjects can be distinguished from adverbials due to their agreement relation to the verb, and due to their semantic usage: they are elicited with the help of *was/wer* 'what/who' questions.

Objects can be distinguished from free adverbials quite easily, since only objects stand in a special relation to the verb: they are arguments and carry a specific thematic role. The differentiation between objects and adverbials that are subcategorized for by the verb is more difficult to make, since these adverbials also fulfill standard criteria for argumenthood.

In the next section, I will turn to the question of the word class into which the boldfaced word forms of example (1) at the beginning of this chapter should be categorized.

2.2. Adverbial adjectives

In referring to the items under investigation as 'adverbial adjectives', I make a clear distinction between form and function: we are interested in items from the word class of adjectives that are used as adverbials. While this terminological choice seems do reflect the majority opinion, cf. Heidolph, Flämig and Motsch (1981:621-622), Eisenberg (1999:220-221), Engel (1996:754) and Pittner (1999:59-60), there also exists an alternative classification in the literature, namely the term 'adjectival adverb' (in German, *Adjektivadverb(i)en*, cf. Helbig and Buscha 2001:313 or Hentschel and Weydt 1994:182). In this section, I will argue for the classification chosen here. As my usage of the term 'adverbial' was already explicated in the last section, we will start here with short definitions of adjectives and adverbs, followed by illustrations of their main characteristics, and finally this will be put together in the section 2.2.3.

2.2.1. Adjectives

A definition for the word class *adjective* is given in (44).[11]

(44)   Adjectives form a lexical category that is defined by the following characteristics: adjectives canonically appear in attributive and predicative position, have comparison forms, and are inflected for gender, number and case as required by agreement with their head noun.

The following data illustrate these properties, cf. (45) for the usage of the adjective *schnell* 'fast' in predicative position, and (46) for the same adjective in attributive position.

(45)   *Der Hund ist **schnell**.*
        the dog   is fast
        'The dog is fast.'

(46)   *der **schnelle** Hund*
        the fast   dog
        'the fast dog'

The comparison forms are the comparative, cf. (47a) and the superlative, cf. (47b), demonstrated in the attributive position.

(47)   a.   *der **schnellere** Hund*
              the faster   dog
              'the faster dog'

        b.   *der **schnellste** Hund*
              the fastest   dog
              'the fastest dog'

Inflection for case, gender and number in agreement with the head noun is shown in (48), (49) and (50), respectively.[12]

(48)   a.   *der   **schnelle** Läufer*
              the.NOM fast.NOM runner.NOM
              'the fast runner'

        b.   *des   **schnellen** Läufers*
              the.GEN fast.GEN runner.GEN
              'the fast runner'

As the contrast between the noun phrase in the nominative case in (48a) and the noun phrase in the genitive case in (48b) shows, the word form of *schnell* 'fast' agrees with the case of the head noun. Agreement for gender is shown in (49), where both noun phrases are in the nominative case. In addition, (49a) is grammatically marked as masculine, whereas the head noun in (49b) is grammatically feminine (in this particular case agreeing with its natural gender).

(49)   a.   *ein   **schneller** Läufer*
              a.MASC fast.MASC runner.MASC
              'a fast runner'

        b.   *eine   **schnelle** Läuferin*
              a.FEM fast.FEM runner.FEM
              'a fast runner'

Finally, the two noun phrases in (50), again both in the nominative case, show number agreement. In (50a), the head noun is singular, whereas in (50b), it is in the plural. Accordingly, the word form of *schnell* 'fast' changes.

(50)   a.   *ein **schneller** Zug*
              a.SG fast.SG   train.SG
              'a fast train'

        b.   ***schnelle** Züge*
              fast.PL   trains.PL
              'fast trains'

Note that agreement plays no role for the adjective in predicative position. Used predicatively, the adjective invariably appears in its short form, i.e., without any inflectional ending, cf. the discussion and examples in section 2.2.3.

2.2.2. Adverbs

German adverbs can be defined as in (51), adopted from Schmöe (2002:159).

(51)   Adverbs form a lexical category characterized
        by the following five properties:
        (i)   Adverbs cannot be inflected.
        (ii)   They can be used as satzglied.
        (iii)   They can carry the sentence accent.
        (iv)   They are mono-lexematic, that is, they are not phrasal.[10]
        (v)   They cannot be used as subjects.[11]

For German, two groups of adverbs can be distinguished. Firstly, there is a group of adverbs that form a closed class and that is commonly subclassified into the four categories of local, temporal, modal and degree adverbs, cf. (52) (cf. e.g. Eisenberg 1999:205).

(52)   local: *oben* 'above', *hinten* 'behind', *hier* 'here'
        temporal: *bald* 'soon', *eben* 'just', *immer* 'always'
        modal: *gern* 'gladly', *kaum* 'hardly', *vielleicht* 'perhaps'
        degree: *sehr* 'very', *ganz* 'completely', *weitaus* 'by far'

Secondly, adverbs can be productively derived from adjectives with the suffix *-weise*, cf. (53).

(53)   *-weise* suffixation:
        intelligent 'intelligent' → *intelligenterweise* 'intelligently'
        arrogant 'arrogant' → *arroganterweise* 'arrogantly'
        normal 'normal' → *normalerweise* 'normally'

As far as their syntactic functions are concerned, derived adverbs and modal adverbs are the most restricted, as they can neither be used predicatively nor attributively, cf. (54) and (55), respectively.

(54)   a.   **der **intelligenterweise** Kämpfer*
             the intelligently   fighter

        b.   **Er ist **intelligenterweise**.*
             he is intelligently

(55)   a.   **der **vielleicht** Kämpfer*
             the perhaps fighter

        b.   **Er ist **vielleicht**.*
             he is perhaps

Of the other adverbs, local and temporal adverbs can be used predicatively
but not attributively, cf. (56) for local adverbs, (57) for temporal adverbs.[15]

(56)   *Er kämpft **hier/dort**.*
        he fights   here/there
        'He fights here/there.'

        a.   **der **hier/dort** Kampf*
             the here/there fight

        b.   *Er ist **hier/dort**.*
             he is here/there
             'He is here/there.'

(57)   *Er kämpft **jetzt/bald/morgen**.*
        he fights   now/soon/tomorrow
        'He fights now/soon/tomorrow.'

        a.   **der **jetzt/bald/morgen**   Kampf*
             the now/soon/tomorrow fight

        b.   *Das Fest ist **jetzt/bald/morgen**.*
             the party is now/soon/tomorrow
             'The party is now/soon/tomorrow.'

Degree adverbs can usually not stand on their own, cf. (58), but rather they
modify other adjectives or adverbs, cf. (59) and (60).

(58)   a.   **Er ist **sehr/höchst/äußerst**.*
             he is very/supremely/utterly

        b.   **der **sehr/höchst/äußerst**   Fridolin*
             the very/supremely/utterly Fridolin

(59) a. *Er ist **sehr/höchst/äußerst** erschöpft.*
          he is very/supremely/utterly exhausted
          'He is very/supremely/utterly exhausted.'
      b. *der **sehr/höchst/äußerst** schöne Fridolin*
          the very/supremely/utterly beautiful Fridolin
          'the very/supremely/utterly beautiful Fridolin'

(60) *Er kämpfte **sehr/extrem/äußerst***
      he fought very/extremely/utterly
      laut/langsam/widerwillig/intelligent.
      loudly/slowly/reluctantly/intelligently
      'He fought very/extremely/utterly loudly/slowly/reluctantly/intelli-
      gently.'

2.2.3. Adjective or adverb?

The question of whether *schnell* 'fast' in examples such as (61) is an adjective
or an adverb cannot be decided on the basis of the criteria given so far.

(61) *Fritz läuft **schnell**.*
      Fritz runs fast
      'Fritz runs fast.'

In this usage, *schnell* 'fast' is not inflected for gender or number, cf. (62).

(62) a. *Sie/Er/Es läuft **schnell**.*
          she/he/it runs fast
          'She/He/It runs fast.'
      b. *Die Leute laufen **schnell**.*
          the people run fast
          'The people run fast.'

In (62a), the morphological form of *schnell* 'fast' stays the same, although
the grammatical gender of each of the pronouns is masculine, feminine and
neuter, respectively. Similarly, the same morphological form of *schnell* 'fast'
is used when the subject is in the plural, as in (62b).
This uninflected morphological form of *schnell* 'fast' used in (61) and (62)
is referred to in German linguistics as *adjectival short form* ('Kurzform', cf.
e.g. Eisenberg 1999:88 or Heidolph, Flämig and Motsch 1981:621) and is
also employed when adjectives are used predicatively, cf. (63).[16]

(63) a. *Sie/Er/Es ist **schnell**.*
          she/he/it is fast
          'She/He/It is fast.'

    b.   *Die Leute   sind **schnell**.*
        the people are fast
        'The people are fast.'

Proponents of the view that *schnell* 'fast' in (61) and (62) is, as far as its word class is concerned, an adjective, argue that adjectives in adverbial function are realized in the adjectival short form, similar to their predicative use.

In contrast, proponents of the view that *schnell* 'fast' in (61) and (62) is an adverb argue that *schnell* 'fast' in these sentences is a derivation via a 0-suffix from the adjective. Since it is viewed as an adverb, it is not surprising that it is uninflected for gender and number, because adverbs cannot be inflected (cf. clause (51i) in the definition of adverbs on page 19). Clearly, this is also a possibility, albeit one which leaves us with two homonymous forms, namely the adjectival short-form and the adverb derived from the adjective. Diachronically, the corresponding word forms in Old and Middle High-German still carried special adverb endings (-o and -e), which have been lost in New High-German (cf. Steinberger 1994:51, Wahrig 1986:32).

Proponents of the adverb analysis sometimes also use crosslinguistic data to argue for their point. In many Indo-European languages, the words corresponding to German adverbial adjectives are morphologically distinct from the adjectives from which they are derived, cf. (64) for English and French.[17]

(64)   a.   English: quick → quickly
        b.   French: rapide → rapidement

However, there are many other languages where this is not the case, for example Dutch, where parallel to German, the same word form is used for the predicative and the adverbial usage of adjectives. Again parallel to the situation in German, it is neither inflected for gender, cf. (65), nor for number, cf. (66).

(65)   a.   *De auto   rijdt **snel**.*
            the car.MASC rides fast
            'The car drives fast.'
        b.   *Het schip   vaart **snel**.*
            the ship.NEUTER goes fast
            'The ship goes fast.'

(66)   a.   *De auto's rijden **snel**.*
            the cars   ride   fast
            'The cars drive fast.'

b. *De schepen varen **snel**.*
the ships   go   fast
'The ships go fast.'

In some languages, we even find that the words serving as manner adverbials agree in case with the agent, cf. (67) from the Australian language Martuthunira (corresponding to (9.136) in Dench (1995), quoted as (20b) in Himmelmann and Schultze-Berndt (2005), who provided the amended translation).

(67)   *ngunhu-ngara pawulu-ngara mir.ta **jarruru-lu** parrungkarri-yangu*
that.NOM-PL child-PL   not slow-EFF shout.at-PASSP
*ngulu   **wartirra-lu***
that.EFF woman-EFF
'These children were shouted at by the woman not slowly (i.e. not softly)'

In (67), both the word form serving as manner adverbial, *jarruru-lu* 'slowly' as well as the noun denoting the agent, *wartirra-lu* 'woman' are in the effective case.

Even in the Indo-European languages in (64) the situation is not as clearcut as it may seem on first analysis, cf. the data from English in (68), reproducing (16b) of Huddleston and Pullum (2002:568).

(68)   a.   He guessed **wrong**.
b.   He acted **wrongly**.

Although in (68a) *wrong* appears without *-ly-* suffix, it is used adverbially. Consequently, Huddleston and Pullum (2002:568) treat *wrong* in (68a) as an adverb, in contrast to its occurrence as an adjective, e.g. in *the wrong decision*, even though there is no special marking. Huddleston and Pullum (2002:568-69) contains more examples where the absence vs. presence of *-ly* does not allow a differentiation between adverb and adjective.

Reference to parallel constructions in other languages is therefore not a suitable tool to decide whether the constituents under investigation are best classified as adjectives or adverbs in German.

2.3. Summary

This discussion on the terminology used in this work fell into two subsections, the first concerned with the syntactic function of the word forms investigated here, the second with their word class.

In the first subsection, I gave a definition of *adverbials* in terms of their specific syntactic function and have shown how this definition allows one a differentiation from the other syntactic functions. It turns out that according to the definition, all the boldfaced words in example (1) of this chapter, repeated as (69), serve as adverbials.

(69)   a.   *Sie hat **laut** gesungen.*
             she has loud sung.
             'She sang loudly.'
        b.   *Der Zug fuhr **schnell**.*
             the train drove fast.
             'The train drove fast'
        c.   *Er löste   die Aufgabe **intelligent**.*
             he solved the problem intelligent.
             'He solved the problem intelligently'

The second subsection was concerned with the question of which word class the boldfaced word forms in (69) belong to. I adopted the view that they are best categorized as adjectives, serving in these sentences as adverbials. The main reason for this is that these words resemble in their morphology the adjectival short form already known from the predicative usage of adjectives. I also pointed out that proponents of the alternative classification as adjectival adverbs argue that the homonymy of adjective and adverb is the result of a 0-derivation.

Nevertheless, it should be clear that whether the boldfaced words in (69) are referred to as *adjectival adverbs* or as *adverbial adjectives* is not critical to the further discussion of syntactic and semantic issues and has no theoretical consequence. Its importance lies rather in giving a clear and consistent way of referring to the words being investigated in this work.

3.   Basic distinctions

As noted at different points, adverbials constitute a heterogeneous category. In this section, I will first discuss to what extent common properties of German adverbial adjectives already allow one to exclude certain adverbial usages on semantic grounds. Secondly, I will discuss a number of set-theoretic properties of adjectives that also interact with their adverbial usages.

3.1.   Class properties of adverbial adjectives

A rough categorization of semantic functions is given in Ernst (2002:9), where a distinction is made between predicational adverbial, participant adverbials, and functional adverbials (cf. also Maienborn and Schäfer 2011, where the term 'participant-oriented adverbial' is used instead of participant adverbial). Prototypical examples of the three types are given in (70).

(70) a.   *Peter läuft **schnell**.* [predicational adverbial]
           Peter runs fast
           'Peter runs fast.'
      b.   *Anna läuft **mit Krücken**.* [participant adverbial]
           Anna runs on crutches
           'Anna runs on crutches.'
      c.   *Anna läuft **wieder**.* [functional adverbial]
           Anna runs again
           'Anna runs again.'

Predicational adverbials express a gradable property, participant-oriented adverbials introduce a new entity, and functional adverbials cover the remaining cases, that is, *wieder* 'again' is neither gradable nor does it introduce a new entity. Adverbial adjectives typically serve as predicationals, as in (70a). They never serve as participant-oriented adverbials, because they do not introduce new arguments, but some of their usages technically correspond to functional usages.

3.2.   Set-theoretic classifications of adjectives

In adjective semantics, especially in the combination with nouns, it is common to differentiate between intersective adjectives and non-intersective adjectives (this section closely follows Partee 1995, 2010). Typical intersective adjectives are given in (71).

(71)   *zwei-beinig* 'two-legged', *radioaktiv* 'radioactive', *krank* 'sick', *rot* 'red', *supraleitend* 'superconductive', *deutsch* 'German'

Assuming that common nouns like e.g. *Mann* 'man' denote sets of individuals, and that the adjectives in (71) likewise denote sets of individuals, their combination can be analysed as the intersection of the two sets, cf. e.g. (72) for the denotation of *kranker Mann* 'sick man'.

(72)   *kranker Mann* 'sick man'
    [[krank]] $= \{x|x \text{ is sick}\}$
    [[Mann]] $= \{x|x \text{ is a man}\}$
    [[kranker Mann]] $= $ [[krank]] $\cap$ [[Mann]]
                 $= \{x|x \text{ is sick and x is a man}\}$

Intersective adjectives therefore allow the inference pattern given in (73).

(73)   Max ist ein kranker Mann.   'Max is a sick man.'
    Max ist ein Linguist.   'Max is a linguist.'
    $\overline{\rightarrow \text{Max ist ein kranker Linguist.}}$ 'Max is a sick linguist.'

Non-intersective adjectives, in contrast, do not show this behavior. A classic example of a non-intersective adjective is *ehemalig* 'former'. If combined with a noun, e.g. in the phrase *ehemaliger Senator* 'former senator', the denotation of the noun phrase is not the intersection of the set denoted by *ehemalig* and the set denoted by *Senator*, cf. (74).

(74)   *ehemaliger Senator* 'former senator'
    [[ehemaliger Senator]] $\neq$ [[ehemalig]] $\cap$ [[Senator]]

Non-intersective adjectives do not allow the inference pattern shown in (73) for intersective adjectives, cf. (75).

(75)   Max ist ein ehemaliger Senator.   'Max is a former senator.'
    Max ist Vorstandsvorsitzender.   'Max is CEO.'
    $\overline{\nrightarrow \text{Max ist ein ehemaliger Vorstandsvorsitzender.}}$ 'Max is a former
    CEO.'

One of the reasons why *former* is such a clear case of non-intersective modification lies in the fact that this adjective is not even subsective, that is, the set of former senators does not form a subset of the set of senators, cf. (76) and the inference pattern in (77).

(76)   *former senator*
    [[former senator]] $\nsubseteq$ [[senator]]

(77)   Max ist ein ehemaliger Senator.   'Max is a former senator.'
    $\overline{\nrightarrow \text{Max ist ein Senator.}}$ 'Max is a senator.'

Between non-subsective adjectives such as *former* and intersective adjectives such as *sick* lies the huge group of subsective adjectives. An adjective like *groß* 'big' seems to belong to this group. Subsective adjectives contrast with non-intersective adjectives in yielding subsets of the sets denoted by whatever they modify, cf. (78) and (79).

(78)   *großer Junge* 'big boy'
        [[großer Junge]] $\subseteq$ [[Junge]]

(79)   Max ist ein großer Junge.   'Max is a big boy.'
        $\to$ Max ist ein Junge.   'Max is a boy.'

On first sight, subsective adjectives also do not allow the inference pattern given in (73) for intersective adjectives, cf. (80).

(80)   Max ist ein großer Junge.   'Max is a big boy.'
        Max ist ein Ringer.   'Max is a wrestler.'
        $\not\to$ Max ist ein großer Ringer. 'Max is a big wrestler.'

Nevertheless, the conclusiveness of (80) for adjectives like *groß* 'big' has been called into question. Partee (1995:330-336) argues that an adjective like *big*, or in her examples, *tall*, is in fact intersective, but context-sensitive and vague.[18]

Her argumentation runs as follows: It is true that adjectives like *tall* and *big* fail the standard test for intersectivity, cf. (80) for *big*. However, the test is inconclusive, because the reason for the inference failure is that the adjective is differently interpreted in the premise and in the conclusion. This different interpretation, in turn, is a result of the inherent vagueness of adjectives such as *big* or *tall* (the context sensitivity or vagueness of these adjectives is frequently discussed, cf. e.g. Kamp 1975, Partee 1995, Heim and Kratzer 1998 and Chierchia and McConnell-Ginet 2000). Something or someone can only be *big* in relation to other things or persons, and these other things or persons are given by the context, either the linguistic or extra-linguistic context, or a combination of both. Thus, assuming no further context, *groß* 'big' in (81a) can be evaluated as setting an elephant into relation to the size standard for elephants. With regard to this size standard, the elephant is judged to be big. In (81b), in contrast, the comparison class in relation to whose size standard the boy is judged to be big consists most likely of other boys, but not of elephants.

(81)   a.   ein großer Elephant   'a big elephant'
           $\approx$ groß für einen Elephanten   'big for an elephant'
     b.   ein großer Junge   'a big boy'
           $\approx$ groß für einen Jungen   'big for a boy'

That it is not the noun phrase which is modified by the adjective alone that influences the interpretation of the adjective can be seen in (82), taken from Partee (1995).

(82)   a.   My 2-year-old son built a really tall snowman yesterday.
       b.   The D.U. fraternity brothers built a really tall snowman last weekend.

Although both sentences talk about tall snowmen, the size standards used to evaluate the adjective differ: We expect the snowman built by the two-year old to be far smaller than the one built by the fraternity. In a similar way, information from previous utterances can influence which size standard is used in evaluation.[19] It seems, however, that the modified noun always plays the most important role in specifying the relevant size standard. That is, intuitively it seems plausible that first the modified noun restricts the possible size standards to size standards for snowmen. In a second step, further contextual information is used to fine-tune that size standard.

The inference in (80) thus fails because, given only the bare noun phrases, the interpretation of *big* is not kept constant. In the premise, *big* is naturally taken as describing Max as big relative to the size standard set by boys. In the conclusion, *big* in its most likely interpretation is evaluated against the size standard of wrestlers. As world knowledge tells us that the latter size standard, on an absolute scale of bigness, is located nearer to the upper end of the scale than for the former, the inference does not hold. If, however, the size standard is kept constant, the inference pattern holds, cf. (83), where the size standard is given by the lowered *for*-phrases.

(83)   Max is a big$_{\text{for boys}}$ boy
       Max is a wrestler
       ―――――――――――――――――――
       → Max is a big$_{\text{for boys}}$ wrestler.

As I will argue in chapter 6, these properties of adjectives also play an important role for their formal analysis when used as adverbials.

3.3.   Sentence and non-sentence adverbials

A well-established distinction within the group of predicational adverbials is that between the usage as a sentence adverbial and the usage as a verb-related adverbial. A classic pair from English is given in (84).

(84)   a.   Rudely, Claire greeted the queen.
        b.   Claire greeted the queen rudely.

In (84a), *rudely* is used as a sentence adverbial: the fact that Claire greeted the queen is judged as rude, regardless of how she greeted her. In (84b), in contrast, the specific way in which Claire greeted the queen is judged as rude; *rudely* serves as a verb-related adverbial.

In German, these two different usages can be morphologically encoded, cf. (85), or one and the same adjective can be used, cf. the two examples with *wirtschaftlich* 'economically' given at the beginning of this chapter.

(85)   a.   *Julia hat **intelligent** geantwortet.*
              Julia has intelligent answered
              'Julia answered intelligently.'
        b.   *Julia hat **intelligenterweise** geantwortet.*
              Julia has intelligently   answered
              'Intelligently, Julia answered.'

Besides sentence adverbials and verb-related adverbials, I introduce a third class, the event-related adverbials. These three classes and their subclasses will be discussed in more details in chapters 2 through 4.

3.4.   Other important semantic properties

Two important semantic properties that play a role in the classification of sentence adverbials as such and the differentiation of the different subclasses are opacity and veridicality.

3.4.1.   Opacity

In extensional systems of logic, it is usually assumed that Leibniz' Law holds: Two coreferential expressions can be freely substituted for one another without changing the truth value of the original expression. Expressions for which this law does not hold are oblique or referentially opaque. Adverbials can be responsible for opaque contexts, cf. (86).

(86)   a.   Necessarily, Sam Peckinpah is Sam Peckinpah.
        b.   Necessarily, Sam Peckinpah is the director of The Wild Bunch.

While (86a) is true (in most systems of logic), (86b) is false, even though Sam Peckinpah and the director of The Wild Bunch are, at least in our world, coreferential. Adverbials can be characterized as to whether they create opaque contexts for all positions in a sentence, for just specific positions, or for no positions at all.

3.4.2.   *Veridicality*

An adverbial is veridical (or factive), if a sentence containing the adverbial entails the sentence without the adverbial. It is nonveridical if there is no such entailment. Some adverbials, e.g. functional adverbials like *never*, are antiveridical, that is, they entail that the sentence without the adverbial is not true; cf. Giannakidou (1999) and also Bonami, Godard and Kampers-Manhe (2004).

4.   Structure of the book

The book falls into eight chapters. Chapter one states the book's aim and scope, in addition providing the basic terminology and fundamental assumptions to be used throughout the rest of the book.

The following three chapters are mostly descriptive in nature and give an overview of the different adverbial usages of adjectives in German: Chapter two characterizes the different readings of adverbial adjectives serving as sentence adverbials. It is rather short, due to the fact that the adjectives themselves only play a minor role here. Instead, deadjectival *weise*-adverbs are frequently employed. Chapter three characterizes the different readings of adverbial adjectives in their verb-related usages. It is more detailed than the previous chapter, since verb-related usages represent the core usages of adverbial adjectives in German. In addition, it is in their usage as verb-related adverbials that they share their position with secondary predicates, from which they can only be kept apart on semantic grounds. This chapter also contains a discussion of possible constraints on verb-adverbial combinations and of the role of negation in the context of verb-related adverbials. Chapter four is concerned with event-related adverbials. This term is used as a cover term for all adverbial usages below the level of sentence adverbials and above the level of verb-related adverbials. In particular, this class consists of mental attitude adverbials on the one hand and event-external adverbials on the other hand. This latter group is discussed in some detail, as the differences between event-external adverbials and manner adverbials are sometimes rather subtle.

Chapter five discusses the syntactic position of event-related and verb-related adverbials. The main thrust of the argumentation is that event-related adverbials are always positioned before the direct object, whereas verb-related adverbials follow the direct object. Chapter six presents the three classical formal approaches to adverbial modification: the operator approach, the argument approach, and the predicate approach. Chapter seven presents a new proposal for the semantic representation of verb-related adverbials, geared in particular towards manner adverbials. It argues that the resulting representation is intuitively more adequate than previous attempts. In addition, it is shown how this representation allows to formally distinguish between event-related and verb-related modification, in turn allowing to make use of the link between the two types of modification and the two different syntactic positions established in chapter five in the derivation of the semantic representation. Chapter eight contains a short summary and outlook.

Chapter 2
The readings of sentence adverbials

1. Introduction

Sentence adverbials constitute a large class which can be classified into a number of subclasses all displaying specific linguistic characteristics. Sentence adverbials have a hierarchically high attachment site; they stand in a relation to or combine with the overall proposition expressed by the rest of the sentence without the adverbial (= the sentential base). Some sort of distinction between sentence adverbials vs. non-sentence adverbials along the lines sketched above can be found in almost any semantic classification of adverbials, although details and further subdivisions may differ to some extent. The subdivision developed in the following draws on previous classifications, especially those by Bartsch (1972), Jackendoff (1972), Bellert (1977), Ernst (1984), Ernst (2002), and Parsons (1990).

Before discussing the different usages of adverbial adjectives as sentence adverbials, two complicating factors need to be mentioned. Firstly, as noted in section 3.3 of chapter 1, German has a group of de-adjectival adverbs that can only be used as sentence adverbials. Secondly, adverbials can be used parenthetically or integrated. Adverbial adjectives can often only occur as sentence adverbials if they are used parenthetically. Both phenomena will be discussed in the following only when relevant.

Each subclass will first be introduced on intuitive grounds and, if available, by some characteristic paraphrases that are indicative of their underlying semantics (for critical remarks on paraphrases, cf. e.g. Jackendoff 1972:50, 52, 57 and Ernst 1984:23-24; for a very elaborate system of paraphrases, cf. Bartsch 1972). Afterwards, each subclass will be characterized in terms of opacity, veridicality and further semantic and inferential properties.

Sentence adverbials can be further subdivided into subject-oriented adverbials, speaker-oriented adverbials and domain adverbials. These three classes are discussed in sections two, three, and four, respectively. The fifth section of this chapter discusses general semantic constraints on adjectives serving as sentence adverbials.

2.   Subject-oriented adverbials

Subject-oriented adverbials assign a specific property to the agent, based on the action as described by the proposition expressed by the sentential base, cf. (1).

(1)   *Peter hat **arroganterweise/idiotischerweise** seine Liebesbriefe*
      Peter has arrogantly/idiotically   his   love.letters
      ins   Netz gestellt.
      on.the net   put
      'Peter arrogantly/idiotically put his love letters on the net.'

In (1), the speaker judges Peter to be arrogant/idiotic, basing his judgment on Peter's action of putting his love letters on the net. In this example, de-adjectival adverbs formed by adding the suffix *-weise* to the adjectival base are used. Typically, these adverbs and not the adjectives constituting the bases are used as subject-oriented adverbials, but see section 2.1 for some exceptions. Sentences containing subject-oriented adverbials allow paraphrases analogous to the one given in (2) for sentence (1), following the pattern in (3), where VERB subsumes the verb itself plus further arguments and modifiers.

(2)   *Es war arrogant/idiotisch von Peter, dass er seine Liebesbriefe*
      It was arrogant/idiotic   of Peter that he his   love.letters
      ins   Netz gestellt hat.
      on.the net   put   has.
      'It was arrogant/idiotic of Peter that he has put his love letters on the net.'

(3)   *Es war ADJ   von SUBJ,   dass SUBJ   geVERBt hat.*
      It was ADJECTIVE of   SUBJECT, that SUBJECT VERBed has.
      'It was ADJECTIVE of SUBJECT, that SUBJECT has VERBed.'

Subject-oriented adverbials are veridical and they have scope over negation: (4a) entails (4b).

(4)   a.   *Peter hat **arroganterweise** nicht zurückgerufen.*
           Peter has arrogantly   not called.back
           'Peter arrogantly didn't call back.'
      b.   *Peter hat nicht zurückgerufen.*
           Peter has not   called.back
           'Peter did not call call back.'

Finally, subject-oriented adverbials appear to be anomalous in questions, cf. (5), which has the flavor of a rhetoric question.

(5)   ?*Hat Peter **arroganterweise** nicht zurückgerufen?*
       has Peter arrogantly   not   called.back

Bellert (1977) relates this behavior to the general observation that we cannot ask a question and assert a proposition in one and the same sentence.

Subject-oriented adverbials are sometimes claimed to create opaque contexts for the direct object position, cf. e.g. Parsons (1990:64). This view is based on data like (6).

(6)   a.   ***Intelligenterweise** hat Peter Ortcutt ermordet.*
            intelligently   has Peter Ortcutt killed
            'Intelligently, Peter killed Ortcutt.'
       b.   [Ortcutt= der Spion 'the spy']
       c.   ***Intelligenterweise** hat Peter den Spion ermordet.*
            intelligently   has Peter the spy   killed
            'Intelligently, Peter killed the spy.'

On first sight, it seems like a typical example of an opaque context: Knowing that Ortcutt has made Peter's life a thoroughly miserable affair, I might judge (6a) to be true. However, not knowing that Ortcutt and the spy are actually one and the same person, I might hold that (6c) is wrong, because I know that Peter wanted to contact a spy for the longest time. Clearly, my judgments of these sentences change if I exchange the respective noun phrase. However, as Wyner (1994:28-29) and Geuder (2000:165-169) point out, these patterns are better explained with reference to context-sensitivity, and subject-oriented adverbials do not create opaque contexts after all. On this view, the key to the patterns is to keep the contexts for the evaluation of Peter's actions constant. Thus, if my base for judging Peter's actions as intelligent is rooted in my firm believe that it is in general intelligent to kill all people that make one's life miserable, then I will also judge (6c) to be true. And the same holds the other way around: if I judge (6c) to be false based on the belief that it is never intelligent to kill spies, then, given that I know (6b), I will judge (6a) to be false, too. The effect here is reminiscent of the effect witnessed in connection with subsective adjectives, cf. the discussion in section 3.2 of chapter 1.

2.1.   Adverbial adjectives as subject-oriented adverbials

As already mentioned, adverbs formed from adjectives by adding the suffix *-weise* are typically used as subject-oriented adverbials, cf. e.g. the adverbs in (1).

But adjectives in their short form can also sometimes serve as subject-oriented adverbials, cf. (7) and (8). In both cases, the adjectives are used non-parenthetically.

(7)   **Taktvoll** *hat er die Tür   geschlossen.*
      tactful   has he the door closed
      'Tactfully, he closed the door.'

(8)   *Sebastian sitzt **tapfer** auf dem Stuhl.*
      Sebastian sits brave on his   chair
      'Sebastian sits bravely in his chair.'

In both cases, the relevant paraphrases are appropriate. The reasons, however, are different. The adjective *taktvoll* 'tactful' tends, due to its lexical semantics, to be interpreted as a subject-oriented adverbial. It often can be found together with verbs that do not allow any typical verb-related reading, cf. *verbergen* 'hide' in (9).

(9)   *Die Bundesregierung   ihrerseits   verbarg   **taktvoll**, dass sie*
      the federal.government on.her.side concealed tactful, that she
      nichts   von diesem Eifer   hält.
      nothing.much of this   eagerness thinks
      'The federal government tactfully hid the fact that it didn't think much of this eagerness.'

For *tapfer* 'brave' in (8), it is the combination with the positional stative *sitzen* 'to sit' that makes an interpretation as a manner adverbial impossible, leaving the interpretation as a subject-oriented adverbial as the most likely interpretation.

An example where a manner interpretation is available for *taktvoll* 'tactful' is given in (10), where *taktvoll* 'tactful' occurs in combination with a verb of saying.

(10)   *Der Minister äußerte sich   sehr **taktvoll** zu dem delikaten Fall.*
       the minister spoke himself very tactful to the delicate case
       'The minister gave very tactful comments on this delicate case.'

Here, *taktvoll* 'tactful' clearly specifies the manner of this minister's commenting, and combining the same sentential base with the corresponding *weise* adverb yields a clear contrast, cf. (11).

(11) **Taktvollerweise** *äußerte sich   der Minister zu dem delikaten Fall.*
      tactfully   spoke himself the minister to the delicate case
      'Tactfully, the minister commented on the delicate case.'

The usage of adjectives as subject-oriented adverbials is rather rare. Thus, for example, it is not possible to use the adjectival bases *idiotic* 'idiotic' and *arrogant* 'arrogant' instead of the derived adverbs in the cases of *idiotischerweise* 'idiotically' and *arroganterweise* 'arrogantly' as they appear in (1), cf. (12).

(12) ***Idiotisch/Arrogant** hat er seine Liebesbriefe ins   Netz gestellt.*
      idiotic/arrogant   has he his   love.letters on.the net put

The reasons for this contrast in behavior between e.g. *taktvoll* 'tactful' and *idiotisch* 'idiotic' as well as *arrogant* 'arrogant' are unclear.

3. Speaker-oriented adverbials

Speaker-oriented adverbials provide a comment by the speaker on the proposition expressed by the sentential base. Examples of this type of adverbials are given in (13).

(13) a. **Ehrlich**, *ich verstehe   überhaupt nicht wovon   du*
          honest I   understand completely not about.what you
          redest.
          talk
          'Honestly, I have no idea what you are talking about.'
      b. **Wahrscheinlich** *liebt sie mich.*
          probably   loves she me
          'She probably loves me.'
      c. **Glücklicherweise** *hat Henrike gute Berater.*
          fortunately   has Henrike good aides
          'Fortunately, Henrike has good aides.'

Following Ernst (2002), they can be further divided into three subgroups, namely speech-act adverbials, epistemic adverbials and evaluative adverbials.

Speaker-oriented adverbials outscope all other scope-bearing elements and therefore cannot occur within the scopes of other adverbials or quantificational noun phrases. Speaker oriented adverbials are ordered relative to each other, obeying the order **speech-act** > **evaluative** > **epistemic**, as exemplified in (14).

(14)   ***Kurzum, bedauerlicherweise*** *hat der Einbrecher den Besitzer*
       briefly,   unfortunately   has the thief   the proprietor
       wahrscheinlich *ermordet.*
       probably   killed
       'To put it briefly, the thief has unfortunately probably killed the proprietor.'

Besides these common characteristics, each subclass has a number of distinctive properties outlined in the following sections.

3.1.   Speech-act adverbials

Speech-act adverbials characterize the speaker's attitude towards the content or the form of what s/he is saying, cf. (15a) and (15b), respectively.[20] They have a metalinguistic function (Mittwoch 1977:183).

(15)   a.   ***Ehrlich/ernsthaft,*** *ich verstehe   überhaupt nicht*
            honest/serious,   I understand completely not
            wovon   du redest.
            about.what you talk
            'Honestly/seriously, I have no idea what you are talking about.'
       b.   ***Kurz,*** *Peter konnte sie nicht überzeugen.*
            brief, Peter could her not   convince
            'In short, Peter did not manage to convince her.'

While all the adverbials in (15) are adjectives in their short-form, at least *ehrlich* 'honest' and *kurz* 'brief', but also some additional adjectives like *offen* 'frank' can occur in combination with the perfect participle *gesagt* 'spoken' (corresponding by and large to the addition of the present participle in English, as in *Honestly speaking, ...*), cf. (16).

(16)   a.   ***Ehrlich/offen*** *gesagt, ich verstehe   überhaupt nicht*
honest/frank   spoken, I   understand completely not
wovon   du   redest.
about.what you talk
'Honestly/frankly speaking, I have no idea what you are talking
about.'

   b.   ***Kurz*** *gesagt,   Peter konnte sie   nicht überzeugen.*
brief spoken, Peter could   her not   convince
'Briefly, Peter did not manage to convince her.'

All of these constructions seem somewhat idiomatic, and for *kurz/kurz gesagt* 'briefly put', German even provides a dedicated speech-act adverb, *kurzum* 'in short', cf. (17).

(17)   ***Kurz*** *(gesagt)/ **kurzum**, du   hast mehr*
Brief (spoken)/briefly,   you have more
Dreck am Stecken   als der ganze restliche
skeletons in the cupboard[idiom] than the whole leftover
Landtag   zusammengenommen.
parliament taken.together
'In short/in a word, you have more skeletons in your cupboard than
all the rest of the parliament taken together.'

Furthermore, speech-act adverbials can appear in explicit performative utterances, cf. (18).

(18)   ***Ehrlich***, *Ich verzeihe Dir.*
honest, I   forgive you
'Honestly, I forgive you.'

As indicated orthographically, speech-act adverbials always occur as parentheticals.

3.2.   Epistemic adverbials

Epistemic adverbials express the speaker's expectation with regard to the truth of the sentential base. Typical representatives of this class are given in (19).

(19)   a.   ***Vielleicht*** *liebt sie mich.*
perhaps   loves she me
'Perhaps she loves me.'

  b. ***Wahrscheinlich*** *liebt sie mich.*
      probably   loves she me
      'She probably loves me.'
  c. ***Sicherlich*** *liebt sie mich.*
      certainly   loves she me
      'She certainly loves me.'

They can be paraphrased according to the pattern given in (20).

(20)   *Es ist vielleicht/wahrscheinlich/sicherlich wahr, dass sie mich*
       it is perhaps/probably/surely   true, that she me
       liebt.
       loves
       'It is perhaps/probably/surely true that she loves me.'

Epistemic adverbials are often discussed under the heading of modal adverbials, and a further distinction is then made between epistemic, alethic,
and deontic modals, in this form probably going back to the discussion in
Lyons (1977:791-832). The term 'alethic modal' is used when talking about
logically necessary or logically contingent circumstances. An example of
an alethic modal is *notwendigerweise* 'necessarily' in *Zwei und zwei sind
notwendigerweise vier* 'Two and two is necessarily four'. The term 'deontic
modal' is used in the context of permission and obligation, as in *Der Bundeskanzler wird notwendigerweise vom Bundestag gewählt* 'Necessarily, the
federal chancellor is elected by the federal parliament'. The term 'epistemic
modal' is used in circumstances where we talk of possibility and necessity as
deriving from things we know about the world, e.g. in *Wenn Licht an ist, ist
er möglicherweise schon da* 'If the light is on, he's possibly already at home'.

   As Bonami, Godard and Kampers-Manhe (2004) point out, only alethic
and deontic readings create opaque contexts for all positions, cf. the following
two examples (21) and (22).

(21)   a. *2 plus 2 ist **notwendigerweise** vier.*
           2 and 2 is necessarily   four
           'Necessarily, two and two makes four.'
       b. *Die Anzahl meiner Implantate   ist vier.*
           the number my.GEN implants.GEN is four
           'The number of my implants is four.'

c. $\not\rightarrow$

*Die Anzahl meiner   Implantate   ist **notwendigerweise***
the number my.GEN implants.GEN is necessarily

vier.
four

'Necessarily, the number of my implants is four.'

(22)   a.   *Der Bundeskanzler   wird **notwendigerweise** vom*
the federal.chancellor gets necessarily   by.the
Bundestag   gewählt.
federal.parliament elected
'Necessarily, the federal chancellor is elected by the federal parliament.'

b.   [A. Merkel= die Bundeskanzlerin 'the federal chancelloress']

c. $\not\rightarrow$

*Angela Merkel wird **notwendigerweise** vom*
Angela Merkel gets necessarily   by.the
Bundestag   gewählt.
federal.parliament elected
'Necessarily, Angela Merkel is elected by the federal parliament.'

On a reading as an epistemic modal, epistemic adverbials do not create opaque contexts, although they might lead to similar effects as discussed in connection with subject-oriented adverbials.

(23)   a.   *Wenn er um 12 Uhr   zu Hause war, hat er*
If   he at 12 o'clock at home was, has he
***notwendigerweise** Angela Merkel noch gesehen.*
necessarily   Angela Merkel still seen
'If he was at home at 12 a.m., he necessarily saw A. Merkel.'

b.   [A. Merkel= die Bundeskanzlerin 'the federal chancelloress']

c. $\rightarrow$

Wenn er um 12 Uhr   zu Hause war, hat er
If   he at 12 o'clock at home was, has he
***notwendigerweise** die Bundeskanzlerin   noch gesehen.*
necessarily   the federal.chancelloress still seen
'If he was at home at 12 a.m., he necessarily saw the federal chancelloress.'

Epistemic adverbials cannot be negated with the help of constituent negation, cf. (24).

(24)   * ***Nicht vielleicht/wahrscheinlich/sicherlich*** *liebt sie mich.*
         not   perhaps/probably/certainly   loves she me
         'Perhaps/probably/certainly she loves me.'

This is especially surprising for a word like *wahrscheinlich* 'probably' which can occur with constituent negation in other usages, e.g. *Eine schnelle Lösung ist nicht wahrscheinlich* 'A quick solution is not probable'. The adjective *wahrscheinlich* 'probable' also has the negative counterpart *unwahrscheinlich* 'improbable', which can likewise not be used, cf. (25a), again a restriction that seems very idiomatic, as the adjective can be used predicatively in copula sentences to make a comment on the proposition in the *dass* 'that'-clause, cf. (25b).

(25)   a.   * ***Unwahrscheinlich*** *liebt sie mich.*
              improbable   loves she me
       b.   *Es ist* **unwahrscheinlich**, *dass sie mich liebt.*
              it is improbable   that she me   loves
              'It is not probable that she loves me.'

Whether expistemic adverbials are veridical or not depends on their lexical meaning and their exact usage. The adverb *notwendigerweise* 'necessarily' in its alethic usage is veridical, all other epistemic adverbials are not veridical.

   While the adjectives and adverbs mentioned so far correspond to the usual suspects standardly classified as epistemic adverbials, other items can also be counted as possible members. Thus, Pittner (1999:112) in addition counts adjectives which relativize propositions to certain sources as epistemics, cf. e.g. (26).

(26)   ***Angeblich*** *hat er den Container mit einer Hand gefangen.*
         alleged   has he the container with one   hand caught
         'Allegedly he caught the container singlehandedly.'

3.3.   Evaluative adverbials

Evaluative adverbials express the opinion of the speaker with regard to the state of affairs expressed by the rest of the sentence, cf. (27).

(27)   *Erfreulicherweise/überraschenderweise hat Kord-Hinrich gute*
         happily/surprisingly   has Kord-Hinrich good
         Berater.
         aides
         'Happily/Surprisingly, Kord-Hinrich has good aides.'

In German, the word forms serving as evaluative adverbials are typically adverbs derived from adjectives through the addition of the suffix -*weise*. They share this behavior with subject-oriented adverbials, cf. the discussion in section 2.

Paraphrases for evaluative adverbials follow the pattern in (28), cf. (27) and its paraphrase in (29).

(28)   *Es ist ADJEKTIV,   dass SUBJEKT OBJECT VERB.*
         it is ADJECTIVE, that SUBJECT OBJECT VERB
         'It is ADJECTIVE, that SUBJECT VERB OBJECT.'

(29)   *Es ist erfreulich/überraschend, dass Kord-Hinrich gute Berater*
         It is happy/surprising   that K-H   good aides
         hat.
         has
         'It is a good thing/surprising that Kord-Hinrich has good aides.'

Just as is the case for the English translation of the paraphrase for *erfreulicherweise* 'fortunately' in (29), this paraphrase pattern is not available for all German evaluative adverbials either, e.g. *glücklicherweise* 'fortunately', where one has to resort to *Es war ein Glück dass ...* 'It was a fortunate thing that ...'.

Two further points need to be mentioned: Firstly, in contrast to subject-oriented adverbials, the judgment expressed via the evaluative adverbial does not attribute a property to the subject, but purely expresses the evaluation of the situation by the speaker. Secondly, as (30) illustrates, evaluatives sometimes come with negative counterparts.

(30)   *Glücklicherweise/unglücklicherweise ist Peter zurück in*
         Fortunately/unfortunately   is Peter back in
         Australien.
         Australia
         'Fortunately/unfortunately, Peter is back in Australia.'

Other such pairs are *erfreulicherweise/unerfreulicherweise* 'fortunately/
unfortunately', *geschickterweise/ungeschickterweise* 'cleverly/clumsily'.
However, this is not a general option, cf. e.g. *dummerweise/*undummerweise*
'foolishly/*unfoolishly', *überraschenderweise/*unüberraschenderweise*
'surprisingly/unsurprisingly'.
   Constituent modification is not possible, cf. (31).

(31)   **Nicht erfreulicherweise/nicht überraschenderweise* hat
      not fortunately/not surprisingly   has
      Kord-Hinrich gute Berater.
      Kord-Hinrich good aides
      Intended:
      'Unfortunately/unsurprisingly, Kord-Hinrich has good aides.'

In contrast to epistemic adverbials, evaluative adverbials are always veridical.
Consequently, they cannot occur in hypothetical contexts, cf. (32).

(32)   **Wenn Sabine Lehrerin   geblieben wäre, wäre sie heute*
      If   Sabine teacheress remained would, would she today
      glücklicherweise/erfreulicherweise unabhängiger.
      luckily/fortunately   more.independent
      *'If Sabine had remained a teacher, she would fortunately/luckily be
      more independent today.'

As Bellert (1977) comments, this is not surprising, since the hypothetical
if ... then ... construction expresses that the proposition expressed by the
main clause can only be true under the conditions given in the preceding but
counterfactual *if*-clause. This clashes with the veridicality of evaluatives.
   Evaluatives are also anomalous in questions, cf. (33).

(33)   **Hat Kord-Hinrich **überraschenderweise** gute Berater?*
      Has Kord-Hinrich surprisingly   good aides

Because of the last two features, work on English evaluative adverbials has
linked them to positive polarity items; cf. Nilsen (2004) and Ernst (2007,
2009).
   As far as opacity is concerned, the pattern displayed by evaluatives is
again best explained by taking recourse to context-sensitivity, as already argued in Bonami, Godard and Kampers-Manhe (2004).

(34)   a.   *Glücklicherweise kam Franz heil nach Hause. (↛b)*
           fortunately   got Franz safe to   home
           'Fortunately Franz made it home safe and sound.'

       b.   [Franz= der Spion 'the spy']

       c.   *Glücklicherweise kam der Spion heil nach Hause.*
           fortunately   got the spy   safe to   home
           'Fortunately the spy made it home safe and sound.'

Just as in the case of subject-oriented adverbials, it seems possible to hold the opinion that (34a) as well as (34c) are true, as long as (34b) is not known. However, again similarly to the situation in the case of subject-oriented adverbials, the two judgments are based on different background assumptions with regard to what is counted as a good thing: If I judge the fact that Franz made it home safe and sound to be a good thing because he is my husband and I need the money he earns in his jobs to finance my high society lifestyle, then the basis for my judgment is that it is in general a good thing if one's husband and financial support stays alive. If this is the basis for the judgment in (34c), I will hold the two sentences to be equally true. Only if I switch the basis for my evaluation will I possibly arrive at a different conclusion. E.g., I could revert to the position that all spies should die, and then, of course, it is not a good thing that Franz returned if he is a spy.

4. Domain adverbials

Domain adverbials restrict the domain in which the proposition expressed by the rest of the sentence is claimed to hold true; cf. Bartsch (1972:62-65), Bartsch (1987),[21] Bellert (1977), and Ernst (2004).

(35)   a.   *Gefühlsmäßig ist Peter kalt.*
           emotionally   he is   cold
           'Emotionally, he is cold.'

       b.   *Wirtschaftlich ist Fritz ein As, aber in sozialer Hinsicht*
           economically is Fritz an ace, but in social   respect
           rücksichtslos.
           ruthless
           'Economically, he is extremely good, but socially, he is ruthless.'

       c.   *Zeitlich paßt es mir nicht.*
           timewise fits it me not
           'It does not fit my schedule.'

Thus, (35a) says that the proposition expressed by the sentential base of *Gefühlsmäßig ist er kalt* is judged to be true when the judgment is restricted to the domain of emotions. Nothing is said about other domains against which coldness could be evaluated, e.g. Peter's body temperature. A simple paraphrase test for these usages consists of the addition of past participles like *gesehen/betrachtet* 'viewed/considered', cf. (36) for (35a).

(36)   ***Gefühlsmäßig** betrachtet ist Peter kalt.*
        emotionally   viewed   is Peter cold
        'As far as emotions are concerned, Peter is cold.'

Domain adverbials do on first sight not appear to be veridical, cf. the pattern in (37).

(37)   a.   ***Deixismäßig** ist dieser Satz   faszinierend.*
              deixis-wise is this   sentence intriguing
              'Deixis-wise, this sentence is intriguing.'
        b.   ↛

              Dieser Satz   ist faszinierend.
              This   sentence is intriguing
              'This sentence is intriguing.'

However, what we witness here is once again best explained as a contextual effect, and the entailment failure in (37) is of a different nature than the entailment failure exemplified by most epistemic adverbials. What happens here is best explained along the following lines: When dropping the domain adverbial, the sentence will still be evaluated from a certain viewpoint. In most cases, this means that the domain will be restricted to some default or contextually salient value. Judging sentences as intriguing from the viewpoint of deixis is, unfortunately, a rather specific restriction of the domain of evaluation, making the non-entailment pattern in (37) intuitively plausible. This situation is another remainder of the importance of context-sensitivity when dealing with modifiers, which already played a crucial role in the discussion of subsective adjectives in section 3.2 in chapter 1, as well as for the behavior of subject-oriented adverbials and some of the speaker-oriented adverbials, the epistemic modals and the evaluative adverbials, discussed in this chapter.

Adjectives often serve as domain adverbials, especially if they are derived from nouns which in turn stand for a specific domain, cf. e.g. (38).

(38)   a.   ***Linguistisch** ist die Software eine Katastrophe.*
            linguistic   is the software a   catastrophe
            'Linguistically, this software is a catastrophe.'
       b.   ***Medizinisch** ist er schon   lange tot.*
            medical   is he already long dead
            'From a medical viewpoint, he has already been dead for quite
            a while.'

Weise-adverbs cannot serve as domain adverbials. According to Pittner
(1999:118), domain adverbials are best analyzed as shortened condi-
tional/participial phrases, cf. (39), the full version of (38a).

(39)   *Wenn man es gefühlmäßig sieht/Gefühlsmäßig betrachtet ist er kalt.*
       If   one it emotionally views/Emotionally seen   is he cold
       'Emotionally, he is cold'

Almost any adjective that can be used as a domain adverbial can also be used
as a method-oriented adverbial, cf. section 4 in chapter 3.

5.   Semantic constraints on possible sentence adverbials

Bartsch (1972:149), in discussing *schnell, langsam, laut* 'fast, slow, loud' and
leise 'quiet' as examples of a single subclass of manner adverbials, remarks
that these words cannot be used to make statements on facts and, as a consequence, are unable to occur in constructions like *It is ADJ, that* .... That
is, these words cannot be used as sentence adverbials. In a similar vein, Ernst
(1984:94-95) notes that some English *-ly* adverbs only occur as verb-related
adverbials (in his terminology, with VP-readings), cf. (40), his (309).

(40)   a.   Several of the mourners were singing **quietly**.
       b.   The goons in the post office handled my package **roughly**.
       c.   The frammis must be held **tightly** in your left hand.
       d.   His bald pate shone **brilliantly** in the noonday sun.

Ernst (1984:94) refers to these adverbs as "'pure' Manner adverbs" (slightly
differing from my usage of the term 'pure manner adverbial', cf. section 2.2
in chapter 3) and offers the following explanation for the absence of usages as
sentence adverbials: All these adjectives refer to perceptible properties. Such
perceptible properties are exactly what facts and propositions do not have,
so that the adjectives simply cannot apply to them. As a consequence of this
feature, these adjectives cannot be used as a base to form *weise*-adverbs.

6. Conclusion

This chapter discussed the most important properties and subclasses of sentence adverbials. In section two, I discussed subject-oriented adverbials, which assign a property to the agent of a sentence based on the evaluation of the speaker of the actions of the agent. They are only seldom realized by adjectives. Instead, adverbs derived from adjectives with the help of the suffix *-weise* are used. Section three discussed speaker-oriented adverbials, which fall into the three subgroups of speech-act, epistemic, and evaluative adverbials. Again, adjectives are rarely used here, but at least for the subgroup of evaluatives, adjective-based *weise*-adverbs are common. Subsection four discussed domain adverbials. Most adjectives that can be used as method-oriented adverbials can also be used as frame adverbials. The fifth section commented on a specific combinatorial restriction: adjectives describing perceivable properties cannot serve as sentence adverbials or as base for corresponding *weise*-adverbs.

Table 1 gives an overview of the usages discussed in this chapter.

Table 1. Adverbial adjectives used as sentence adverbials

type of sentence adverbial		example sentence and free English translation
subject-oriented		*Taktvoll hat Peter die Tür geschlossen.* 'Tactfully, Peter closed the door.'
speaker-oriented	*speech-act*	*Kurz, Peter konnte sie nicht überzeugen.* 'Briefly put, Peter coudn't convince her.'
	epis-temic	*Sicherlich liebt sie mich.* 'Surely she loves me.'
	eval-uative	*Dummerweise liebt sie mich.* 'Unfortunately she loves me.'
domain		*Wirtschaftlich liegt Deutschland am Boden.* 'Economically, Germany has hit rock bottom.'

Chapter 3
The readings of verb-related adverbials

1. Introduction

German adverbial adjectives are prototypically used as verb-related adverbials. In contrast with sentence adverbials, they only appear in the adjectival short form, morphological derivations with -*weise* cannot be used. As verb-related adverbials, adjectives show a dazzling variety of usages. Thus, all the adverbials in (1) are verb-related:

(1)   a.   *Sie hat **laut** gesungen.*
                she has loud sung
                'She sang loudly.'

        b.   *Er löste die Aufgabe **intelligent**.*
                he solved the problem intelligent
                'He solved the problem intelligently.'

        c.   *Dieses Problem ist nur **wirtschaftlich** zu lösen.*
                this   problem is only economical   to solve
                'This problem can only be solved economically.'

        d.   *Uta liebt ihn **unheimlich**.*
                Uta loves him uncanny
                'Uta loves him unbelievably.'

The four adverbials have three things in common: they can be elicited with *Wie?* 'How?', they are all veridical, and they do not create opaque contexts. In spite of these commonalities, they have very different semantics: *Laut* 'loudly' in (1a) specifies the sound volume of the singing. *Intelligent* 'intelligently' in (1b) can either be taken to specify the way in which a solution was achieved, e.g. by a series of intelligent steps, or it characterizes the solution arrived at. *Wirtschaftlich* 'economically' in (1c) specifies the means or the methods that need to be employed to arrive at a solution, whereas *unheimlich* 'uncannily' specifies the degree of Uta's love.

    In addition to these adverbial usages, adjectives can also be used as depictives or as resultatives, leading at times to sentences that are either ambiguous or perhaps vague, cf. e.g. (2).

(2)   a.   *Julia ging   **traurig** durch   die Stadt.*
              Julia walked sad   through the town
              'Julia walked sad/sadly through the town.'
       b.   *Bolli schmückte den Weihnachtsbaum **elegant**.*
              Bolli decorated the Christmas.tree   elegant
              'Bolli decorated the Christmas tree elegant/elegantly.'

Thus, (2a) can mean that Julia was sad when she walked through the town, or that the way she walked looked like she was sad, and it could also be the case that both readings are true of the same situation. (2b) is standardly interpreted as expressing that the Christmas tree is elegantly decorated as a result of Bolli's actions, but could also be interpreted as characterizing Bolli's manner, e.g. his moves in decorating the Christmas tree, as elegant.

Before proceeding to a detailed differentiation of all these usages, it is helpful to first present the general conceptualization behind the relationship between the meaning contribution of the different adjectives and that of the verb. Leaving the formal implementation for chapter 7, I assume that the verb introduces an event variable, standing for some event. The term *event* is here used in a wide sense, corresponding to the term eventuality as introduced in Bach (1986). That is, an event is the cover term for states as well as non-states, e.g. processes, accomplishments, and achievements. The usages of adjectives interact with or contribute to a specification of this eventuality in different ways, and the eventuality itself might yield itself for these kind of interactions in different ways. Thinking about the relations to the eventuality provides a straightforward dividing line between verb-related adverbials and secondary predicates. Secondary predicates provide predications over participants of the eventuality, cf. e.g. the stock examples in (3), where in (3a) nudeness is predicated of the subject Uta, and in (3b), rawness of the object meat, respectively.

(3)   a.   *Uta sitzt **nackt** in der Badewanne.*
              Uta sits naked in the bathtub
              'Uta is sitting naked in the bathtub.'
       b.   *Roland isst Fleisch **roh**.*
              Roland eats meat   raw
              'Roland eats meat raw.'

If they do not target the participants of an event, what then is the target of verb-related adverbials? I propose that they target specific aspects within the conceptual structure of the events in question (this idea is largely based on

Geuder 2006, cf. the discussion in section 6 of this chapter and the discussion in chapter 7). The idea becomes clearer when we apply it to the four introductory examples in (1).

Thus, the sentence (1a) describes a singing event. The conceptual structure of this event can be described in considerable detail, and one of these details consists in the fact that singing involves the emission of sounds, and that sounds come with a certain sound volume. The adverbial *laut* 'loudly' specifies this sound volume, that is, it specifies a specific aspect, a specific conceptual coordinate of the complex cognitive structure that represents a singing event. Similarly, the event of problem solving described in (1b) comes with a complex internal structure, and the adverbial *intelligent* 'intelligently' can target different conceptual coordinates within this structure. Depending on the target chosen, e.g. either the solution produced, or the path chosen to arrive at that solution, different readings result. Sentence (1c) describes the solving of a problem, and problem-solving typically involves a specific method or technique. *Wirtschaftlich* 'economically' indicates the domain that this method or technique is drawn from. And, finally, in (1d), the adjective *unheimlich* 'unbelievably' targets the intensity dimension inherent to the predicate. While I will refer to conceptual dimensions and events in this chapter in the description of the different readings, I will discuss these concepts in more detail in chapter 7, also providing an overview of the idea in the recent literature.

This chapter starts with the discussion of manner adverbials, followed by a section on degree adverbials, and a section on method-oriented adverbials. Section 5 focuses on secondary predicates and the differences between verb-related adverbials and secondary predication. Section 6 investigates the nature of verb-adverbial combinatorics. The relationship between verb-related adverbials and negation is discussed in section 7.

2. Manner adverbials

2.1. Introduction

The term 'manner adverbials' or its German translation equivalent, *Adverbiale der Art und Weise*, is used for a rather heterogeneous group of adverbials, cf. (4), where all the bold-faced words serve as manner adverbials.

(4) a. *Peter hat **laut/leise/schnell/langsam**   gesungen.*
         Peter has loudly/quietly/quickly/slowly sung
         'Peter sang loudly/low/quickly/slowly.'

    b.   *Peter hat **elegant/hölzern/wunderbar** vorgetragen.*
        Peter has elegant/wooden/wonderful   presented.
        'Peger presented [his talk] elegantly/woodenly/wonderfully.'
    c.   *Peter hat sich   **intelligent/geschickt** verteidigt.*
        Peter has himself intelligently/skillfully defended
        'Peter defended himself intelligently/skillfully.'

One feature that all these adverbials have in common is that they all can be questioned with the help of a *Wie?* 'How?'-question, cf. e.g. the question-answer pair in (5) for (4b).

(5)   a.   *Wie hat Peter vorgetragen?*
        how has Peter presented
        'How did Peter's presentation go?'
    b.   ***Elegant/Hölzern/Wunderbar.***
        elegant/wooden/wonderful
        'Elegantly/Woodenly/Beautifully.'

However, as mentioned in section 1, this question typically works for all verb-related adverbials, and can also be used for other types of adverbials, e.g. for instrumentals, cf. (6), or for secondary predicates, cf. (7).

(6)   a.   *Wie hat Fritz die Räuber aufgehalten?*
        how has Fritz the robbers held.back
        'How did Fritz hold back the robbers?'
    b.   ***Mit einem Trick.***
        with a   trick
        'With a trick.'
(7)   a.   *Wie hast du den Fisch gegessen?*
        how has you the fish   eaten
        'How did you eat your fish'
    b.   ***Roh.***
        raw
        'Raw.'

Paraphrase tests do a better job in singling out the class of adverbials in (4), the most reliable one, the *Wie-das-ist*-paraphrase, is given in (8), corresponding to [*s*] in Bartsch (1972:150).

(8)   *Wie-das-ist*-paraphrase:

        Wie SUBJECT VERB, das ist ADJ.
        how SUBJECT VERB that is ADJ
        'The way SUBJECT VERB is ADJ.'

The application of this paraphrase is illustrated in examples (9) through (11), modeled after (10), an example from Bartsch (1972:150). In all cases, the b-sentences give the paraphrases for the a-sentences.

(9)   a.   *Petra singt **laut**.*
           Petra sings loud
           'Petra sings loudly.'
     b.   *Wie Petra singt, das ist laut. ($\approx$ a)*
           how Petra sings, that is loud
           'The way Petra sings is loud.'

(10) a.   *Petra tanzt **wunderbar**.*
           Petra dances wonderful
           'Petra dances wonderfully.'
     b.   *Wie Petra tanzt, das ist wunderbar. ($\approx$ a)*
           how Petra dances, that is wonderful
           'The way Petra dances is wonderful.'

(11) a.   *Petra tanzt **elegant**.*
           Petra dances elegant
           'Petra dances elegantly.'
     b.   *Wie Petra tanzt, das ist elegant. ($\approx$ a)*
           how Petra dances, that is elegant
           'The way Petra dances is elegant.'

(12) a.   *Peter verteidigt sich   **intelligent**.*
           Peter defends   himself intelligent
           'Peter defends himself intelligently.'
     b.   *Wie Peter sich   verteidigt, das ist intelligent. ($\approx$ a)*
           how Peter himself defends,   that is intelligent
           'The way Peter defends himself is intelligent.'

This paraphrase does not work for instrumentals, because they cannot appear in predicative position, and it does not work for the adjectives serving as secondary predicates, which can principally occur in predicative position, but do not attribute the property they express to the correct referent anymore.

Incidentally, another paraphrase test that seems rather trivial does in fact lead to an interesting conceptual distinction: the paraphrase with the help of the prepositional phrase *auf ADJEKTIV Art und Weise* 'in an ADJECTIVE manner', the *In-ADJ-manner*-paraphrase, following the pattern in (13).

(13)   *In-ADJ-manner*-paraphrase:

> *SUBJEKT VERB* auf *ADJ* Art und Weise
> SUBJECT VERB on ADJ manner
> 'SUBJECT VERB in ADJ manner.' [22]

The successful usage of (13) is illustrated in (14) and (15), where the b-sentences give good paraphrases of the a-sentences.

(14)   a.   *Petra tanzt* **wunderbar**.
              Petra dances wonderful
              'Petra dances wonderfully.'

        b.   *Petra tanzt   auf wunderbare Art und Weise.*
              Petra dances on wonderful   manner
              'Petra dances in a wonderful manner.'

(15)   a.   *Franz hat den Text* **oberflächlich** *gelesen.*
              Franz has the text cursory   read
              'Franz read the text cursorily.'

        b.   *Franz hat den Text auf oberflächliche Art und Weise gelesen.*
              Franz has the text on superficial   manner   read
              'Franz read the text in a cursory manner.'

In contrast, this paraphrase does not yield good results for some adverbial adjectives that are usually seen as core instances of manner modification, e.g. *laut/leise* 'loudly/quietly' and *schnell/langsam* 'quickly/slowly'. This can be seen via a direct comparison of the *Wie-das-ist*-paraphrase and the *In-ADJ-manner*-paraphrase for sentences containing theses adverbials, cf. (16) for *laut/leise* 'loudly/quietly' and (17) for *schnell/langsam* 'quickly/slowly'.

(16)   a.   *Ephraim hat das Lied* **laut/leise** *gesungen.*
              Ephraim has the song loud/quiet sung
              'Ephraim sang the song loudly/quietly.'

        b.   *?Ephraim hat das Lied auf laute/leise Art und Weise gesungen.*
              Ephraim has the song on loud/quiet manner   sung
              'Ephraim sang the song in a loud/quiet manner.'

c.   *Wie Ephraim das Lied gesungen hat, das war laut/leise.*
     how Ephraim the song sung   has, that was loud/quiet
     'The way in which Ephraim sang the song was loud/quiet.'

(17)   a.   *Kord ist **schnell/langsam** gelaufen.*
            Kord is quick/slow   ran
            'Kord ran quickly/slowly.'

       b.   ?*Kord ist auf schnelle Art und Weise gelaufen.*
            Kord is on quick   manner   ran
            'Kord ran in a quick manner.'

       c.   *Wie Kord gelaufen ist, das war schnell/langsam.*
            how Kord run   is, that was quick/slow
            'The way in which Kord ran was quick/slow.'

As the comparison between examples (16b) and (16c) and (17b) and (17c) shows, both *laut/leise* 'loudly/quietly' and *schnell/langsam* 'quickly/slowly' sound strange with the *in-ADJ-manner*-paraphrase, while the *Wie-das-ist*-paraphrase is unproblematic. An attractive explanation for this lies in the one-dimensionality of these adjectives: *laut/leise* 'loud/quiet' specify only the sound volume, *schnell/langsam* 'fast/slow' specify only the speed, whereas the usage of adjectives such as *wunderbar* 'wonderful' involves a more complex interaction with the conceptual structure associated with the event. The difference becomes apparent when we again consider the simplified conceptual structures introduced above: If someone dances wonderfully, it is not a single aspect or a single dimension of the dancing which is specified as *wunderbar* 'wonderful'. Instead, we express that the manner of dancing as a whole is *wunderbar* 'wonderful', while what exactly is responsible for this effect is left open but typically results from the interplay of several parameters or dimensions of the dancing, e.g. the movements and facial expressions of the dancers, or the alignment of the dancing moves to the rhythm etc. A similar point can be made with regard to *oberflächlich lesen* 'read cursorily' in (15): there are many possibilities to read a text in such a way that one only gets a superficial impression of its contents, the exact specification of these possibilities is left open. This effect-character of multidimensional manner modification is also noted by Bartsch (1972:149) in discussing her Mod_1-subclass: "These manner specifications are not provided by a direct description of the manner of a process or of an action, but rather by an indirect characterization of the consequences arising from the manner in which the process or action is performed" Bartsch (1976:152). As Bartsch points out, these consequence can also be expressed with the help of constructions involving the manner-adverbial proform *so* and a consecutive clause, cf. her example in (18).

(18)   a.   *Er arbeitet **erfreulich**.*
            he works   pleasing
            'He works to the pleasure (of all of us).'
       b.   *Er arbeitet so, dass man sich   freut.*
            he works   so, that   one   oneself enjoys
            'He works in a way (such) that one is happy.'

Whether this one-dimensionality is a good reason to put words such as *schnell* 'fast' or *langsam* 'slowly' in a special class of adverbials, as hinted at in Dik (1975), will be left open here. I will come back to this point in the formalization in chapter 7.

Besides the distinction between adverbials targeting only one specific dimension and adverbials targeting multiple but unspecific dimensions, a further distinction can be made between adverbials that stand in a special relation to the agent of the sentence, and those that do not, cf. e.g. (19a) vs. (19b).

(19)   a.   *Peter hat **laut/leise/schnell/langsam/wunderbar/greulich***
            Peter has loud/quiet/wonderful/dreadful
            gesungen.
            sung
            'Peter sang loudly/low/wonderfully/dreadfully.'
       b.   *Peter hat sich   **intelligent/geschickt** verteidigt.*
            Peter has himself intelligent/skillful   defended
            'Peter defended himself intelligently/skillfully.'

In the following, I refer to the adverbials in (19b) as pure manner adverbials, and to those in (19a) as agent-oriented manner adverbials. I will discuss the two groups separately in sections 2.2 and 2.3, respectively.

2.2.   Pure manner adverbials

The term 'pure manner adverbial' is used to indicate that the semantic contribution of this adverbial type to the sentence meaning is restricted to the specification of the manner in which the action referred to by the verbal predicate is carried out.[23] Some examples of pure manner adverbials are given in (20).

(20)   a.   *Klaus singt **laut/leise/schnell/langsam**.*
            Klaus sings loud/quiet/quick/slow
            'Klaus sings loudly/quietly/quickly/slowly.'
       b.   *Klaus tanzt   **wunderbar/hölzern/elegant**.*
            Klaus dances beautiful/wooden/elegant
            'Klaus dances beautifully/woodenly/elegantly.'

The one-dimensional manner adverbials in (20a) are clear instances of pure manner adverbials, since they exclusively refer to a parameter internal to the event concept expressed by the verb.

On the other hand, adjectives like those in (20b), which were argued not to be one-dimensional above, are nevertheless also pure manner adverbials, because they target the manner by itself and do not make any reference to other participants of the event.

Note that for most adjectives discussed as one-dimensional there seem to exist other adjectives from the same word field that differ from these in exactly this respect. That is, besides sound or speed, they specify some other dimensions or aspects of the event, resulting in a more complex modification, cf. the usage of *lautstark* and *lauthals* instead of *laut* 'loudly' in (21a) and of *flink* and *hurtig* instead of *schnell* 'quickly' in (21b).

(21)   a.   *Klaus singt **lautstark/lauthals**.*
            Klaus sings at.the.top.of.his.voice/vociferously
            'Klaus sings at the top of his voice/vociferously.'
       b.   *Klaus klettert **flink/hurtig**.*
            Klaus climbs swift/lightfooted
            'Klaus climbs swiftly/lightfooted.'

A further difference between these adjectives and *laut* 'loudly', *leise* 'quietly', *schnell* 'quickly', *langsam* 'slowly' is that the latter can specify the sound volume of all eventualities, whereas *lautstark* 'at the top of one's voice' *lauthals* 'vociferously' *flink* 'swift' *hurtig* 'lightfooted' are much more restricted. For example, all four seem to require an animate agent, cf. the contrast between (22) and (23).

(22)   a.   *Der Stein rollt   **laut/leise**   den Berg runter.*
            the stone rolled loud/quiet the hill   down
            'The stone rolled down the hill loudly/quietly.'

b. *Der Stein rollt **schnell/langsam** den Berg runter.*
    the stone rolled quick/slow   the hill   down
    'The stone rolled down the hill quickly/slowly.'

(23) a. **Der Stein rollt **lautstark/lauthals**   den Berg*
          the stone rolled at.the.top.of.his.voice/vociferously the hill
          runter.
          down

      b. **Der Stein rollt **flink/hurtig**   den Berg runter.*
          the stone rolled swift/lightfooted the hill   down

However, this animacy requirement is not a general requirement for multi-dimensional manner adverbials, cf. the two corpus-examples in (24).[24]

(24) a. *Die Flügeltüren   im   Porsche schwingen **elegant** nach*
          The gull-wing.doors in.the Porsche swing   elegant to
          vorn,   und gewähren Einblick ins   Cockpit.
          the.front, and allow   a.view   into.the cockpit
          'The gull-wing doors in the Porsche swing elegantly to the front
          and allow a view of the cockpit.'

      b. *Wir sehen ja, daß die Marktwirtschaft im   Kapitalismus*
          We see   yes, that the market.economy in.the capitalism
          ***wunderbar** funktioniert.*
          beautiful   functions
          'It is clear to see that the market economy functions beautifully
          inside capitalism.'

In (24a), the gull-wing doors are neither animate, nor do they need to be reinterpreted as personified entities, the sentence is fine as it is, with *elegant* 'elegantly' specifying the manner of the doors' movement. Similarly, the market economy in (24) is inanimate, but *wunderbar* 'wonderfully' can be used.

2.3.   Agent-oriented manner adverbials

All the boldfaced words in (25) serve as agent-oriented manner adverbials. They express that an action is executed in a way one would expect of someone who is ADJ. That is, *to solve a problem intelligently* means to solve a problem in a way an intelligent person would solve this problem.

(25) a. *Petra löst   das Problem **intelligent/geschickt**.*
          Petra solves the problem intelligent/skillful
          'Petra solves the problem intelligently/skillfully.'

b.   *Sebastian hat Arnd **fies/gemein** getreten.*
    Sebastian has Arnd nasty/mean kicked
    'Sebastian kicked Arnd nastily/meanly.'

Agent-oriented manner adverbials show all the characteristics of manner adverbials discussed in section 2. They differ from pure manner adverbials in that the highest ranked argument of sentences containing agent-oriented manner adverbials must always have control over the action denoted by the verbal predicate, cf. (26).

(26)   a.   *Der Stein rollte **laut/leise/schnell/langsam**   den Abhang*
            The stone rolled loudly/quietly/quickly/slowly the hill
            runter.
            down
            'The stone rolled loudly/quietly/quickly/slowly down the hill.'
      b.   **Der Stein rollte **intelligent/geschickt**   den Abhang runter.*
            The stone rolled intelligently/skillfully the hill   down
            'The stone rolled intelligently/skillfully down the hill.'

Agent-oriented manner adverbials allow the addition of an agentive *von*-phrase to the basic pattern of the *Wie-das-ist*-paraphrase introduced in section 2.1, cf. the pattern in (27) and the paraphrases for sentences (28) and (29), contrasting with the examples (30) and (31), where this paraphrase does not work (cf. Bartsch 1972:150-153 for this pattern).

(27)   *Es ist ADJ von X, wie X etwas   tut.*
      It is ADJ of X, how X something does
      'It is ADJ of X, how X does something.'

(28)   a.   *Peter verkaufte seine Bücher **klug**.*
            Peter sold   his   books prudent
            'Peter sold his books prudently.'
      b.   *Es war klug   von Peter, wie er seine Bücher verkaufte. (≈a)*
            it was prudent of Peter, how he his   books sold
            'It was prudent of Peter, how he sold his books.'

(29)   a.   *Peter löste   das Problem **geschickt**.*
            Peter solved the problem skillful
            'Peter solved the problem skillfully.'

b. *Es war geschickt von Peter, wie er das Problem löste. (≈ a)*
    It was skillfull   of   Peter, how he the problem solved
    'It was prudent of Peter, how he solved the problem.'

(30)   a. *Petra tanzt **wunderbar**.*
           Petra dances wonderful
           'Petra dances wonderfully.'

       b. *?Es ist wunderbar von Petra, wie sie tanzt. (≉a)*
           it is wonderful of   Petra, how she dances
           'It is wonderful of Petra, how she dances.'

(31)   a. *Der Reifen knallt **laut**.*
           The tire   bangs loud
           'The tire bangs loudly.'

       b. *?Es ist laut von dem Reifen, wie er knallt. (≉a)*
           It is loud of   the   tire,   how he bangs
           'It is loud of the tire how it bangs.'

The fact that this paraphrase cannot be used for (31) does not depend on
whether or not the subject can act volitionally, cf. (32).

(32)   a. *Petra singt **laut**.*
           Petra sings loud
           'Petra sings loudly.'

       b. *?Es ist laut von Petra, wie sie singt. (≉a)*
           it is loud of   Petra how she sings
           'It is loud of Petra, how she sings.'

Although *laut* 'loudly' is used here in combination with a volitional subject,
the paraphrase remains inappropriate.

This paraphrase also allows the distinction between agent-oriented adverbials and those pure manner adverbials which require control/animate agents,
as discussed in the previous section, cf. the examples in (33).

(33)   a. **Es war lauthals   von Peter, wie er schrie.*
           it was vociferous of   Peter, how he screamed

       b. **Es war flink von Peter, wie er lief.*
           it was swift of   Peter, how he ran

The conceptual differences between these adverbials and agent-oriented adverbials is that when interpreting *elegant* and *wunderbar* as pure manner adverbials one does so without recourse to the properties of the agent. That is, an action is specified as being *elegant* or *wunderbar*, because we judge aspects of the action itself as elegant or wonderful, not because it is executed in a way that we would expect of someone who is elegant or wonderful.

The agent-orientedness of these adverbials is also responsible for the different behavior in the corresponding predicative uses of the adjective in combination with an event-nominalization as the subject, cf. the patterns in (34) and (35) in contrast to (36), taken from Bartsch (1972:151-153).

(34)   *Der Fluss fließt **träge**.* *(→a, b)*
    the river flows sluggish
    'The river flows sluggishly.'

    a.   *Das Fließen des Flusses ist träge.*
        the flowing of the river is sluggish
        'The flow of the river is sluggish.'

    b.   *Das Fließen ist träge.*
        the flowing is sluggish
        'The flow is sluggish.'

(35)   *Petra tanzt **schön**.* *(→a, b)*
    Petra dances beautiful
    'Petra dances beautifully.'

    a.   *Petras Tanzen ist schön.*
        Petra's dancing is beautiful
        'Petra's dancing is beautiful.'

    b.   *Das Tanzen ist schön.*
        the dancing is beautiful
        'The dancing is beautiful.'

(36)   *Peter schreibt **sorgfältig**.* *(→a, ↛ b)*
    Peter is.writing careful
    'Peter is writing carefully.'

    a.   *Peters Schreiben ist sorgfältig.*
        Peter's writing   is careful
        'Peter's writing is careful.'

    b. ??*Das Schreiben ist sorgfältig.*
        the writing   is careful
        'The writing is careful.'

As the contrast between (36) and the preceding examples shows, in uses where the adjective serves as the predicative adjective in a copula construction and is predicating over the referent of an event-nominalization, the agent needs to be explicitly expressed in the subject noun phrase when the predication semantically resembles agent-oriented manner modification.

2.4.   Further orientations

In addition to the two subgroups introduced in the previous two sections, Platt and Platt (1972) introduce another subgroup, namely experiencer-oriented manner adverbials, cf. the two examples in (37), their (31) and (41), where in (37a) the experiencer is the direct object, in (37b) the experiencer is the subject referent Joe.

(37)   a.   Joe kissed Aggie **thrillingly**.
       b.   Joe got up **painfully**.

Whereas the German translation equivalent to (37b) uses a prepositional phrase for the adverbial, cf. (38), the translation equivalent to (37a) employs an adjective, cf. (39).

(38)   *Joe stand **unter Schmerzen** auf.*
       Joe stand under pain   up
       'Joe got up under pain.'

(39)   *Joe hat ihn **aufregend** geküßt.*
       Joe has him stimulating kissed
       'Joe kissed him stimulatingly.'

Unsurprisingly, these usages allow yet another variant of the *Wie-das-ist*-paraphrase, establishing the link to the experiencer, cf. (40).

(40)   *Es war aufregend für sie, wie Fritz sie geküsst hat.*
       it was exciting   for her, how Fritz her kissed   has
       'It was exciting for her, how Fritz kissed her.'

In German, experiencer-orientation typically occurs with participle-based adjectives in the first state, cf. (41).[25]

(41)   a.   *Peter hat uns **anregend/stimulierend** unterhalten.*
            Peter has us inspiring/stimulating   entertained
            'Peter entertained us inspiringly/stimulatingly.'

b. *Die Leipziger   haben heute*
the people.from.Leipzig have   today
***enttäuschend/faszinierend** gespielt.*
disappointing/fascinating   played
'Leipzig played disappointingly/fascinatingly today.'

c. *Er hat **beleidigend** mit   dem Mädchen gesprochen.*
he has insulting   with the   girl   talked
'He talked insultingly to the girl.'

In all these cases, the experiencer is not the subject-referent, but adjectives are not restricted to non-subject experiencers, cf. (42).

(42)   *Fritz mußte **schmerzhaft** feststellen, dass ein Marathon kein*
Fritz had.to painful   realize,   that a   marathon no
Kindergeburtstag ist.
children's.party   is
'Fritz painfully had to realize that a marathon is not a children's birthday party.'

Another point shown by (42) is that, as so often with adverbials, we have some rather idiomatic usages, e.g., the expression *schmerzhaft feststellen* 'painfully realize' is possible, although the German *schmerzhaft* cannot be used for its English translation equivalent *painfully* in (37b), where instead the prepositional phrase *unter Schmerzen* 'under pain' was used.

3.   Degree adverbials

Following Bolinger (1972:160-165), degree adverbials can be differentiated with respect to inherent or extensible modification, cf. (43).

(43)   a.   *Peter schwitzt **sehr**.* [inherent modification]
Peter sweats   very
'Peter sweats very much.'

b.   *Peter schwitzt **viel**.* [extensible modification]
Peter sweats   much
'Peter sweats a lot.'

Sehr 'very' in (43a) specifies the intensity of the sweating, whereas *viel* 'much' in (43b) specifies the extent of sweating, that is, the amount of Peter's sweating is specified. In the following, I will concentrate on inherent modification, as this represents the prototypical case of degree modification.

In German, the lexeme *sehr* 'very' is the universal modifier for inherent degree modification. It can modify adjectives, adverbs, or verbs, cf. (44).

(44)   a.   *der **sehr** große Erfolg*
               the very big   success
               'the very big success'
        b.   *Uta ist **sehr** schnell gelaufen.*
               Uta is very fast   run
               'Uta ran very fast.'
        c.   *Uta hat ihn **sehr** vermisst.*
               Uta has him very missed
               'Uta missed him very much.'

Besides *sehr* 'very', usually classified as adverb or particle, adjectives can also occur in these three usages, cf. (45).

(45)   a.   *der **fürchterlich/unglaublich/unbeschreiblich** große Erfolg*
               the terrible/unbelievable/indescribable   huge success
               'the terribly/unbelievably/indescribably huge success'
        b.   *Uta ist **fürchterlich/unglaublich/unbeschreiblich** schnell*
               Uta is terrible/unbelievable/indescribable   fast
               gelaufen.
               run
               'Uta ran terribly/unbelievably/indescribably fast.'
        c.   *Uta hat ihn **fürchterlich/unglaublich/unbeschreiblich***
               Uta has him terrible/unbelievable/indescribable
               vermisst.
               missed
               'Uta missed him terribly/unbelievably/indescribably.'

How can we distinguish between adjectives used as degree adverbials and adjectives used as manner adverbials? As mentioned in section 1, degree adverbials can also be questioned with *Wie?* 'How?'. Even some of the paraphrases for manner adverbials can be used for degree adverbials. Thus, the *Wie-das-ist*-paraphrase introduced in section 2.1 can in most cases be used, cf. (46).

(46)   a.   *Peter liebt sie **unglaublich**.*
               Peter loves her unbelievable
               'Peter loves her unbelievably'

b. *Wie Peter sie liebt, das ist unglaublich. (≈ a)*
how Peter she loves, that is unbelievable
'How Peter loves her, that is unbelievable.'

Trivially, the *in a manner*-paraphrase cannot be used, cf. (47). (47b) is a fully grammatical and understandable sentence, but it does not express a degree meaning anymore. With respect to this paraphrase, degree adverbials thus pattern with one-dimensional manner adverbials.

(47) a. *Peter liebt sie **unglaublich**.*
Peter loves her unbelievable
'Peter loves her unbelievably.'
b. Peter liebt sie auf unglaubliche Art und Weise. (≉ b)
Peter loves her on unbelievable manner
'Peter loves her in an unbelievable manner.'

The similar behavior of degree adverbials and one-dimensional manner adverbials is not surprising if we again consider the underlying conceptual structures. Thus, degree expressions are one-dimensional in the same sense, that is, they target a single conceptual dimension, in the cases discussed so far, the intensity dimension.

Two further questions that arise when comparing adjectives used as degree adverbials to adjectives used as manner adverbials are the following: First, what are the contexts that allow degree modification and which adjectives can be used in degree modification? Second, are there ambiguities where one and the same adjective-verb combination can give rise to either a manner or a degree reading? These two questions will be addressed in the following two sections.

3.1. Contexts and constraints for degree modification

Degree adverbials are not restricted to state verbs like *lieben* 'love', but can be combined with all four Vendlerian verb classes (cf. Löbner and Stamm 2005 for this observation). In (48), *unglaublich* 'unbelievable' occurs as a degree modifier in connection with a state, cf. (48a), an activity, cf. (48b), an achievement, (48c), and an accomplishment, (48d).

(48) a. *Sie ähneln sich **unglaublich**.*
They resemble each.other unbelievable
'They resemble each other unbelievably.'

    b.   *Wir haben **unglaublich** gelacht, gestern   Abend in der*
        we have   unbelievable laughed, yesterday evening in the
        Kneipe.
        bar
        'Yesterday evening in the bar, we laughed unbelievably.'

    c.   *Ich habe ihn **unglaublich** erschreckt.*
        I   have him unbelievable frightened
        'I frightened him unbelievably.'

    d.   *Gestern   habe ich mich **unglaublich** verirrt.*
        Yesterday have I   me   unbelievable lost
        'Yesterday, I got lost unbelievably.'

There does not seem to be any specific interaction between the lexical item serving as a degree adverbial and these classes, as *unglaublich* can easily be replaced with any of the other items discussed as degree adverbials in the previous section, nor is there any noticeable class-type restriction.

3.2.   Degree-manner ambiguities

Some adjectives can be used either as degree adverbials or as manner adverbials, others allow only one of the two usages. An example of an adjective that can be used either as a degree or a manner adverbial is *unglaublich* 'unbelievable'. Its usage as a degree adverbial was exemplified in (48). An example of its usage as a manner adverbial is given in (49). The source of the example is its free English translation, which corresponds to (8) in Ernst (1984:24).

(49)   *Sie hat die Karten **unglaublich** ausgespielt.*
        she has the cards   unbelievably put.down
        'She put the cards down unbelievably.'

Sentence (49) can be used to describe a wide variety of situations. Typically, it is taken to mean that the playing of the cards, i.e. their sequence or, in card games like e.g. poker, the accompanying gestures, ideally support the aims of the player. Thus, we have a clear manner usage of the adjective, and other manner adverbials can appear here without problems, cf. (50).

(50)   *Sie hat die Karten **clever/vorhersagbar** ausgespielt.*
        she has the cards   clever/predictable   put.down
        'She put the cards down cleverly/predictably.'

In addition, (49) is not ambiguous, but only has a manner reading, and the *in-ADJ-manner*-paraphrase can be used successfully in all cases. Therefore, this sentence can also be used to illustrate that some lexemes can never occur as manner adverbials, e.g. the above-mentioned *sehr* or adjectives like *ziemlich* 'rather', cf. (51).

(51)   *Sie hat die Karten **sehr/ziemlich** ausgespielt.*
         she has the cards   very/rather   put.down

To sum up this section on degree adverbials: Degree adverbials differ from manner adverbials in specifying an intensity dimension that comes with specific verbal predicates. In addition, although many adjectives can serve as degree adverbials, they always target the very same intensity dimension and are therefore as a class very homogeneous. As long as the verb provides an intensity dimension, degree adverbials are compatible with all verb classes. Their wide distribution sometimes gives rise to ambiguities between manner and degree adverbials. Nevertheless, conceptually, the two usages are always easily told apart.

4.   Method-oriented adverbials

Method-oriented adverbials specify specific methods or principles which are employed in executing the action described by the verbal predicate, cf. the examples in (52).

(52)   a.   *Alma hat die Pflanzen **biologisch** kategorisiert.*
              Alma has the plants   biological categorized
              'Alma categorized the plants biologically.'
         b.   *Noam hat die Daten **linguistisch** ausgewertet.*
              Noam has the data   linguistically evaluated
              'Noam evaluated the data linguistically.'
         c.   *Dirk hat seine CDs **alphabetisch** sortiert.*
              Dirk has his   CDs alphabetically arranged
              'Dirk arranged his CDs alphabetically.'

All sentences in (52) can be rephrased so that the methods and principles are mentioned explicitly, cf. (53).

(53)   a.   *Alma hat biologische Methoden/Prinzipien benutzt, um*
            Alma has biological   methods/principles   used   in.order
            die Pflanzen zu kategorisieren.
            the plants   to categorize
            'Alma used biological methods/principles to categorize the
            plants.'

      b.   *Noam hat die Daten mit   Hilfe linguistischer*
            Noam has the data   with help linguistic.GEN
            Methoden/Tests   ausgewertet.
            methods/tests.GEN analyzed
            'Noam analyzed the data with the help of linguistic meth-
            ods/tests.'

      c.   *Dirk hat seine CDs nach der Reihenfolge des*
            Dirk has his   CDs after the order   the.GEN
            Alphabets   sortiert.
            alphabet.GEN sorted
            'Dirk sorted his CDs after the order of the alphabet.'

Adjectives derived from nouns that refer to fields of science can very frequently be used as method-oriented adverbials, cf. e.g. *biologisch* 'biologi-
cal' and *linguistisch* 'linguistical' in the previous examples, which are derived
from the nominal bases *Biologie* 'biology' and *Linguistik* 'linguistics'.

Method-oriented adverbials share some properties with manner adverbials, in particular, they can also be elicited with the help of *Wie?* 'How?'
Partially, they also allow the *in-ADJ-manner*-paraphrase, cf. (54) for (53b).

(54)   *Noam hat die Daten auf linguistische Art und Weise ausgewertet.*
        Noam has the data   on linguistic   manner   evaluated
        'Noam evaluated the data in a linguistic manner/way.'

To set them apart from manner modification, the *Wie-das-ist*-paraphrase introduced in section 2.1 is more reliable. It cannot be used for method-oriented
adverbials, cf. (55).

(55)   a.   ??*Wie Alma die Pflanzen kategorisiert, das ist biologisch.*
              how Alma the plants   categorizes,   that is biological
              'The way Alma categorizes the plants is biological.'

      b.   ??*Wie Noam die Daten auswertet, das ist linguistisch.*
              how Noam the data   evaluates, that is linguistical
              'The way Noam evaluates the data is linguistical.'

   c. ??*Wie Dirk seine CDs sortiert hat, das war alphabetisch.*
       how Dirk his CDs sorted has, that was alphabetical
       'The way Dirk arranged his CDs was alphabetical.'

When the noun root does not denote a field of science, this often leads to readings which are very close to instrumentals, cf. (56).

(56)   *Sie haben den Konflikt **diplomatisch/wirtschaftlich** gelöst.*
       they have the conflict diplomatical/economical   solved
       'They solved the conflict diplomatically/economically, i.e. with diplomatic/economic methods.'

Typically, the adjectives that can occur as method-oriented adverbials can also be used as domain adverbials, cf. section 4 in chapter 2.

5. Verb-related adverbials and secondary predication

Adjectives serving as manner adverbials need to be distinguished from secondary predicates, with whom they share the same form. Secondary predication can be expressed either through resultatives or depictives. These two groups will be discussed in turn.

5.1. Resultatives

Resultatives can be sub-classified in *control-* and *raising-resultatives* (cf. for discussion and literature Lüdeling (2001:148-155)). Control-resultatives introduce a further predication over one of the arguments of the verbs, cf. (57), her (209).

(57)   *Der Prinz streicht die Tür rot.* [control]
       the prince paints   the door red
       'The prince paints the door red.'

Raising-resultatives change the argument structure of the verb, cf. the examples in (58), again from her (209).

(58)   *Der Prinz streicht den Eimer leer.* [raising]
       the prince paints   the bucket empty
       'The prince paints the bucket empty.'

Streichen 'to paint' is a transitive verb taking an agentive subject and a patient as the direct object, as in *John strich sein Zimmer* 'John painted his room',

the same structure that actually occurs in (57). However, in (58), the direct
object does not denote what is being painted but the source for the paint used
in the painting; the addition of the standard direct object is impossible. Since
raising resultatives clearly differ structurally from adverbial-constructions, I
will not discuss them further in the following. Control-resultatives are more
interesting in this respect, especially those where the secondary predication
is over the object and not the subject, cf. the additional examples in (59).

(59)   a.   *Er putzte   die Böden **blank**.*
              he cleaned the floors shining
              'He cleaned the floors till they shone.'
        b.   *Er malte   die Wand **blau**.*
              he painted the wall   blue
              'He painted the wall with blue color.'
        c.   *Er schmirgelte   die Schwerter **glatt**.*
              he sandpapered the swords   smooth
              'He sandpapered the swords so they were smooth.'
        d.   *Er kochte die Kartoffeln **gar**.*
              he cooked the potatoes   done.
              'He cooked the potatoes so that they are good'

While resultatives share with verb-related adverbials that they can be elicited
with *Wie?* 'how?', all the cases discussed so far are all conceptually clearly
distinguishable from adverbial modification. As the name *resultatives* suggests, the key semantic feature of these constructions is that the secondary
predication expressed by the adjective obtains as a direct result of the event
described in the respective sentence. In all of the examples in (59), the resultative predication holds of the referent of the direct object, cf. e.g. the pattern
for (59b) in (60).

(60)   a.   *Er malte   die Wand **blau**.*
              he painted the wall   blue
              'He painted the wall blue'.
        b.   *Er malte   die Wand, so dass die Wand blau ist. ($\approx$ a)*
              he painted the wall, so that the wall   blue is
              'He painted the wall, so that as a result, the wall is blue.'

This kind of paraphrase pattern is not available for sentences containing manner adverbials, cf. e.g. (61).

(61) a. *Er malte   die Wand **schnell**.*
          he painted the wall   quick
          'He painted the wall quickly.'

      b. *Er malte   die Wand, so dass die Wand schnell ist. (≠a)*
          he painted the wall,   so that the wall   quick   is
          'He painted the wall, so that as a result, the wall is quick.'

In addition, the *Wie-das-ist*-paraphrase and the *In-ADJ-manner*-paraphrases
cannot be used for resultatives, cf. (62b-c) for (62a).

(62) a. *Er putzte   die Böden **blank**.*
          he scrubbed the floors shining
          'He scrubbed the floors shining.'

      b. *Wie er die Böden putzte,   das war **blank**. (≠a)*
          how he the floors scubbed, that was shining
          'The way he scrubbed the floors was shining.'

      c. *??Er putzte   die Böden auf blanke Art und Weise. (≠a)*
          he scrubbed the floors on shining manner
          'He scrubbed the floors in a shining manner.'

Due to this mutual incompatibility, resultatives and manner adverbials are
usually easily distinguishable. Cases where a distinction is more difficult are
discussed in the next section.

5.2. Ambiguities and blends

Consider the sentence in (63) and the two interpretations given in (64), already visible in the two choices available for the English translation.[26]

(63) *Julia schmückte die Festtafel **elegant**.*
      Julia decorated the table   elegant
      'Julia decorated the table elegant/elegantly.'

(64) a. *Die Art und Weise, wie Julia den Tisch dekorierte, war*
          the manner,   how Julia the table decorated, was
          elegant.
          elegant
          'The way Julia decorated the table was elegant.'

      b. *Die Dekoration des   Tisches   war elegant.*
          the decoration the.GEN table.GEN was elegant
          'The decoration of the table was elegant.'

In the reading paraphrased in (64a), *elegant* 'elegant' serves as a manner adverbial (e.g. Julia's movements etc. were elegant). In contrast, if (64b) follows from (63), *elegant* 'elegant' is a secondary predicate. In this reading, the manner of Julia's movements is not characterized. Both readings are conceptually distinct and a single reading of the adverbial that combines the two readings is not possible.

This type of secondary predication differs from resultatives and depictives as discussed in the previous section in that the object over which *elegant* predicates is not given in the sentence itself. Therefore, I refer to them here as *implicit resultatives*.[27] Referring to them as a class of their own is justified by the fact that there are cases where an adjective can only be used as an implicit resultative and is not available for a manner reading nor a control resultative reading, cf. e.g. (65), (8a) in Geuder (2000:23), where it is neither the manner that is heavy nor the cart that is heavy as a result.

(65)   *Sie   beluden den Wagen **schwer**.*
        They loaded the cart   heavy
        'They loaded the cart until it was heavily loaded.'

If we look for a paraphrase that encompasses both the standard resultatives and the implicit resultative, then the best option is to use the *Zustandspassiv* 'stative passive', that is all regular resultatives in (59) as well as the implicit resultatives discussed in this section entail sentences which describe a resultant state that holds of the object and is formed with the help of the *Zustandspassiv*, cf. the examples in (66) and (67).

(66)   a.   *Fritz strich   die Wand **blau**. (→ b)*
              Fritz painted the wall   blue
              'Fritz painted the wall blue.'
        b.   *Die Wand ist blau gestrichen.*
              the wall is blue painted
              'The wall was painted blue.'

(67)   a.   *Sie   beluden den Wagen **schwer**. (→ b)*
              they loaded the cart   heavy
              'They loaded the cart until it was heavy.'
        b.   *Der Wagen ist schwer beladen.*
              the cart   is heavy loaded
              'The cart is heavily loaded.'

This paraphrase, however, is also appropriate for many instances where a distinction between manner adverbial and resultative does not seem to be possible anymore, cf. the examples in (68), (69), and (70).

(68) *Peggy hat das Zelt **schlampig** aufgebaut.*
     Peggy has the tent sloppily   put.up
     'Peggy put up the tent half-assedly.'

(69) *Arnd hat das Schaufenster **liebevoll** dekoriert.*
     Arnd has the display   lovingly decorated
     'Arnd decorated the display lovingly.'

(70) *Frieda hat das Buch **kongenial** übersetzt.*
     Frieda has the book congenial translated
     'Frieda congenially translated the book.'

I will adopt the term 'blend' from Quirk et al. (1985:560) to refer to these usages where the disctinction between manner and resultative interpretation is impossible.[28] Besides the *Zustandspassiv*-entailment that they share with the resultative, they also allow all the regular manner adverbial paraphrases, cf. e.g. (71) for (68), where the manner-paraphrases are given in (71a) and (71b), and the *Zustandspassiv*-entailment in (71c) .

(71) a. *Wie Peter das Zelt aufgebaut hat, das war schlampig.*
        How Peter the tent put.up   has, that was half-assedly
        'The way Peter put up the tent was half-assedly.'
    b. *Peter hat das Zelt auf schlampige Art und Weise aufgebaut.*
        Peter has the tent in.a sloppy   manner   put.up
        'Peter put up the tent in a sloppy manner.'
    c. *Das Zelt ist schlampig aufgebaut.*
        The tent is sloppy   put.up
        'The tent is put up carelessly.'

The usages classified here as blends partially overlap with a class of adverbials introduced in Eckardt (1998:160), the so-called *adverbs of degree of perfection*. Thus, for Eckardt, *schlampig* 'sloppily' in (68), which adapts her (7), falls into this class, as well as e.g. *perfekt* 'perfectly' and *mittelgut* 'moderately well', cf. (72), her (1) and (5).

(72) a. *Olga spielte die Sonate **perfekt**.*
        Olga played the sonata perfect
        'Olga played the sonata perfectly.'

> b. *Paul hat den Handstand **mittelgut** ausgeführt.*
> Paul has the handstand moderately.well executed
> 'Paul executed the handstand moderately well.'

Just as the *schlampig*-sentence, the two sentences in (72) satisfy the two standard tests for manner adverbials, cf. the paraphrases in (73) and (74).

(73) a. *Wie Olga spielt, das ist perfekt.*
How Olga plays, that is perfect
'The way Olga plays is perfect.'

b. *Olga spielt auf perfekte Art und Weise.*
Olga plays on perfect manner
'Olga plays in a perfect manner.'

(74) a. *Wie Paul den Handstand ausführt, das ist mittelgut.*
how Paul the handstand executes, that is moderately.good
'The way Paul executed the handstand is moderately good.'

b. *Paul führt den Handstand auf mittelgute*
Paul executes the handstand on moderately-good
Art und Weise aus.
manner   verb-particle
'Paul executes the handstand in a moderately good manner.'

However, the two sentences in (72) do not support the *Zustandspassiv*-entailment, for the simple reason that they do not create stable result states. Eckardt (1998:161) argues that these adverbs "say something about the degree of perfection to which a certain action has been performed". This suggests that they form a subgroup within the group of manner adverbials whose defining characteristic is a common scale on which they map, namely some perfection-scale. However, in the case of the adverbials given by Eckardt, there seems to be no common single scale on which they are mapped. Consequently, its members can co-occur without any semantic clashes, cf. e.g. (75).

(75) *Gaspar hat die Sonate **perfekt** gespielt, allerdings nicht **schön**.*
Gaspar has the sonata perfect played, but   not beautiful
'Gaspar played the sonata perfectly, but not beautifully.'

Therefore, all the adverbials Eckardt calls 'degree of perfection adverbs' can be subsumed under either the group of manner adverbials or, if applicable, blends between manner adverbials and resultatives.

5.3.   Depictives

Depictives express secondary predications over either the object or the subject, cf. (76), where *roh* 'raw' in (76a) serves as an object depictive and *nackt* 'nude' in (76b) serves as a subject depictive.

(76) a. *Er isst das Fleisch **roh**.*
        he eats the meat   raw
        'He eats the meat raw.'
     b. *Er isst das Fleich **nackt**.*
        he eats the meat   nude
        'He eats the meat nude.'

Depictives can be paraphrased with the help of a temporal subordinate clause introduced by *während* 'while', cf. (77) for the object depictives and (78) for subject-depictives.

(77) *Er isst das Fleisch, während das Fleisch roh ist.*
     he eats the meat   while   the meat   raw is
     'He eats the meat while it is raw.'

(78) *Er isst das Fleisch, während er nackt ist.*
     he eats the meat,   while   he nude is
     'He eats the meat, while he is nude.'

This temporal connection, that is, the co-temporality of the state encoded by the depictive and the event or state described in the embedding sentence is one of the the key properties of depictives, cf. e.g. Rothstein (2003:565-567) and clearly distinguishes them from resultatives. The other key property discussed by Rothstein (2003:567-569) is the shared argument constraint, i.e. the requirement that the referent of a depictive predicates also serves as an argument of the main verb.

The *Wie-das-ist-* and the *In-ADJ-manner*-paraphrases cannot be used, cf. (79) and (80).

(79) a. *Er isst das Fleisch **roh**.*
        he eats the meat   raw
        'He eats the meat raw.'
     b. *Wie er das Fleisch isst, das ist roh. ($\neq$a)*
        how he the meat   eats, that is raw
        'The way he eats the meat is raw.'

c.   *Er isst das Fleisch auf rohe Art und Weise. (≉ a)*
he eats the meat   on raw manner
'He eats the meat in a raw manner.'

(80)   a.   *Er isst das Fleich **nackt**.*
he eats the meat   nude
'He eats the meat nude.'

b.   *Wie er das Fleisch isst, das ist nackt. (≉a)*
how he the meat   eats, that is nude
'The way he eats the meat is nude.'

c.   *Er isst das Fleisch auf nackte Art und Weise. (≉a)*
he eats the meat   on nude   manner
'He eats the meat in a nude manner'

Due to this difference in possible paraphrases, the distinction between depictives and manner adverbials is in most cases unproblematic.

In the same way, agent-oriented adverbials can be distinguished from depictives. In addition, the different inference patterns can be exploited, cf. (81) vs. (82), both examples adapted from Bartsch (1972:152).

(81)   a.   *Er flüchtete **geschickt** aus dem Lager. (→ a,b)*
he fled   ingenious from the camp
'He fled ingeniously from the camp.'

b.   *Sein Handeln war geschickt.*
his   acting   was ingenious
'His act was ingenious.'

c.   *Sein geschicktes Handeln ...*
his ingenious acting
'His ingenious act ...'

(82)   a.   *Er flüchtete **krank** aus dem Lager. (↛ a,b)*
he fled   sick   from the camp
'He fled sick from the camp'

b.   *Sein Handeln war krank.*
his   acting   was sick
'His act was sick.'

c.   *Sein krankes Handeln ...*
his sick   acting
'His sick act ...'

The distinction between manner adverbials and depictives becomes more subtle when the adjectives characterize a mental state, e.g. adjectives like *traurig* 'sad', *nervös* 'nervous' or *freudig* 'happy'. For these *psychological adjectives* all three paraphrases seem to work, cf. (83):

(83)   *Gudrun ging   **traurig** nach   Hause.*
        Gudrun walked sad(ly) towards home
        'Gudrun went home sad' or 'Gudrun sadly went home'

    a.   *Gudrun ging   nach Hause, während sie traurig war.*
        Gudrun walked to   home, while   she sad   was
        'Gudrun walked home while she was sad.'

    b.   *Wie Gudrun nach Hause ging,   das war traurig.*
        how Gudrun to   home walked, that was sad
        'The way Gudrun walked home was sad.'

    c.   *Gudrun ging   auf traurige Art und Weise nach Hause.*
        Gudrun walked on sad   manner   to   home
        'Gudrun walked home in a sad manner.'

Geuder (2000, 2004) shows in detail that the two readings of e.g. *traurig* 'sad' as a depictive or as a manner adverbial nevertheless can be told apart: The manner reading is *opaque* with respect to the real mental state of the agent, whereas on the depictive interpretation, it is exactly this mental state about which is predicated. In other words, when *traurig* in (83) is interpreted as a depictive, then we know that Gudrun is sad. When *traurig* serves as a manner adverbial, it is something in the way she walks or she carries herself while walking that makes us deduce that she must be sad. In that case, we simply do not know whether Gudrun is really sad or not. As the translation indicates, in English the different usages can sometimes be told apart via the absence or presence of the *-ly* suffix. Clear instances of usages of psychological adjectives as manner adverbials are cases where the subject is inanimate, cf. e.g. (84).

(84)   *Das Buch endete sehr traurig.*
        the novel ended very sad
        'The novel ended very sadly.'

A third possible interpretation discussed by Geuder (2000), that as a *transparent adverbial*, will be discussed in more detail in chapter 4.

6.   Adverbial adjectives and the verb-adverbial combinatorics

Whereas sentence adverbials are largely unrestricted when it comes to their combination with verbs, verb-related adverbials are in several ways restricted as far as their possible combinations with specific verbs are concerned. These interactions cover a large spectrum, starting from the fact that some verbs subcategorize for adverbials, cf. (85) and the discussion in section (18) of chapter 1.

(85)   *Jane wohnt billig/teuer.*
       Jane lives   cheap/expensive
       'Jane lives cheap/expensive.'

At the other end of the spectrum, we have adverbial-verb combinations that are hard if not impossible to interpret because of the specific lexical semantics of the items involved, cf. (86a) vs. (86b).

(86)   a.   *Peter singt **schnell/langsam/laut/leise/wunderbar**.*
            Peter sings fast/slow/loud/soft/wonderful
            'Peter sings fast/slowly/loudly/softly/wonderfully.'
       b.   *Peter singt **oberflächlich/intelligent/geschickt**.*
            Peter sings cursory/intelligent/skillful
            'Peter sings cursorily/intelligently/skillfully.'

While the sentences in (86a) can be easily interpreted, this is next to impossible for the sentences in (86b): What should cursory, intelligent, or even skillful singing refer to? In addition, we have many combinations which have a very idiomatic flavor, e.g. the football-examples in (87).

(87)   *den Ball **flach/hoch** spielen*
       the ball low/high   play
       'to play/keep the ball low/high'

Adjectives like *flach/hoch* 'low/high', which specify physical properties, are normally not available as manner adverbials (other examples include e.g. *viereckig* 'rectangular' or *dünn* 'thin').

   While this topic as a whole is far too complex to do justice within this work, I will focus on one issue that regularly comes up in semantic analyses of adverbial modification in the context of event semantics, namely the impossibility of combining manner adverbials with stative verbs. The data is often interpreted as evidence for a distinction between verbs that come with an event argument and other verbs that do not come with an event argument, cf. e.g. Katz (2003) or Maienborn (2005).

In this section, I want to present the most important data and argue for a position proposed in Geuder (2006), who argues that the restricted combinatorics is simply a consequence of the general interaction between verb-related adverbial and the conceptual structure of the verbs involved.

6.1. Statives that allow manner modification

Prototypical examples of manner adverbials do not combine with all statives, cf. (88a) for *ähneln* 'resemble', (88b) for *heißen* 'be called' and (88c) for *besitzen* 'own' (cf. the examples in Maienborn 2003a:89).

(88)   a. **Paul ähnelt   laut/wunderbar Romy Schneider.*
             Paul resembles loud/wonderful Romy Schneider

      b. **Paul ähnelt   elegant/intelligent Romy Schneider.*
             Paul resembles elegant/intelligent Romy Schneider

(89)   a. **Das Unihochhaus   heißt   jetzt laut/wunderbar*
             The University skyscraper is.called now loud/wonderful
             Cityhochhaus.
             City Skyscraper

      b. **Das Unihochhaus   heißt   jetzt elegant/intelligent*
             The University skyscraper is.called now elegant/intelligent
             Cityhochhaus.
             City Skyscraper

(90)   a. **Jochen besitzt laut/wunderbar viel   Geld.*
             Jochen owns loud/wonderful much money

      b. **Jochen besitzt elegant/intelligent viel   Geld.*
             Jochen owns elegant/intelligent much money

A subgroup of statives, the *positionals* (this term is taken from Dik 1975), combines with manner adverbials. Typical positionals are verbs like *sitzen* 'sit' *stehen* 'stand', *liegen* 'lie' , *hocken* 'squat' and *hängen* 'hang'.[29] Below are some example sentences for positionals in combination with manner adverbials.

(91)   a.   *Christian steht **ruhig/hippelig/elegant** an der Theke.*
            Christian stands quiet/figdety/elegant   at the bar
            'Christian stands at the bar quietly/fidgetly/elegantly.'
       b.   *Ralf liegt **elegant/wunderbar** auf dem Sofa.*
            Ralf lies elegant/wonderful on the couch
            'Ralf lies on the couch elegantly/wonderfully.'
       c.   *Emma sitzt **kerzengerade/hippelig** auf dem Stuhl.*
            Emma sits erect/fidgety   in the chair
            'Emma sits in her chair erectly/fidgetly. '

Despite the above examples, it is clear that positionals are for principled reasons more restricted in their combinatorial possibilities than e.g. process verbs. Thus, although it is possible to combine adjectives like *laut/leise* 'loud/ quiet' with positionals, cf. e.g. (92), they do not get manner readings here, but are interpreted as depictives or with associated readings (for associated readings, cf. section 3.2.3 in chapter 4).

(92)   *Christian steht **laut/leise** an der Theke.*
       Christian stands loud/quiet at the bar
       'Christian stands at the bar loudly/quietly.'

Adjectives that require dynamic change, e.g. *schnell* 'fast' or *langsam* 'slow', or Dik's example *rhythmisch* 'rhythmical', cannot combine with positionals at all, cf. e.g. (93).

(93)   **Sebastian sitzt **rhythmisch** auf dem Stuhl.*
       Sebastian sits rhythmical in his chair

Dik accounts for this data by arguing that manner adverbials at the very least require the sentence subject to have some control over the activity expressed by the verbal predicate. This corresponds to the distinction between *schnell* 'fast' and e.g. *flink* 'swift' as discussed in section 2.2. Whether or not a manner adverbial requires dynamic change can then be used for further subclassification.

According to Maienborn (2003a:88-90), manner adverbials[30] can also, apart from positionals, combine with a group of further statives, e.g. *schlafen* 'sleep', *ruhen* 'relax', *warten* 'wait', *glänzen* 'gleam', *kleben* 'stick', *ankern* 'anchor', *parken* 'park' (cf. Maienborn (2003a:54)).

Maienborn refers to these types of statives (including positionals) as *Davidsonian statives* (D-statives). According to Maienborn (2005), they differ from the stative verbs like *ähneln* 'resemble', *heißen* 'be called', and *besitzen* 'own' discussed at the start of this section in that they (a) can appear as infinitive-complements of perception verbs, (b) allow for local modifiers, and (c) allow for manner modification.

In the following, I will exemplarily discuss *schlafen* 'sleep' and *glänzen* 'gleam' in combination with adverbial adjectives. The most important difference between these two verbs and the positionals is that the agent does not have control over the action described by the verbal predicate. This has direct consequences for the possible combinations with adverbial adjectives, cf. (94) for *schlafen* 'sleep', adapted from (72) in Maienborn (2003a:90).

(94)   a.   *Henrike hat **gut/schlecht** geschlafen.*
              Henrike has good/bad   slept
              'Henrike slept well/badly.'

        b.   *Henrike hat **ausgezeichnet/wunderbar** geschlafen.*
              Henrike has superb/wonderful   slept
              'Henrike slept superbly/wonderfully.'

        c.   *Henrike hat **fest/tief**   geschlafen.*
              Henrike has thick/deep slept
              'Henrike was fast asleep.'

        d.   *Henrike hat **ruhig/unruhig** geschlafen.*
              Henrike has calm/uneasy   slept
              'Henrike slept calmly/uneasily.'

None of the adverbials in (94) requires control, and just as with the one-dimensional adverbials (*laut/leise/schnell/langsam*), the *In-ADJ-manner*-paraphrase does not yield good results, cf. (95) for the pair *gut/schlecht* 'well/badly' in (94a).

(95)   *?Henrike hat auf gute/schlechte Art und Weise geschlafen.*
        Henrike has on good/bad   manner   slept
        'Henrike slept in an good/bad manner.'

What exactly is it that the individual adjectives predicate of? The answer seems easiest for *fest/tief*: They serve as degree adverbials, specifying the intensity of the sleeping. As far as their meanings are concerned, they are interchangeable and very conventionalized. They can even be used together in coordination for an intensifying effect, cf. (96).

(96)   *Die süßen Kinder   schliefen **tief und fest**.*
        the sweet children slept   deep and thick
        'The sweet children were fast asleep.'

What about the other modifiers? *Gut/schlecht* 'good/bad' and *ausgezeich-net/wunderbar* 'superb/wonderful' all seem to target the same dimension, quality of sleep, with a mapping ranging from *schlecht* 'bad' via *gut* 'good' to *wunderbar/ausgezeichnet* 'wonderful/superb'. In all cases, the evaluation of the quality of sleep is based on the judgement of the sleeper, that is, if I feel wonderful in the morning, I must have slept wonderfully. For the final pair, *ruhig/unruhig* 'calm/uneasy', the target dimension still is the quality of sleep, but the basis for evaluation is an outside observer, that is, one sleeps restless when one tosses and turns during one's sleep, and this is taken as an indication of the quality of the sleeping.

The verb *glänzen* 'gleam' seems to be even further restricted in its combinatorics, some possible verb-related adverbials are given in (97), cf. (6c) in Maienborn (2007).

(97)   *Die Perlen glänzten **matt/hell/rötlich/feucht**.*
        The pearls gleamed dull/bright/reddish/moist
        'The pearls were gleaming dully/brightly/reddishly/moistly.'

Geuder (2006) contains a detailed discussion of this example, using it to demonstrate that we can establish a link between the number of possible modifiers and the complexity of the concept associated with the verbal predicate. Thus, when we compare *glänzen* 'gleam' to *leuchten* 'shine', we observe that they can largely combine with the same modifiers, but differ e.g. in that the latter does not combine with *feucht* 'moist', cf. (98).

(98)   **Die Lampe leuchtete **feucht**.*
        the lamp   shone   moist

Sketching a conceptual structure for *leuchten* and *glänzen*, he shows that we can easily find target dimensions for the modifiers that are shared by both verbs, e.g. the brightness and the color dimension of the emitted light, along with dimensions capturing the force of the emission etc. Where the two concepts differ, however, is that *glänzen* 'gleam' expresses a very specific way of light emission, the emission of light by way of reflection from a surface. And it is this surface that is targeted by the modifier *feucht* 'moist'. Since this component is absent from the structure of the concept *leuchten* 'shine', the modifier cannot be interpreted.

An account along these lines seems to be fully compatible with all the data discussed so far: The more complex the internal structure of the concepts associated with the verbal predicates, the more possible targets for modification are available. The less complex the internal structure, the less targets are available. Below, we will see whether we can use the same reasoning to explain the behavior of those verbs that are usually claimed to be unavailable for manner modification.

6.2. Mannerless statives

If we finally consider the group of verbs that is left, prototypical statives like *wissen* 'know', *glauben* 'believe', *lieben* 'love' and *hassen* 'hate', the first thing to note is that they appear in combination with adjectives which clearly express more than simple degree modification, cf. the examples in (99).

(99) a. *Jane weiß die Antwort **genau**.*
    Jane knows the answer exact
    'Jane knows the answer exactly.'

  b. *Christian glaubt **fest** an ihre Unschuld.*
    Christian believes firm in her innocence
    'Christian believes firmly in her innocence.'

  c. *Kord-Hinrich liebt/hasst sie **bedingungslos**.*
    Kord-Hinrich loves/hates her unconditional
    'Kord-Hinrich loves/hates her unconditionally/
    unquestioningly.'

  d. *Anton ähnelt ihr nur **oberflächlich**.*
    Anton resembles her only superficial
    'Anton resembles her only superficially.'

Nevertheless, they do not seem to correspond to standard manner modification, either. This can be seen by looking at the *In-ADJ-manner-* and the *Wie-das-ist*-paraphrases, which are not possible for (99a-b), cf. (100) and (101).

(100) a. ??*Jane weiß die Antwort auf genaue Art und Weise.*
     Jane knows the answer on exact manner
     'Jane knows the answer in a sure manner.'

   b. ??*Wie Jane die Antwort weiß, das ist genau.*
     how Jane the answer knows, that is exact
     'The way Jane knows the answer is exact.'

(101)   a. ??*Christian glaubt   auf feste Art und Weise an ihre Unschuld.*
          Christian believes on firm manner   at her innocence
          'Christian believes in her innocence in a firm manner.'
    b. ??*Wie Christian an ihre Unschuld glaubt,   das ist fest.*
        how Christian at her innocence believes, that is solid
        'The way Christian believes in her innocence is solid/
        unshakable.'

In fact, *fest glauben* 'believe firmly' in (101) seems semantically closer to
degree modification, corresponding to a very high degree, e.g. *fest glauben*
expresses a deeper belief than *sehr glauben* 'believe very much'.

It is more difficult to see this in the case of (99c) and (99d), cf. the paraphrases in (102) and (103).

(102)   a. *Er liebt/hasst sie auf bedingungslose Art und Weise.*
        he loves/hates her on unconditional   manner
        'He loves/hates her in an unconditional manner.'
    b. *Wie er sie liebt/hasst, das ist bedingungslos.*
        how he her loves/hates, that is unconditional
        'The way he loves/hates her is unconditional.'

(103)   a. *Er ähnelt   ihr auf oberflächliche Art und Weise.*
        he resembles her on superficial   manner
        'He resembles her in a superficial manner.'
    b. *Wie er ihr ähnelt,   das ist oberflächlich.*
        how he her resembles, that is superficial
        'The way he resembles her is superficial.'

According to the paraphrases, both occurrences are instances of manner modification. All in all, the data does not convincingly support a view that there
is somewhere a principled distinction between verbs coming with an event
argument and those that don't, and this position therefore requires additional
accounts for all this variation (cf. Katz (2008) for the most recent attempt
of such a detailed account). In contrast, it is fully compatible with the argumentation of Geuder (2006) outlined at the end of the previous section: there
is a cline in conceptual complexity, so that the concept associated with the
verb *wissen* 'know' is less complex than that associated with the verb *hassen*
'hate', which in turn is less complex than that associated with *schlafen* 'sleep'
and so on.[31]

7.   Verb-related adverbials and negation

Many of the verb-related adverbials cannot have scope over sentence negation, cf. the manner adverbials in (104) and (105).

(104)   a.   *Peter hat **wunderbar** nicht getanzt.*
             Peter has wonderful not   danced
       b.   *Peter hat nicht **wunderbar** getanzt.*
             Peter has not   wonderful danced
             'Peter did not dance wonderfully.'

(105)   a.   *Frieda hat **laut** nicht gesungen.*
             Frieda has loud not   sung
       b.   *Frieda hat nicht **laut** gesungen.*
             Frieda has not   loud sung
             'Frieda did not sing loudly.'

In both examples, the linear ordering **manner adverbial** > **negation** leads to ungrammaticality, cf. (104a) and (105a), while the order **negation** > **manner adverbial** is acceptable.

As far as the meaning of these constructions is concerned, this behavior seems straightforward. If, as I have argued throughout, a manner adverbial targets a conceptual dimension of an event, then there needs to be an event that provides an appropriate dimension. However, if the verbal predicate is under the scope of negation, then there is no such event that could provide this dimension.[32]

Nevertheless, some manner adverbials can scope over negation, cf. (106).

(106)   *Hans hat **geschickt** die Frage   **nicht** beantwortet.*
         Hans has skillfully the question not   answered
         'Hans has skillfully not answered the question.'

In this section, I focus on two issues. Firstly, what is the relationship between negation, the adverbial, and the sentential base. Secondly, I discuss those cases where verb-related adverbials take scope over negation and offer an explanation for their behavior.

In order to discuss these issues, it is helpful to use the distinction between replacive and non-replacive negation introduced in Jacobs (1991:586). The defining characteristic of replacive negation is that it is necessarily connected with the replacement of at least part of the negated content.[33] A good diagnostic for whether something constitutes replacive negation is the usage of German *sondern* vs. *aber* in follow-up phrases: *sondern*-phrases follow replacive negation, *aber*-phrases cannot follow.

(107)   a.   *Fritz hat das Lied nicht LAUT gesungen, sondern leise.*
                Fritz has the song not   loud   sung,   but   quiet
                'Fritz did not sing the song loudly, but quietly.'
         b.   ??*Fritz hat das Lied nicht LAUT gesungen, aber leise.*
                Fritz has the song not   loud   sung,   but   quiet
                'Fritz did not sing the song loudly, but quietly.'

Prosody plays an important role in the evaluation of these sentences, as it allows the conversion of the linear order of words that can be used for non-replacive negation into a replacive negation. For the two sentences in (107), for example, it is the main stress on *laut* that makes an interpretation of the negation as replacive negation the most natural reading.

7.1.   Negation, adverbials, and the sentential base

All verb-related adverbials discussed so far are veridical, and sentences with verb-related adverbials clearly entail the sentential base, cf. (108), where (108a) entails (108b).

(108)   a.   *Petra singt **laut**.*
                Petra sings loud
                'Petra sings loudly.'
         b.   *Petra singt.*
                Petra sings
                'Petra sings.'

In combination with sentence negation, cf. (109), the placement of the main stress determines whether any implicational relationship between the sentences containing a negation and manner modification and the sentential base is felt.

(109)   a.   *Petra singt nicht **laut**.*
                Petra sings not   loud
                'Petra does not sing loudly.'
         b.   *Petra singt.*
                Petra sings
                'Petra sings.'

If the main stress falls on *nicht* 'not', cf. (110a), the a-variants do not seem to imply the b-variants. However, if the manner adverbial bears main stress, cf. (110b), the b-variants seem to be implied.

(110) a. *Petra singt NICHT laut.*
           Petra sings not   loud
           'Petra does NOT sing loudly'
       b. *Petra singt nicht LAUT.*
           Petra sings not   loud
           'Petra does not sing LOUDLY.'

Discussing parallel data in English, Bellert (1977:339) explicitly mentions main stress on the manner adverb as a prerequisite for the implication relationships.

However, the exact nature of this implicational relationship is not clear. Especially, it is not clear whether this implication is an entailment, in effect turning the sentential base into a presupposition, or whether it is something weaker than an entailment. Here, I follow the standard distinction that if we can judge that *A implies B* on the basis of the truth-conditional content of A, then *A entails B*, whereas if the reasons for the judgment concern pragmatics, e.g. conversational strategies, speaker/hearer expectations etc., then B is an implicature of A (the term is from Grice (1975), and I use it for all those phenomena he classes as conversational implicatures.).

This question is addressed in some detail in Jacobs (1982:175-177), whose example sentence involving adverbials is reproduced in (111), his (3.112b), where *heimlich* 'secretly' functions, according to my classification, as a mental-attitude adverbial (cf. the discussion in chapter 4).

(111) *Luise bewundert Dr. No nicht HEIMlich.*
       Luise admires   Dr. No not   secretly
       'Luise does not admire Dr. No secretly'

Jacobs investigates the relationship between (111) and (112), his (3.112c), where *irgendwie* replaces the manner adverbial.

(112) *Luise bewundert Dr. No irgendwie.*
       Luise admires   Dr. No in.some.way
       'In some way, Luise admires Dr. No.'

(112), in turn, semantically entails (113), leading back to the pattern of interest.

(113)   *Luise bewundert Dr. No.*
         Luise admires   Dr. No
         'Luise admires Dr. No.'

Jacobs argues quite convincingly that the implication from (111) to (112) is a conversational implicature in the sense of Grice (1975). Jacobs's argumentation rests on the principle that "[d]as Erfülltsein von Wahrheitsbedingungen nicht-ambiger Sätze kann nicht angezweifelt oder als unsicher dargestellt werden, wenn man gleichzeitig die fraglichen Sätze als sicher zutreffend behaupten will, [...]" [the satisfaction of truth conditions of un-ambiguous sentences cannot be questioned or be portrayed as doubtful, if at the same time the sentences in question are asserted to be true] (Jacobs 1982:176).

    Thus, the discourse in (114) is ungrammatical, because the proposition that *Luise admires Dr. No* is doubted, while at the same time the proposition that *Luise secretly admires Dr. No* is asserted. Because the latter entails the former, the juxtaposition of the two sentences is impossible, cf. (114), his (3.114).

(114)   *Ich bin mir nicht sicher, ob Luise Dr. No bewundert. Sicher ist aber: Sie bewundert ihn **HEIMlich**. Wenn sie jemand bewundert, tut sie das nämlich immer **heimlich**.*
         'I am not sure whether Luise admires Dr. No. One thing is sure, though: she admires him secretly. When she admires somebody, she always does it in secret.'

In contrast, no such clash arises in (115), his (3.116), where the negation is added to the sentence containing the adverbial.

(115)   *Ich bin mir nicht sicher, ob Luise Dr. No **irgendwie** bewundert. Sicher ist aber: Luise bewundert Dr. No nicht **HEIMlich**. Wenn sie jemand bewundert, dann läßt sie es nämlich alle Welt wissen.*
         'I am not sure whether Luise admires Dr. No in some way. One thing is sure, though: she does not admire him secretly. When she admires somebody, she always lets the whole world know.'

In (115), the doubting of the proposition that *Luise admires Dr. No in some manner*, which in turn entails *Luise admires Dr. No*, does not clash with the assertion that *Luise does not admire Dr. No secretly*. This shows that the sentence containing the negation does not entail the proposition expressed by the sentential base, i.e. that Luise admires Dr. No, but only conversationally implicates it.

As (116) and (117) show, the effect is not limited to mental attitude adverbials, but holds for standard manner adverbials, too.

(116) *Ich bin mir nicht sicher, ob Petra singt. Sicher ist aber: Sie singt* **LAUT**. *Wenn sie singt, tut sie das nämlich immer* **laut**.
'I am not sure that Petra sings. One thing is sure, though: she sings loudly. When she sings, she always sings loudly'

(117) *Ich bin mir nicht sicher, ob Petra* **irgendwie** *singt. Sicher ist aber: Sie singt nicht* **LAUT**. *Wenn sie singt, dann singt sie nur* **leise**.
'I am not sure that Petra sings in some manner. One thing is sure, though: she does not sing loudly. When she sings, she sings only quietly'

Jacobs also provides an explanation why the availability of the conversational implicature is intertwined with the placement of main stress, that is, why, of the pair in (118), repeated from (110), only (118a) conversationally implicates that Petra sings, while (118b) does not.

(118) a. *Petra singt nicht* **LAUT**.
Petra sings not   loud
'Petra does not sing loudly'

       b. Petra singt NICHT **laut**.

In (118a) the adverb constitutes/is the focus of the *nicht* 'not', the carrier of the negation (*Negationsträger*), but in (118b), this is not the case. According to Jacobs (1982:177-179), the focusing of an expression by negation points to the possibility that the replacement of the focused material will yield a description of a state of affairs which could not be negated any more in the specific context.

7.2. Verb-related adverbials with scope over negation

As mentioned in the beginning of section 7, many verb-related adverbials never have scope over negation, cf. (119) and (120), repeated from (104a) and (105a).

(119)   *Peter hat **wunderbar** nicht getanzt.*
Peter has wonderful   not   danced

(120)   *Frieda hat **laut** nicht gesungen.*
Frieda has loud not   sung

Other verb-related adverbials, however, can have scope over negation, cf. (121), repeated from (106).

(121)   *Hans hat **geschickt** die Frage   **nicht** beantwortet.*
Hans has skillful   the question not   answered
'Hans has skillfully not answered the question.'

The first thing to note is that (121), but also its variant where *geschickt* 'skillful' is positioned adjacent to the negation, cf. (122), is ambiguous between a sentence adverbial reading and a verb-related adverbial reading.

(122)   *Hans hat die Frage   **geschickt nicht** beantwortet.*
Hans has the question skillful   not   answered
'Hans has skillfully not answered the question.'

Both sentences can receive two interpretations. One is a reading of *geschickt* as a subject-oriented modifier, cf. the English paraphrase in (123).

(123)   It was clever of Hans that he did not answer the question.
[subject-oriented]

On the interpretation given in (123), *geschickt* serves as a subject-oriented adverbial. On this usage, *geschickt* is synonymous with *geschickterweise* 'cleverly', its unambiguous adverb cognate, cf. (124).

(124)   *Hans hat **geschickterweise** die Frage   **nicht** beantwortet.*
Hans has cleverly   the question not   answered
'Cleverly, Hans did not answer the question.'

The other reading is given in (125a) and conveys the same meaning as (125b).

(125)   a.   How Hans did not answer the question, that was clever.
b.   It was clever of Hans how he talked without answering the question.

The reading of (106) given in (125), is a manner reading. This interpretation seems also to be the preferred one for (122). However, in contrast to the regular cases of manner modification, it is not the activity denoted by the verbal predicate whose manner is specified. What is specified by *geschickt* 'skillfully' seems to be the 'not_answering', which itself denotes a specific activity. Or rather, there is some activity, which is executed skillfully, which allows the subject to uphold the state of not_having_answered. On this reading the sentence in (106) conveys the same meaning as the sentence in (126), containing lexically negative verbs, i.e. verbs that form converses with negated verbs (e.g. here *eine Frage nicht beantworten* 'to not answer a question' ⇔ *einer Frage ausweichen* 'to dodge a question').

(126) *Hans ist **geschickt** der Frage   ausgewichen.*
       Hans is skillfully the question dodged
       'Hans skillfully dodged the question.'

This usage of the negation marker in combination with the verb is marked, as can be seen from the following datum from a newspaper, cf. (127), where *nicht* 'not' was printed in italics to reflect the markedness of the construction.[34]

(127) *Doch das Publikum hing an seinen Lippen und begann nach dem einstündigen Vortrag, fleißig Fragen zu stellen, die er so virtuos* nicht *beantwortete, dass niemand es merkte.*
       'But he had the audience in his grip, and after the one-hour talk they started asking questions which he so virtuoso *not* answered that no one noticed.'

Note that the markedness of this construction is not due to an occurrence of replacive negation. This is confirmed by the fact that it is impossible to insert a *sondern*-phrase in the last part of the sentence, cf. (128).

(128) ??*die   er so virtuos nicht beantwortete, **sondern umging**, dass*
       which he so virtuoso not answered,   but   dodged, that
       niemand es merkte.
       no.one it noticed
       'which he so virtuoso not answered, but dodged, that no one even noticed.'

More evidence for this analysis of *geschickt* 'skillfully' comes from the comparison of the paraphrases possible for (128) to the paraphrase available for sentences containing adverbials that clearly can outscope sentence negation, e.g. mental-attitude adverbials such as *absichtlich* 'on purpose', cf. (129) (for more on mental attitude adverbials, cf. chapter 4).

(129)   *Hans hat die Frage*   **absichtlich nicht** *beantwortet.*
        Hans has the question on.purpose not   answered
        'Hans did not answer the question on purpose.'

Sentence (129) can be paraphrased with the help of (130a), the paraphrase for subject-oriented adverbials, but not with the help of the agent-oriented version of the *Wie-das-ist*-paraphrase, cf. (130b).

(130)   a.   *Es war absichtlich von Hans, dass er die Frage*   *nicht*
           it was on.purpose of   Hans, that he the question not
           beantwortet hat. ≈ *(129)*
           answered   has
           'It was on purpose (of Hans) that he did not answer the question.'
     b.   *Es war absichtlich von Hans wie er die Frage*   *nicht*
           it was on.purpose of   Hans how he the question not
           beantwortet hat. ≉ *(129)*
           answered   has
           'It was on purpose (of Hans) how he did not answer the question.'

The pattern for the *geschickt-not*-sentences is exactly opposite, cf. (131) and the two paraphrases (132a) and (132b).

(131)   *Hans hat die Frage*   **geschickt nicht** *beantwortet.*
        Hans has the question skillful   not   answered
        'Hans did skillfully not answer the question.'

(132)   a.   *Es war geschickt von Hans, dass er die Frage*   *nicht*
           it was skillful   of   Hans, that he the question not
           beantwortet hat. ≉ *(131)*
           answered   has
           'It was skillful (of Hans) that he did not answer the question.'

  b. *Es war geschickt von Hans, wie er die Frage nicht*
    it was skillful of Hans, how he the question not
    beantwortet hat. ≈ (131)
    answered has
    'It was skillful (of Hans) how Hans did not answer the question.'

Only (132b) is a paraphrase of the intented reading of the sentence, while (132a) paraphrases the subject-oriented reading of *geschickt* 'skillfully'.

 Additional evidence for this analysis comes from cases where the negated verbal predicate is not usually associated with certain activities. For these sentences, a manner reading is not so readily available, cf. (133) and (134).

(133) a. *Hans hat **geschickt** den Knoten gelöst.*
     Hans has skillfully the knot untied
     'Hans skillfully untied the knot.'
    b. *Hans hat **geschickt** den Knoten **nicht** gelöst.*
     Hans has skillfully the knot not untied
     'Cleverly, Hans did not untie the knot.'

(134) a. *Hans hat **geschickt** geschrieben.*
     Hans has skillfully written
     'Hans wrote skillfully.'
    b. *Hans hat **geschickt nicht** geschrieben.*
     Hans has cleverly   not   written
     'Cleverly, Hans did not write.'

For both (133) and (134), a manner reading is only possible if an activity is construed that is used to uphold the state of not_untying_the_knot and not_writing, respectively. Such a reading might be possible for (133b) in situations where someone is supposed to untie a knot and in fact pretends to do so, but in reality does everything he can to not untie it. For (134b), it is hard to imagine what a possible situation could be that makes this sentence a plausible description of an active covert avoidance of an action.

 At the beginning of section 7, I argued that the impossibility of manner adverbials to take scope over negation can be explained semantically: if the manner adverbial precedes the negation, then no process or activity where a manner can be specified is available. The patterns for *geschickt* 'skillful' show one exception to this rule, since here the negated verb is associated with a specific activity, and a manner can be specified.

8.   Conclusion

This chapter discussed the verb-related adverbial usages of adjectives, their difference to secondary predications, and some issue relating in particular to manner adverbials, namely, the relation between manner modifiers and specific verb classes and the relationship between manner modification and negation.

In section 1, I argued that although all verb-related adverbials share some properties, the several subgroups make very different kinds of meaning contributions to their host sentences. In addition, they must be kept apart from secondary predications, which, just like verb-related adverbials, can be questioned with *Wie?* 'how?'. I argued that the key to grasp the differences between these modifiers is to think about the different places within the conceptual structures of the events denoted by the verbal predicates to whose specification the adverbials contribute.

Section 2 introduced manner adverbials and their most important paraphrases, the *Wie-das-ist-* and the *In-ADJ-manner*-paraphrases. In addition, I argued for the distinction between one-dimensional and multi-dimensional manner adverbials. Furthermore, I distinguished between pure and agent-oriented adverbials.

Section 3 gave a short overview of degree modification, arguing that the most important characteristics of degree modification are 1. its dependence on some kind of intensity scale provided by the verb and 2. its restriction to just one scale, even when different lexical items are used to express the degree modification.

Section 4 discussed method-oriented adverbials, a subclass of verb-related adverbials dominated by de-nominal adjectives and specifying the source of the methods or means used.

Section 5 discussed secondary predications, especially with regard to their differences from verb-related adverbials. As it turned out, adjectives can be ambiguous between resultative and manner adverbials as well as depictive and manner adverbials, the latter especially holds for psychological adjectives. In addition, the term 'blend' was introduced for those usages where resultative and manner meaning are indistinguishably entwined.

Section 6 focused on the often discussed incompatibility between stative predicates and verb-related modifiers. In a nutshell, I argued, adapting an idea by Geuder (2006), that the most promising approach to explain this data lies in turning to the conceptual structures associated with the events referred to in the respective sentence, and not in a principled distinction between the formal properties of stative and non-stative predicates.

Section 7 discussed several issues concerning verb-related adverbials and negation. 7.1 focused on the relationship between manner adverbials within the scope of negation and the un-negated sentential base, arguing with Jacobs (1982) that this involves conversational implicatures. Section 7.2 discussed cases where manner adverbials can have scope over negation, arguing that this is only possible if the negated verbal predicate can be interpreted as a specific activity whose manner is then modified.

For convenience, tabe 2 gives an overview of the verb-related usages of adverbial adjectives, and table 3 gives an overview of the usages of adjectives as secondary predicates discussed in this chapter.

Table 2. Verb-related usages of adverbial adjectives

type of verb-related adverbial	example sentence and free English translation
pure manner	*Peggy tanzt schön.* 'Petra dances beautifully.'
agent-oriented manner	*Peggy argumentiert geschickt.* 'Peggy argues skillfully.'
degree	*Peggy liebt Martin unheimlich.* 'Peggy loves Martin unbelievably.'
method-oriented	*Peggy argumentiert linguistisch.* 'Peggy argues linguistically.'

Table 3. Adjectives as secondary predicates

type of secondary predication	example sentence and free English translation
resultative	*Peggy streicht die Wand blau.* 'Peggy paints the wall blue.'
depictive [subject]	*Peggy streicht die Wand nackt.* 'Peggy paints the wall nude.'
depicte [object]	*Peggy isst das Fleisch nackt.* 'Peggy eats the meat raw.'
implicit resultative	*Peggy belädt den Wagen schwer.* 'Peggy loads the cart heavily.'

Chapter 4
Event-related adverbials

Whereas the verb-related adverbials discussed so far targeted internal aspects of the events denoted by the verbal predicates, this chapter investigates adverbial usages that, though clearly relating to the event introduced by the verbal predicate, do so in a much more indirect way, so that the internal characteristics of the event that are contributed by the verbal predicate are not the target of the modification.

In the first section, mental-attitude adverbials as well as transparent adverbials are introduced and discussed, especially in contrast to depictives. The second section focuses on event-external adverbials. This name is intended to catch the intuition that these usages involve more or even different events than the event introduced by the verbal predicate. The group is rather heterogeneous, comprising inchoative readings of some adjectives, holistic usages, as well as modification of complex events. In the third section, the semantics behind the *wobei-* 'in doing so'-paraphrase is investigated, leading to the introduction of another usage, the associated readings.

1. Mental-attitude adverbials

Mental-attitude adverbials describe the attitude of the agent with regard to the activity described by the verbal predicate, cf. the examples in (1).[35]

(1) a. *Martha geht **widerwillig** zur Schule.*
         Martha goes reluctant   to   school
         'Martha goes to school reluctantly.'
     b. *Fritz schummelt **absichtlich**.*
         Fritz cheats   intentional
         'Fritz cheats intentionally.'
     c. *Der Mann spielt **heimlich** Fußball.*
         The man   plays secret   soccer
         'The man secretly plays soccer.'

Widerwillig 'reluctant' in (1a) does not primarily characterize the manner of going to school, but Martha's attitude towards going to school. That this attitude has repercussions on the manner of going is secondary. *Absichtlich* 'intentional' in (1b) describes the attitude of the agent with respect to the decision to cheat.[36] Finally, *heimlich* 'secret' functions in a more complex way. Not the mental attitude or mental state of the agent is secret; rather, the agent intends to keep his actions secret. Mental-attitude adverbials are agent-oriented, but in contrast to the agent-oriented manner adverbials discussed in section 2.3 in chapter 3, they have scope over negation, cf. (2), where (2a) implies (2b).

(2)   a.   *Martha geht **widerwillig/absichtlich/heimlich** nicht zur Schule.*
Martha goes reluctant/intentional/secret   not   to   school
'Martha reluctantly/on purpose/secretly does not go to school.'

       b.   *Martha geht nicht zur Schule.*
Martha goes not   to   school
'Martha does not go to school.'

The *Wie-das-ist-* and the *in-ADJ-manner*-paraphrases, introduced in the previous chapter as paraphrases for manner adverbials, do not work for mental-attitude adverbials, cf. (3).

(3)   *Jürgen zielt **widerwillig/absichtlich/heimlich** daneben.*
Jürgen aims reluctant/intentional/secret   off.target
'Jürgen reluctantly/intentionally/secretly aims off target.'

       a.   *Wie Jürgen daneben zielt, das ist*
how Jürgen off.target aims, that is
widerwillig/absichtlich/heimlich. (≠a)
reluctant/intentional/secret
'How Jürgen aims off target, that is reluctant/intentional/secret.'

       b.   *?Jürgen zielt auf widerwillige/absichtliche/heimliche*
Jürgen aims on reluctant/intentional/secret
Art und Weise daneben. (≠a)
manner   off.target
'Jürgen aims off target in a reluctant/intentional/secret manner.'

In contrast, just as the verb-related adverbials discussed in the previous chapter, mental-attitude adverbials can be elicited with the help of *Wie?* 'How?', cf. (4).

(4)   a.   *Wie hat er das Kind geschlagen?*
how has he the child hit
'How did he hit the child?'

b. ***Widerwillig/absichtlich/heimlich.***
reluctant/intentional/secret
'Reluctantly/intentionally/secretly.'

Using the *How?*-question also allows one to distinguish mental-attitude adverbials from sentence adverbials. In addition, the standard paraphrases for sentence adverbials do not work for mental-attitude adverbials, cf. e.g. (5), where (5b) is an attempt to use the paraphrase for subject-oriented adverbials for the mental-attitude adverbial in (5a).

(5)   a.   *Fritz ist **widerwillig** zur Schule gegangen.*
Fritz is reluctant   to school gone
'Fritz went to school reluctantly.'

        b.   *?Es war widerwillig von Fritz, daß er zur Schule gegangen ist.*
It was reluctant   of Fritz, that he to school gone   has
'It was reluctant of Fritz, that he went to school.'

1.1. Mental-attitude adverbials and opacity

The English translation equivalent of *absichtlich*, *intentionally*, has figured very prominently in the discussion of adverbials and opacity. Thomason and Stalnaker (1973) argue that *intentionally* creates opaque contexts for the object position, basing their argumentation on (6), their (68).

(6)   a.   Oedipus **intentionally** married Jocasta.
        b.   Jocasta is Oedipus' mother.
        c.   Therefore, Oedipus **intentionally** married his mother.

According to them, the inference in (6) is logically not valid, that is, we cannot deduce (6c) from (6a) and (6b). As it stands, this argument is hardly convincing; the inference from (6a-b) to (6c) seems straightforward. On the other hand, a sentence like (7), discussed by Eckardt (2003), her (13), can receive a non-contradictory interpretation.

(7)   Oedipus **intentionally** married Iocaste, but did not **intentionally** marry his mother.

How can we explain all this? Bonami, Godard and Kampers-Manhe (2004), discussing a parallel example from French,[37] observes that the inference in (6) fails because "we are dealing with an imperfect information state. [...] the evaluation is sensitive to the information state of an agent mentioned in the sentence, whereas agentive adverbs [subject-oriented adverbials] are sensitive to the information state of the discourse participant" (Bonami, Godard and Kampers-Manhe 2004:23). But this does not really seem sufficient to explain the pattern, and especially it does not explain why the inference in (6) as well as the sentence in (7) seems OK. What seems to happen is that (6) is fine because the proper name and the definite description can receive a specific interpretation, that is, they are interpreted as referring to the very same specific referent in both cases. In contrast, if we take *his mother* on a non-specific reading, then the reference does not seem to go through, because on that reading it is the specific intension that is the target of the intention and not the specific referent. And on this latter reading, (7) makes perfect sense. That it is the specific-non-specific distinction that is relevant is supported by data like the sentences in (8), where non-specific readings are pragmatically likely. Assuming (8a) and (8b) are given, the inference to (8c) does not seem to be valid.

(8)　　a.　Oedipus **intentionally** married a princess.
　　　　b.　The princess is a liar.
　　　　c.　Therefore, Oedipus **intentionally** married a liar.

Mental-attitude adverbials therefore create opacity for their direct objects, but on a specific reading, the opacity vanishes.[38]

1.2.　Mental-attitude adverbials vs. secondary predication

Mental-attitude adverbials predicate of the agent of the predication expressed by the sentential base of the sentence and thus share an important property with subject depictives, cf. *nackt* 'nude' and *betrunken* 'drunk' in (9).

(9)　　a.　*Martha geht **nackt** zur Schule.*
　　　　　　Martha goes nude to   school
　　　　　　'Martha goes to school nude.'
　　　　b.　*Martha geht **betrunken** zur Schule.*
　　　　　　Martha goes drunk   to school
　　　　　　'Martha goes to school drunk.'

In most cases, the distinction between mental-attitude adverbials and depictives is unproblematic. Whereas mental-attitude adverbials are closely connected to the event expressed by the verbal predicate, depictives are independent of this event, as evidenced by *nackt* 'nude' and *betrunken* 'drunk' in (9).

The difficulties arise when the adjectives themselves denote a mental state, cf. the psychological adjectives in (10).

(10)   *Martha geht **traurig/wütend** zur Schule.*
Martha goes sad/angry   to   school
'Martha goes to school sad/sadly/angry/angrily.'

Principally, the two sentences in (10) are three-way ambiguous: As agent-oriented manner adverbials, *traurig* 'sad' and *wütend* 'angry' specify the manner of Martha's going to school. Whether she is in fact sad or angry is irrelevant. As depictives, the adjectives express that Martha's being sad/angry is co-temporal with her going to school. Finally, there is a reading on which the adjectives specify Martha's state of mind while at the same time establishing a relationship between this state of mind and the event of going to school. These usages will be discussed in detail in section 1.3.

In contrast to subject depictives, mental-attitude adverbials and resultatives can always be easily distinguished. However, sometimes ambiguities arise. Eckardt (1998) discusses such a case of ambiguity, cf. (11), her (24).

(11)   *Sarah belud   den Wagen **unsicher** mit   Holz.*
Sarah loaded the cart   uncertain with wood
'Sarah loaded the cart uncertainly with wood.'
   a.   Sarah loaded the cart with wood in a manner that showed that she was not certain whether or how this was to be done (The load itself might have been stable).
   b.   Sarah loaded the cart with wood in such a way that the load was insecurely fixed on the cart afterwards (Sarah herself was quite confident about her action).

(11) has two readings: In its first reading, paraphrased in (11a), *unsicher* 'uncertain' is interpreted has a mental attitude adverbial. On the second reading, paraphrased in (11b), *unsicher* 'uncertain [also: unsecure]' is interpreted as an implicit resultative: not the load nor the manner are unsecure, but the cart is unsecurely loaded, that is, the Zustandspassiv-Entailment discussed in section 5.2 of chapter 3 holds.

1.3.   Transparent adverbials

As mentioned in section 5.3 of chapter 3, adjectives that characterize a mental state can serve either as a depictive or as a manner adverbial, cf. *traurig* 'sad(ly)' in (12).

(12)   *Sabine ist **traurig** nach   Hause gegangen.*
       Sabine is sad   towards home walked
       'Sabine walked home sad/sadly.'

As Geuder (2004) argues at length, these adjective posses one further reading, because they can function as transparent adverbials, a term adapted from his *transparent adverbs*. (13) is an example of a transparent adverbial where this reading is actually the preferred reading.[39]

(13)   *Peter erkannte **traurig**, dass er der einzige Überlebende war.*
       Peter realized sad,   that he the sole   survivor   was
       'Peter sadly realized that he was the sole survivor.'

A manner reading is not available for *traurig* 'sad' in (13), because there simply is no sad manner of realizing something. Similarly, *traurig* 'sad' in (13) is not just a depictive, since the relationship between Peter recognizing his status and his sadness cannot be reduced to co-temporality. On the contrary, his sadness his linked to the recognition of his status. On its preferred interpretation, (13) means that it is the recognition that he is the sole survivor that causes his sadness. Geuder's rationale for calling these adverbial usages *transparent* is that they are not opaque with regard to the mental state of the subject, that is, they cannot be reduced to just a manner reading.

What is the difference between a transparent adverbial and the examples of mental attitude adverbials in (1)? In the terminology used here, transparent adverbials are simply a subgroup of mental attitude adverbials, a view which is, as far as I can see, compatible with the usage of the term *mental attitude adverb* in Ernst (2002). Geuder (2004), who argues explicitly against the account of Ernst (2002), distinguishes between *transparent adverbs* and *intentional adverbs*. *Intentional adverbs* "denote attitudes by virtue of their lexical content" Ernst (2002:146), e.g. *reluctantly, willingly*, and *intentionally*. Geuder argues, on the basis of English data, that intentional adverbs differ from transparent adverbs because they have different readings in different positions. In addition, they have a different semantics, cf. (14), his (38).

(14)   a.   I **angrily** forwarded the letter to my solicitor.
       b.   I **reluctantly** forwarded the letter to my solicitor.

Commenting on this pair, Geuder states that "the thing that angers me is not my forwarding the letter. In contrast to this, the forwarding is indeed what constitutes the objective of my reluctance [...]" (Geuder 2004:146-147). Although I agree with Geuder's observation, I will leave it open whether this justifies establishing transparent adverbials as a separate class from mental attitude adverbials, all the more so since they will not play a large role in the semantic analysis to follow in chapter 7.

The important point made by Geuder (2004), and this is an observation also made in Ernst (1984, 2002), is that one and the same word can either serve as a manner adverbial or a mental attitude adverbial, depending on whether it is opaque or transparent with respect to the actual mental state of the agent.

1.4. Transparent adverbials, depictives and negation

Pittner (1999:105, 115) notes that if depictives have scope over the sentence negation, they are interpreted as shortened adverbial clauses, with a causal, conditional, concessive or some other clausal relation to the embedding sentence, cf. (15), Pittner's (117a), and (16), her (134).

(15)   *Er kam **krank** nicht aus   dem Urlaub zurück.*
          he came sick   not   from the holiday back
          'Sick, he did not return from his vacations.'

(16)   *Hans ist **krank** nicht zur Arbeit gegangen.*
          Hans is sick   not   to   work   went
          'Sick, Hans did not go to work.'

The most natural interpretation of (15) is that his sickness was the cause of his not coming back from his vacations. Similarly, for (16), Hans did not go to work because he was sick.

In these cases we therefore get a clear connection between the predication contributed by the secondary predicate and the negated sentential base, presenting almost the mirror image of the relationship between the predication of a transparent adverbial and the sentential base. That is, while in the case of the transparent adverbials, e.g. *traurig* 'sad' in (13), the event described by the sentential base causes the sadness, it is the state described by the secondary predicate that causes the negated event in (16) and (15). We find the same effect for the standard examples of depictives, cf. (17), the negated variants of example (76) in chapter 3.

(17)   a.   *Er isst das Fleisch **roh** nicht.*
           he eats the meat   raw not
           'He doesn't eat the meat, because it is raw.'
    b.   *Er isst das Fleich **nackt** nicht.*
           he eats the meat   nude not
           'He doesn't eat the meat, because he is nude.'

As (17a) shows, these kinds of readings even arise for object depictives.

If it is difficult to establish a causal or other salient connection between the predication contributed by the adjective and the negated sentential base, the sentences appear correspondingly odd, cf. (18).

(18)   *Uta ist **gutgelaunt**   nicht zur   Party gegangen.*
    Uta is in.a.good.temper not   to.the party went
    'In a good temper, Uta did not go to the party.'

For (18), the most likely interpretation is a concessive reading: although she was in a good mood, Uta did not go to the party.

2.   Event-external adverbials

The term 'event-external adverbials' is here used as a cover term for a rather large number of different usages which are in some ways very much like manner adverbials. They differ from manner adverbials in that they are not directly connected to the event predicated over by the verbal predicate. I.e., they either specify the time-span leading up to the event introduced by the verbal predicate, or they make a predication over the event introduced by the verbal predicate in a very holistic manner, or they predicate over an event that is in other aspects more complex than the event introduced by the verbal predicate. I will focus on three subclasses: inchoative readings, holistic usages, and modifiers of complex/inferred events.

Many distinctions made in this section are inspired by or adapted from the works of Frey and Pittner, but my usage of the term 'event-external adverbials' does not correspond to their usage of *event-external adjunct*, cf. Frey (2003), but rather to a class they refer to either as *event-internal adjuncts* in Frey (2003) or as *ereignisbezogene Adverbiale/event related adverbials* in Pittner (1999:106-108) and Frey and Pittner (1998, 1999).

2.1. Inchoative readings of *schnell* and *langsam*

Adjectives like *schnell* 'fast' and *langsam* 'slow' have usages where they target eventualities different from the ones introduced by the verbal predicate. Since the usage of *langsam* 'slow' is rather idiosyncratic, I will start with a discussion of *schnell* 'quick' in the sentences in (19).

(19) a. *Roland hat **schnell** die Reißleine gezogen.*
          Roland has fast   the rip.cord   pulled
          'Roland quickly pulled the plug.'
      b. *Wir sind **schnell** gegangen, weil   die Party total*
          we are   quick   left,   because the party totally
          langweilig war.
          boring   was
          'We quickly left, because the party was a total bore.'
      c. *Der Zug fuhr **schnell** langsamer.*
          the train drove quickly slower.
          'Quickly, the train slowed down.'

The semantic function of *schnell* 'quick' in all three sentences in (19) is to specify the time span from a given reference point to the beginning of the activity denoted by the verb as short. It does not directly specify the event introduced by the verbal predicate, nor does it target the internal structure of that event.

In this usage, *schnell* 'quick' can therefore easily be combined with statives and achievements, cf. (20).

(20) a. *Frieda wußte die Antwort **schnell**.*
          Frieda knew the answer quick
          'Quickly, Frieda knew the answer.'
      b. *Bolli heiratete Julia **schnell**.*
          Bolli married   Julia quick
          'Bolli quickly married Julia. (Context: they had known each other for only two weeks.)'

The event-external reading of *langsam* 'slow' is exemplified by (21).

(21) *Mach **langsam** die Tür zu!*
       close slow   the door PART
       'It is high time you close the door!'

(21)   **Langsam** fuhr er schneller.
  slow drove he faster
  'Slowly, he began to go faster.'

The event-external reading of *langsam* 'slow' has, as the translation shows, a very idiosyncratic meaning, and in this it differs from *schnell* 'quick', where the different readings are closely related, though its usage is also highly conventionalized.

2.2.   Holistic usages

The holistic usages of verb-related adverbials are those that refer to one single event as a whole, even if that event itself consists of a number of separate subevents or repetitions of the same event-type. I will first consider cases where authors have tried to make a differentiation between the activity referred to by the verbal predicate and the individual subevents constituting this event. In the second section, I will discuss cases where quantified direct objects lead to holistic modifications of repetitions of the same event.

2.2.1.   *Holistic usages and the internal structure of the event*

Maienborn (2003a) uses the two sentences in (22), her (82), to argue for a distinction between a holistic interpretation and a subevent-oriented interpretation.

(22) a. *Jochen schmückte **schnell** den Weihnachtsbaum.*
    Jochen decorated   quick   the Christmas.tree
    'Jochen quickly decorated the Christmas tree.'
  b. *Jochen schmückte den Weihnachtsbaum **schnell**.*
    Jochen decorated the Christmas.tree   quick
    'Jochen decorated the Christmas tree quickly.'

According to Maienborn (2003a:93), (22a) is two-way ambiguous. On one reading, it is interpreted as in (23), which corresponds to the readings of *schnell* discussed in the previous section. The second reading is paraphrased in (24).

(23) The distance in time between some contextual reference point and the beginning of the decoration event was short.

(24) The duration of Jochen's decorating_the_Christmas_tree was short.

In its purest form, the holistic interpretation thus specifies only the speed dimension of the decorating event, in effect saying that the decorating took only a short amount of time. As Maienborn (2003a:93-94) points out, it does not say anything about the speed at which the subevents involved in decorating the tree (e.g. application of ornaments, fixation of the candles and whatnot) unfolded.

This holistic interpretation can be contrasted with a non-holistic interpretation, illustrated by Maienborn (2003a:94) with (22b), the same sentence with a different word order (more on this point in chapter 5) in (25).[40]

According to Maienborn, the preferred interpretation of *schnell* 'quick' in (22b) is that *schnell* 'quick' "evaluates the length of the subevents of processes and accomplishments; [...]. The interpretation of (22b) on this reading is that Jochen executed the discrete acts which constitute the decoration of a Christmas tree (application of ornaments, fixation of the candles and distribution of tinsel) quickly, while the event as a whole might well have taken its time" (Maienborn 2003a:93-94) [my translation].

Maienborn is right in saying that one can conceptually distinguish between the modification of subevents and the modification of the event as a whole. But *schnell* 'quick' cannot be used to illustrate this feature. Even if, as Maienborn says, the whole event might well have taken its time, it will still be judged as quickly. I will come back to this issue below.

Interestingly, Tenny (2000), who analyzes the adverbial usages of *quickly* in English, argues for a three-way distinction that seems to exactly mirror Maienborn's proposal.

According to Tenny (2000), *quickly* can be used either as a rate adverbial or as a manner adverbial. In turn, the usage as a rate adverbial falls into two distinct subclasses: a higher reading, corresponding to the inchoative reading discussed above, and a lower reading. In addition, she also assumes a manner reading. She illustrates the difference between the lower rate reading ('true rate modification') and the manner reading ('pure manner modification') with (25), her (66), where the respective interpretations are given in (25a) and (25b).

(25)   Kazuko moved **quickly** to the window.

   a.   Kazuko moved her body in quick motions while progressing to the window, although her traversal of the path to the window may not have been a fast one.

   b.   Kazuko's traversal of the path to the window was fast.

The two different interpretations of (25) as (25a) and (25b) are not very convincing. Although it is true that a verb such as *move to* allows, in a similar way as e.g. *swim* and *run*, modification of the path of movement, as well as of the manner of the movement (cf. the section on *Zweibewegungsverben* 'double-movement verbs' in Engelberg 2000:294-299), *quickly* is not a good candidate to demonstrate such a difference. On the contrary, a *quick* manner of movement does, in the case of swimming, usually directly correlate with a *quick* traversal of the path in question. This is not to say that the situation does not exists, that is, one can easily imagine someone being in the water and making fast movements but not moving forward at all. But this would not be referred to with *swimming fast*. This must have occured to Tenny, too, as she herself states that "the pure manner reading [paraphrased in (25a)] is odd" (Tenny 2000:322).

As far as I can tell, both Maienborn and Tenny have the same distinction between a holistic and a non-holistic reading in mind. In both cases, they use *quickly* or its German equivalent to make their case, and this is what makes the examples unconvincing, because the two usages are not truly independent: I cannot execute all the subevents fast, but end up with the hole event being executed slowly. This accounts for the oddness of a sentence like (26), with *schnell* in a holistic interpretation.

(26)   ??*Jochen hat **schnell** den Weihnachtsbaum **langsam** geschmückt.*
       Jochen has fast   the Christmas.tree   slow   decorated

A better illustration of what both authors must have had in mind is given in Engelberg's discussion of double-movement verbs, which he analyses as referring to events which in turn consist of two sub-events, one being the translatory movement involved, the other one the movements of the event-participant. As Engelberg argues, while *elegant* 'elegant' in (27a), his (30a), targets the movements of the event-participant, *ohne Umwege* 'without detours' in (27b), his (30b), targets the translatory movements, cf. the respective paraphrases.

(27)   a.   *Sie schwamm **elegant** zum   gegenüberliegenden Beckenrand.*
             she swam   elegant to.the opposing   pool.edge
             'She elegantly swam to the other side of the pool.'
             ≈ She moved with elegant swimming movements to the other
             side of the pool.

b. *Sie schwamm **ohne** **Umwege** zum gegenüberliegenden*
   she swam   without detour to.the opposing
Beckenrand.
pool.edge
'She swam directly to the other side of the pool'
≈ She moved directly with swimming movements to the other
side of the pool.

This example works, because the modifiers clearly target different aspects of the event. While Engelberg analyses it as consisting of two sub-events, it could also be described by the distinction introduced in the discussion of *quickly*: one modifier modifies the whole event holistically, the other predicates of all the subevents.

Pittner (1999:107) argues that *schön* 'beautiful' can also occur as an event-external adverbial[41] that targets the event holistically, cf. (28), her (122a).

(28)   *Sie hat **schön** das Bild gemalt.*
        she has beautiful the painting painted
        'She nicely painted the painting.'

I agree with Pittner that these usages somehow target the event described by the verb in a holistic way, although I am not exactly sure how to explain the semantics of this usage. Pittner (1999:107) writes that the event "*schön* (ruhig, friedlich o.ä.) ablief" [took place *beautifully*, i.e. quietly, peacefully etc.]. In addition, it often has positive consequences for the agent or some other participant mentioned in the sentence, cf. the two examples in (29).

(29)   a.   *Die Kinder haben **schön** im Garten gespielt und wir*
           the children have beautiful in.the garden played and we
           konnten in Ruhe Kaffeetrinken.
           could   in peace coffee.drink
           'The children went off to play in the garden, allowing us to have coffee in peace.'
    b.   *Peggy hat **schön** ihre Steuererklärung gemacht, und ich*
           Peggy has beautiful her tax.return   made,   and I
           hab Alien geguckt.
           have Alien watched
           'Peggy did her tax return, and I watched Alien.'

In (29a), the children's playing proceeds smoothly, and the fact that the children play in the garden is seen as positive for the party interested in drinking coffee. In (29b), Peggy is fully engulfed in the specific activity of doing her taxes, and this fact is seen as positive not only for her, but also for the agent in the coordinated sentence (note that this aspect is not reflected in the free English translation).

2.2.2.   Quantified direct objects

If the objects in a sentence contain quantification, this often leads to very clear differences between holistic and non-holistic readings. A classic example is given in (30).[42]

(30)   a.   Sam **carefully** sliced all the bagels.
        b.   Sam sliced all the bagels **carefully**.

Syntactically, the two sentences differ in that *carefully* in (30a) has scope over the quantified direct object *all bagels*, whereas in (30b) it is the other way around. In addition, as Lakoff (1972:section IX-A fn. 2) points out, (30a) is compatible with (31). In contrast, (30b) is not compatible with (31).

(31)   Sam sliced some of the bagels **carelessly**.

The easiest analysis of this contrast is to assume that *carefully* in (30a) is used as a subject-oriented adverbial (in the literature alternatively referred to as 'sentential reading', 'sentence adverb(ial)' or 'clausal reading'). In contrast, in (30b) it occurs with a manner reading, cf. (32) with the repeated examples and the appropriate paraphrases.[43]

(32)   a.   Sam **carefully** sliced all the bagels. [subject-oriented reading]
              ≈ It was careful of Sam that he sliced all the bagels.
        b.   Sam sliced all the bagels **carefully**. [manner reading]
              ≈ The way in which Sam sliced all the bagels, that was careful.

In order to verify this analysis, it is insightful to look at the German translation equivalents of (30) (cf. Bartsch 1972:168-172, which I used as the source for the German versions of the sentences under discussion). As has been mentioned several times, German allows the formation of sentential adverbials with the help of the suffix *-weise*. However, *sorgfältigerweise* necessarily has syntactic scope over a quantified direct object. With respect to the scope in relation to the direct object, German thus offers three variants: *sorgfältig* before or after the direct object, cf. (33a) and (33b), and *sorgfältigerweise* with scope over the direct object, cf. (34a).[44]

(33) a. *Sam schnitt **sorgfältig** alle Brötchen.*
          Sam sliced careful   all rolls
          'Sam carefully sliced all rolls.'

      b. *Sam schnitt alle Brötchen **sorgfältig**.*
          Sam sliced all rolls   careful
          'Sam sliced all rolls carefully.'

(34) a. *Sam schnitt **sorgfältigerweise** alle Brötchen.*
          Sam sliced carefully   all rolls
          'Carefully, Sam sliced all rolls.'

      b. **Sam schnitt alle Brötchen **sorgfältigerweise**.*
          Sam sliced all rolls   carefully

The linearizations that start with the preposed adverbial add nothing new as far as scope is concerned. (35a) seems semantically to correspond to (33a), and (35b) corresponds to (34a).

(35) a. ***Sorgfältig** schnitt Sam alle Brötchen.*
          careful   sliced Sam all rolls
          'Sam carefully sliced all rolls.'

      b. ***Sorgfältigerweise** schnitt Sam alle Brötchen.*
          carefully   sliced Sam all rolls
          'Carefully, Sam sliced all rolls.'

The translation equivalent to the English word order **direct object**$_{quantized}$ **> manner adverbial** is the parallel German linearization **direct object**$_{quantized}$ **> manner adverbial**, that is (30b) corresponds to (33b). The English sentence with the word order **manner adverbial > direct object**$_{quantized}$ can be translated into German either as (33a) or as (34a).

The remaining question is whether there are any differences in meaning between the two German sentences (33a) and (34a), which share the word order but differ in that one sentence employs the adjectival short form, the other the *-weise*-derivation. (36) repeats the German version of the pair for convenience.

(36) a. Sam schnitt **sorgfältig** alle Brötchen.
      b. Sam schnitt **sorgfältigerweise** alle Brötchen.

Bartsch (1972:168) gives the two paraphrases in (37) for (36a).

(37)   a.   *Sam handelte insofern sorgfältig, als er **alle** Brötchen schnitt.*
           Sam acted   insofar careful,   as he all rolls   sliced
           'Sam acted careful in as far as he sliced all rolls.'
           [Bartsch's emphasis]
       b.   *Sam handelte sorgfältig, indem er alle Brötchen schnitt.*
           Sam acted   careful   in.that he all rolls   sliced
           'Sam acted careful in that he sliced all rolls.'

If the meaning of (36a) is captured by these two paraphrases, Bartsch writes, there is no discernible difference between the meaning of (36a) and the meaning of (36b). In turn, this means that the meaning difference between the two linear orders in English, cf. (30a) and (30), is in fact that in (30a) the adverbial functions as a subject-oriented adverbial, in (30) as a manner adverbial.

The situation does not seem to be as simple as this, though. Thus, Eckardt (1998) argues that there is an interpretational difference between (38a) and (38b), her (1),[45] even if the sentential reading (in her terminology, evaluative reading) is excluded.

(38)   a.   Alma picked each worm **carefully** out of the salad.
       b.   Alma **carefully** picked each worm out of the salad.

Eckardt notes the following difference in meaning: "For (38b) [her 1a] to be true, it is enough that Alma's care was devoted to each single worm picking. We get the feeling that the care was directed, for example, towards not hurting the worm. In sentence (38a) [her 1b] Alma's care focusses on some overall task. While she might be indifferent with respect to the health of the single worm, she is concerned about the state of the salad" (Eckardt 1998:9).

It is not clear to me to what extend this observation captures the intuition of native speakers.[46] If we turn to the German translation equivalents, these exact readings do not seem to be available, cf. (39).

(39)   a.   *Klara hat jeden Wurm **sorgfältig** aus   dem Salat entfernt.*
           Klara has every worm careful   from the salad removed
           'Klara removed every worm carefully from the salad.'
       b.   *Klara hat **sorgfältig** jeden Wurm aus   dem Salat entfernt.*
           Klara has careful   every worm from the salad removed
           'Klara carefully removed every worm from the salad.'

One problem is that *sorgfältig* does not correspond in all respects to *carefully*. That is, there is no reading of (39a) where one gets the feeling that the care was directed towards not hurting the worm. If such a reading is intended, a different adverbial, namely *vorsichtig* 'cautious', is more likely to be used, cf. (40).

(40)   *Klara hat jeden Wurm **vorsichtig** aus   dem Salat entfernt.*
        Klara has every worm cautious   from the   salad removed
        'Klara removed every worm cautiously from the salad.'

Even with *vorsichtig* 'cautious', Eckardt's example interpretation remains difficult, perhaps for pragmatic reasons (who cares about the health of the worms when cleaning a salad!).

   Although I doubt that the exact readings mentioned by Eckardt are available in either English or German, there still seems to be something to her observation. To see this, consider the different preferences for on the one hand, the *Wie-das-ist*-paraphrase, and, on the other hand, a paraphrase with *wobei*, as shown in (41), again associated with their preferred linear order (the *wobei*-paraphrase will be discussed in detail in section 3).

(41)   a.   *Klara hat jeden Wurm **sorgfältig** aus   dem Salat entfernt.*
              Klara has every worm careful   from the   salad removed
              'Klara carefully removed every worm from the salad'
        (i)   *Wie Klara jeden Wurm aus   dem Salat entfernt hat,*
               how Klara every worm from the   salad removed has,
               das war sorgfältig. (preferred paraphrase)
               that was careful
               'The way in which Klara picked each worm from the salad was careful.'
        (ii)   *Klara hat jeden Wurm aus   dem Salat entfernt,*
               Klara has every worm from the   salad removed,
               wobei   sie sorgfältig war. (dispreferred paraphrase)
               in.doing.so she careful   was
               'Klara picked every worm from the salad. In doing so, she was careful.'

b.   *Klara hat **sorgfältig** jeden Wurm aus   dem Salat entfernt.*
Klara has careful   every worm from the   salad removed.
'Klara carefully removed every worm from the salad'
(i)   *Wie Klara jeden Wurm aus   dem Salat entfernt hat,*
how Klara every worm from the   salad removed has,
das war sorgfältig. (questionable paraphrase)
that was careful
'The way in which Klara picked each worm from the salad was careful.'
(ii)   *Klara hat jeden Wurm aus   dem Salat entfernt,*
Klara has every worm from the   salad removed,
wobei   sie sorgfältig war. (preferred paraphrase)
in.doing.that she careful   was
'Klara picked every worm from the salad. In doing so, she
was careful.'

It thus turns out that we can in fact distinguish two different adverbial readings of *sorgfältig* 'carefully', a manner reading, and a second reading, which
I will refer to as an 'associated reading' (the term is adapted from the term
'associative sense' in Cresswell 1985:187; for more on associated readings,
cf. section 3.2.3). While the manner readings are preferably linked to a position after the direct object, the associated readings preferably occur in the
pre- direct object position.

The quantificational scope seems to go well together with other cases with
more or less established different readings, cf. (42).

(42)   a.   *Thomas hat jedes Brötchen **schnell** geschmiert.*
Thomas has every roll   quick   buttered
'Thomas buttered every roll quickly'
b.   *Thomas hat **schnell** jedes Brötchen geschmiert.*
Thomas has quick   every roll   buttered
'Thomas quickly buttered every roll'

(42a) is preferably interpreted with a manner reading, that is, the agent might
have had breaks in between the preparation of the individual rolls, while (42b)
is either inchoative, holistic, or both.

Quantificational scope cannot override the word order for adverbials that
appear only after the direct object, cf. the patterns for the method-oriented
adverbial *alphabetisch* 'alphabetical' in (43).

(43) a. *Thomas hat alle seine CDs **alphabetisch** sortiert.*
      Thomas has all his CDs alphabetical sorted
      'Thomas keeps his CDs in alphabetical order.'
   b. ??*Thomas hat **alphabetisch** alle seine CDs sortiert.*
      Thomas has alphabetical all his CDs sorted

The usage of quantified direct objects in sentences containing manner adverbials thus appears to be quite consistent: Whenever no other reading alternative is available, the surface scope is used for interpretation. For some adjectives, e.g. *sorgfältig* 'careful', this leads to rather subtle reading differences.

2.2.3. Modifiers of complex events

What I describe here as modifiers of complex events are actually variants of the holistic usage; the only difference is that in these cases, the complex event is build up analytically due to the involvement of additional verb-related modifiers. The classic example of a non-mental attitude verb-related adverbial to take scope over another verb-related adverbial is the following sentence from Parsons (1972:131):

(44) John **painstakingly** wrote **illegibly**.

Crucially, Parsons (1972) notes that (44) requires that "the illegibility of the writing was at least one of the things John was taking pains to do" (Parsons 1972:p. 131). That is, *painstakingly* does not specify the manner of the writing, but rather specifies the manner of the writing_illegibly.

The German translation equivalent of (44), given in (45), shows the same semantic scope effect as the English sentence.

(45) *Fritz hat **sorgfältig unleserlich** geschrieben.*
      Fritz has painstaking illegible written
      'Fritz painstakingly wrote illegibly.'

A similar phenomenon is exhibited by the German sentence in (46).

(46) *Hans hat **geschickt** die Frage **dumm** beantwortet.*
      Hans has skillful the question stupidly answered
      'Hans skillfully answered the question stupidly.'

This sentence can only be successfully interpreted if the stupidity of the answer was one of the things in which Hans showed his skill.

A context that makes the intented reading of (46) clearer is given in (47).[47]

(47)   *Auch nach sieben Tagen Einzelhaft hat Hans die Fragen **so geschickt** dumm beantwortet, dass niemand auf die Idee gekommen wäre, dass er die Antworten aus dem Effeff kannte.*

'Even after seven days of solitary confinement did Hans answer the questions so craftily stupidly, that no one could possibly suspect that he knew the answers off pat.'

As noted by Peterson (1997:241), the English adverb *carefully* also exhibits semantic scope effects, cf. (48), his (47).

(48)   John **carefully** buttered toast **quietly**.

Peterson argues that (48) has one interpretation that is synonymous with *John was careful in buttering (to butter the) toast quietly*. Such an interpretation is possible, as Peterson argues, if we imagine a situation where "John took care to be *quiet* while performing his task, but *not* that he took care in his buttering–i.e., that he buttered sloppily" (Peterson 1997:241).

I am not sure what the German translation equivalent of (48), with the reading Peterson has in mind, should be. As noted in section 2.2.2, *carefully* can be translated in its usage as a manner adverbial into German either with *sorgfältig* or with *vorsichtig*. With both adverbials, the interpretation seems to correspond to the interpretation of the corresponding sentence where *leise* 'quietly' would appear in conjunction with the other adjective. I.e., there is no meaning difference between the two sentences in (49) and the sentence in (50), and the two sentences in (49) actually sound somewhat odd.

(49)   a.   ?*Franz hat Brote **vorsichtig/sorgfältig leise** geschmiert.*
             Franz has toasts careful/cautious   quiet buttered

        b.   ?*Franz hat **vorsichtig/sorgfältig** Brote **leise** geschmiert.*
             Franz has careful/cautious   toasts quiet buttered

(50)   *Franz hat **vorsichtig/sorgfältig** und **leise** Brote geschmiert.*
        Franz has careful/cautious   and quiet toasts buttered
        'Franz buttered toasts carefully/cautiously and quietly.'

A possible reason that makes the reading intended by Peterson difficult is its pragmatic anomaly: buttering toasts is a quiet activity in the first place and demands no special efforts from the agent to be executed quietly.

Note that these instances of sentences containing two adverbials differ from those discussed in Ernst (2002), cf. (51), his (6.91).

(51) a. They play **quietly well**, but get rambunctious when we have more lively games.

  b. She runs **slowly correctly**, but loses her form when she speeds up.

In both examples, the first adverbial presents a precondition for the application of the second. Thus, (51a) expresses the same meaning as (52a), (51b) the same as (52b).

(52) a. When we have quiet games, they play well, but they get rambunctious when we have more lively games.

  b. When she runs slowly she runs correctly, but loses her form when she speeds up.

In contrast, the first set of manner adverbials in the earlier examples do not express such preconditions. In German, adjectives can be used to express such preconditions, but they are then usually fronted, as in (53).

(53) ***Langsam** läuft sie **richtig**, aber wenn sie schneller wird,*
  Slowly runs she correctly, but when she faster becomes,
  beginnt sie Fehler zu machen.
  starts she mistakes to make
  'Slowly she runs correctly, but when she speeds up, she starts making mistakes.'

3. The *wobei*-paraphrase

Bartsch (1972:151) uses paraphrases involving *wobei*- 'in doing so' to establish a subgroup of adverbials, cf. her example in (54).[48]

(54) a. *Petra kocht **sorgfältig**.*
  Petra cooks careful
  'Petra is cooking carefully.'

b. *Petra kocht, wobei   sie sorgfältig ist. (≈ a)*
Petra cooks, in.doing.so she careful   is
'Petra is cooking; in doing this she is careful.'

This paraphrase has been brought back into the discussion by Frey and Pittner (1999) and seems to work for many of the event-related adverbials. In addition, it is also available for depictives, cf. (55).

(55)   a. *Er malt   das Bild   **nackt.***
He paints the picture nude
'He paints the picture nude.'
b. *Er malt   das Bild,   wobei   er nackt ist. (≈ a)*
he paints the picture, in.doing.so he nude is
'He paints the picture, in doing so, he is nude.'

The *wobei*-paraphrase brings together a quite heterogeneous group of usages. The aim of this section is to get a better understanding of what property it is that this paraphrase targets. To start with, it is helpful to compare this paraphrase to the standard *während*-paraphrase used for depictives, before turning to the issue of the interrelation between event-related adverbials and this paraphrase.

3.1.   *Wobei* vs. *während*

The *wobei*-paraphrase can be used for depictives, and if so used, yields paraphrases that seem as good as (if not equivalent in meaning to) the paraphrases using *while*-paraphrases, cf. (56).

(56)   a. *Er malt   das Bild   **nackt.***
he paints the picture nude
'He paints the picture nude.'
b. *Er malt   das Bild,   während er nackt ist. (≈ a)*
he paints the picture, while   he nude is
'He paints the picture while he is nude.'
c. *Er malt   das Bild,   wobei   er nackt ist. (≈ a)*
he paints the picture, in.doing.so he nude is
'He paints the picture, in doing so, he is nude.'

One reason why *während* and *wobei* are interchangeable in this specific context is that the *wobei*-paraphrase is only possible when the participant of the event described by the *wobei*-sentence also occurs as a participant of the event described in the main clause. This restriction corresponds to the shared argument constraint on depictives (Rothstein 2003:567-569). *Während* is not subject to this constraint, as can be seen by comparing (57a) and (57b).

(57)   a.   *Ich schlief, während die Kinder arbeiteten.*
             I   slept,   while   the kids   worked
             'I slept, while the kids were working.'
       b.   **Ich schlief, wobei   die Kinder arbeiteten.*
             I   slept,   in.doing.so the kids   worked

However, since depictive always fulfill this condition, this difference between *wobei* and *während* becomes irrelevant.

A second important difference between *wobei* and *während* seems likewise irrelevant for depictives. This difference, discussed in Bartsch (1972:151-152), concerns the following minimal pairs (cf. Bartsch 1972:152 and Bartsch 1976:155):

(58)   a.   *Der Stein rollt den Berg   hinunter, wobei   er sich*
             the stone rolls the mountain down,   in.doing.so he himself
             überschlägt.
             somersaults
             'The stone is rolling down the mountain, in doing so it somer-saults.'
       b.   **Der Stein rollt den Berg   hinunter, während er sich*
             the stone rolls the mountain down,   while   it itself
             überschlägt.
             somersaults

(59)   a.   *Er trinkt, wobei   er schlürft.*
             he drinks, in.doing.so he slurps
             'He drinks, in doing so he slurps.'
       b.   **Er trinkt, während er schlürft.*
             he drinks while   he slurps

Bartsch writes: "Die Konjunktion 'wobei' soll hier von 'während' unter-schieden werden dadurch, daß durch die Relation zwei Aspekte eines Vor-gangs oder zwei Vorgänge zu einem Vorgang oder Handlungs-Vorgang ver-bunden werden, wogegen durch 'während' zwei Ereignisse oder Umstände zueinander in Relation gestellt werden" (Bartsch 1972:151-152) ["The con-junction 'wobei' ('at which, in doing so') should be kept apart from 'während' ('while'). In the case of 'wobei' the relation combines two aspects of a process or two processes into a single process or action, while in the case of 'während' a relation is established between two events or circumstances" Bartsch (1976:155).]

Given this description, it turns out that depictives after all seem to go beyond mere co-temporality and a shared argument constraint, although, as Bartsch's formulations show, it is hard to define exactly what this 'going beyond' is supposed to consist of. Dölling (2003:535) writes that depictives introduce states that are "to be considered a concomitant circumstance (of secondary import) to this process [the process characterized by the verbal predicate]". A similar observation seems to motivate Rothstein (2003:569) when, discussing the example of *John drove the car drunk*, she writes that "we assert that there is a sum of two events, [...], which do not just occur at the same time but which are inextricably attached to each other [...]", although I do not think that co-temporality and participant-connectedness, the two conditions she invokes, capture this inextricable attachment.

The *wobei*-paraphrase also works for object depictives, cf. (60), although the English *in doing so* cannot be used here anymore and *while* has to be used.

(60)　　a.　*Er isst das Fleisch roh.* [Object depictive]
　　　　　　 he eats the meat   raw
　　　　　　 'He eats the meat raw.'
　　　　b.　*Er isst das Fleisch, wobei   das Fleisch roh ist. (≈ a)*
　　　　　　 he eats the meat,   in.doing.so the meat   raw is
　　　　　　 'He eats the meat, in doing so [while], the meat is raw.'

This is not surprising, because object depictives need to fulfill the same conditions as subject depictives.

3.2.　Event-related adverbials and the *wobei*-paraphrase

3.2.1.　*Mental-attitude adverbials and the* wobei-*paraphrase*

All in all, the *wobei*-paraphrase delivers unclear results for mental-attitude adverbials. It never works for psychological adjectives that belong to the subclass of transparent adverbials. The reason is obvious: the paraphrase fits the depictive readings of these adjectives, which brings with it the co-temporality that is absent from transparent adverbials. For the traditional core group of mental-attitude adverbials, that is, for *absichtlich* 'intentional', *heimlich* 'secret', and *widerwillig* 'reluctant', we get mixed results. This paraphrase works for *widerwillig* 'reluctant', cf. (61), where (61b) provides a paraphrase for (61a).

(61) a. *Peter ist ihr **widerwillig** gefolgt.*
    Peter is her reluctant   followed
    'Peter followed her reluctantly.'
  b. *Peter ist ihr gefolgt, wobei er widerwillig war.*
    Peter is her followed, in.doing.so he reluctant   was
    'Peter followed her. In doing so, he was reluctant.'

In contrast, it does not work for the other two adjectives, cf. (62).

(62) a. *Martha zog Peter **absichtlich/heimlich** an den Haaren.*
    Martha pulled Peter on.purpose/secretly   at the hairs
    'Martha on purpose/secretly pulled Peter's hair.'
  b. ??*Martha zog Peter an den Haaren, wobei sie*
    Martha pulled Peter at the hairs,   in.doing.so she
    ***absichtlich/heimlich** war.*
    intentional/secret   was

Again, the reason is rather trivial: in predicative positions, the two adjectives do not allow predications over the mental state of the subject referent of copula sentences.

3.2.2. *The* wobei-*paraphrase and event-external modification*

The behavior of the *wobei*-paraphrase with respect to the different subgroups of event-external modification is rather straightforward. The paraphrase does not work for the inchoative usage of *schnell* 'quick' and *langsam* 'slow'. Again, this is not surprising, because they specify the time leading up to the event described by the verbal predicate, whereas the *wobei*-paraphrase describes something that is co-temporal to the event introduced by the verbal predicate of the main clause.

  On the other hand, the paraphrase works fine for the holistic readings of *schnell* 'quick', cf. (63), again with (63b) paraphrasing (63a).

(63) a. *Jochen schmückte **schnell** den Weihnachtsbaum.*
    Jochen decorated quickly the Christmas.tree
    'Jochen quickly decorated the Christmas tree.'

b.   *Jochen schmückte den Weihnachtsbaum, wobei   er*
Jochen decorated the Christmas.tree,   in.doing.so he
schnell war. (≈ a)
quick was
'Jochen decorated the Christmas tree. In doing so, he was
quick.'

The paraphrase is also appropriate for all holistic readings involving quantification, cf. (64) and (65).

(64)   a.   *Klara hat **sorgfältig** jeden Wurm aus   dem Salat entfernt.*
Klara has careful   every worm from the   salad removed
'Klara carefully removed every worm from the salad'

b.   *Klara hat jeden Wurm aus   dem Salat entfernt, wobei*
Klara has every worm from the   salad removed, in.doing.so
sie sorgfältig war. (≈ a)
she careful   was
'Klara picked every worm from the salad. In doing so, she was
careful.'

(65)   a.   *Thomas hat **schnell** jedes Brötchen geschmiert.*
Thomas has quickly every roll   buttered
'Thomas quickly buttered every roll'

b.   *Thomas hat jedes Brötchen geschmiert, wobei   er schnell*
Thomas has every roll   buttered,   in.doing.so he quick
war. (≈ a)
was
'Thomas buttered every roll, being quick in doing so.'

And finally, the pattern yields acceptable paraphrases for the adverbials involved in complex modification, cf. (66) and (67).

(66)   a.   *Fritz hat **sorgfältig   unleserlich** geschrieben.*
Fritz has painstaking illegible   written
'Fritz painstakingly wrote illegibly.'

b.   *Fritz hat **unleserlich** geschrieben, wobei   er **sorgfältig***
Fritz has illegible   written,   in.doing.so he careful
war. (≈ a)
was
'Fritz wrote illegibly, in doing so, he was careful.'

(67)　a.　*Hans hat **geschickt** die Frage   **dumm** beantwortet.*
　　　　Hans has skillful   the question stupidly answered
　　　　'Hans skillfully answered the question stupidly.'

　　　b.　*Hans hat die Frage   **dumm** beantwortet, wobei   er*
　　　　Hans has the question stupid answered,   in.doing.so he
　　　　***geschickt** war. (≈ a)*
　　　　skillful   was
　　　　'Hans answered the question stupidly, in doing so, he was skill-
　　　　ful.'

3.2.3.　The wobei-*paraphrase and associated readings*

As it stands, we have seen that the *wobei*-paraphrase works for a large number
of event-related adverbials. If we look at verb-related adverbials, it appears
that the paraphrase does not work, cf. the examples in (68), (69), and (74).

(68)　a.　*Robert hat Stella **wunderbar** geführt.*
　　　　Robert has Stella wonderful led
　　　　'Robert led Stella wonderfully.'

　　　b.　*Robert hat Stella geführt, wobei   er wunderbar war. (≉ a)*
　　　　Robert has Stella led,   in.doing.so he wonderful was
　　　　'Robert led Stella, in doing so, he was wonderful.'

(69)　a.　*Friedrich hat das Buch **oberflächlich** gelesen.*
　　　　Friedrich has the book cursory   read
　　　　'Friedrich read the book cursorily.'

　　　b.　*Friedrich hat das Buch gelesen, wobei   er oberflächlich*
　　　　Friedrich has the book read,   in.doing.so he cursory
　　　　war. (≉ a)
　　　　was
　　　　'Friedrich read the book, in doing that, he was cursory.'

(70)　a.　*Petra löst   die Aufgabe **intelligent**.*
　　　　Petra solves the problem intelligent
　　　　'Petra solves the problem intelligently.'

　　　b.　*Petra löst   die Aufgabe, wobei   sie intelligent ist. (≉ b)*
　　　　Petra solves the problem, in.doing.so she intelligent is
　　　　'Petra solves the problem, in doing so, she is intelligent.'

The most interesting piece of data relating to the *wobei*-paraphrases on the one hand and manner adverbials on the other hand are contrasting pairs like the following, (71) and (72).

(71)   a.   *Fritz hat die Marseillaise **laut** gesungen.*
             Fritz has the Marseillaise loud sung
             'Fritz sang the Marseillaise loudly.'
       b.   *Fritz hat die Marseillaise gesungen, wobei   er laut war.*
             Fritz has the Marseillaise sung,   in.doing.so he loud was
             ($\not\approx$ a)

             'Fritz sang the Marseillaise. In doing so, he was loud.'

(72)   a.   *Fritz hat Isolde **laut** verfolgt.*
             Fritz has Isolde loud followed
             'Fritz loudly followed Isolde.'
       b.   *Fritz hat Isolde verfolgt, wobei   er laut war. ($\approx$ a)*
             Fritz has Isolde followed, in.doing.so he loud was
             'Fritz followed Isolde. In doing so, he was loud.'

Why is the *wobei*-paraphrase not appropriate for (71), but appropriate for (72)? Following up on an observation made by Cresswell (1985:186-189) in the discussion of the semantics of the adverb *audibly*, I assume that in (71) it is the singing itself which is specified as loud and therefore the source of the loudness. In contrast, the activity of following does not come with an inbuilt loudness dimension, and what exactly causes the loudness of the following is left open. It might be an event that is more or less closely connected to the following event, but it might also be an event that has strictly speaking little to do with the following. That is, if I follow somebody and clap my hands in doing so in order to let my friends know where I am, this can be successfully described by (72). I use the term 'associated readings', which was already mentioned in the discussion of example (41) in section 2.2.2, for adverbial usages that allow these readings. Another example with *laut* 'loud' that gives rise to an associated reading is given in (73).

(73)   *Peter repariert **laut** das Radio.*
        Peter repairs   loud the radio
        'Peter noisily repairs the radio.'

Again, a repairing event does not come with an internal structure that offers a loudness-dimension, what causes the loudness is some associated event. A reflex of this is that imperatives in which the speaker ask the addressee to put an end to loud activities are, in the case of associated readings, preferably given in copula-predicative form, e.g. *Sei doch mal leise!* 'Be quiet!', and not with the corresponding main verb (*Reparier doch mal leise* 'Repair quietly!').

At least some adjectives seem to allow this paraphrase freely even if used as a manner adverbial, cf. *sorgfältig* in (74).

(74)   a.   *Petra löst   die Aufgabe sorgfältig.*
            Petra solves the problem careful
            'Petra solves the problem carefully.'
       b.   *Petra löst   die Aufgabe, wobei   sie sorgfältig ist. (≉ a)*
            Petra solves the problem, in.doing.so she careful   is
            'Petra solves the problem, in doing so, she is careful.'

The reason seems to lie in the lexical semantics of *sorgfältig* 'careful', which seem far more strictly defined in terms of the ways and manners in which somebody acts, so that a person is characterized as *sorgfältig* 'careful' on account of him acting *sorgfältig* 'careful'. Compare this to the situation with *intelligent* 'intelligent', which, when used predicatively, always characterizes a property that is somehow conceptualized as inherent to a person and not necessarily related to the way somebody acts.

Note that although the positions lead to differences in preferred paraphrases, they are often semantically or pragmatically closely related. The simultaneous use of direct opposites in the two positions in one single sentence is in general not acceptable, cf. the two examples in (75) (For cases where this is possible, cf. chapter 5).

(75)   a.   *??Er hat **laut** das Lied **leise** gesungen.*
            he has loud the song quiet sung
            'He loudly sang the song quietly.'
       b.   *??Er hat **sorgfältig** das Buch **unachtsam** durchgearbeitet.*
            he has careful   the book careless   worked.through
            'He carefully worked through the book carelessly.'

4.   Summary

In this chapter, I discussed in detail the class of event-related adverbials. The feature that connects the different subclasses presented here is that they semantically clearly relate to events, and not to higher entities like facts or propositions. On the other hand, they do not access aspects or dimensions internal to the structure of the event characterized by the verbal predicate.

Mental-attitude adverbials and transparent adverbials were linked to attitudes towards executing an event or states of mind resulting from the event described by the verbal predicate. Event-external usages comprise three distinct subclasses: inchoative readings, holistic readings, and modifications of complex events. In addition, adverbials with associative readings can also be seen as a subgroup of event-external adverbials. This last group was distinguished from verb-related adverbials by allowing the *wobei*-paraphrase, which was discussed in detail in the third section of this chapter.

Chapter 5
The syntactic position of manner adverbials

1. Introduction

In the preceding chapters, I discussed the different semantic distinctions holding for German verb-related and event-related adverbial adjectives. The aim of this chapter is to investigate to what extent specific readings of verb-related adverbials are tied to specific syntactic configurations, either with regard to the absolute syntactic positions in a sentence or with regard to the adverbial's position relative to other elements in a sentence. It has been mentioned repeatedly that adverbial adjectives are prototypically used as verb-related adverbials, and within this subgroup, manner adverbials constitute the bulk of the examples discussed so far. The position of manner adverbials has also been the object of intense discussion in the literature on the syntactic positions of adverbials, and I will therefore focus on this subgroup and the claims made in relation to this group. The main weakness of the previous analyses lies in failing to distinguish carefully between lexical items that can either serve as manner adverbials, and hence constitute a case of verb-related modification, or the same lexical items being used as event-related adverbials.

I argue that event-oriented adverbials always precede the direct object, whereas verb-related adverbials follow the direct object. This claim is the natural consequence of looking at previous accounts of the base positions on the basis of the reading distinctions established in chapters 3 and 4.

The position of adverbials in German has been the topic of intensive investigation. Frey and Pittner, as a team and solo, have worked on the positioning of adverbials in general, cf. Frey and Pittner (1998, 1999), Frey (2003), Pittner (2004).[49] Maienborn (1996, 2001) has investigated the relationship between syntactic position and semantic interpretation of locative adverbials, Eckardt (1998, 2003) has been concerned with the syntactic position of manner adverbials.

The chapter is organized as follows: In section 2, I introduce the diagnostics that can be used to establish syntactic positions of adverbials. Section 3 looks more closely at the relationship between adverbial position and focus projection, showing that focus projection alone cannot decide the issue of the base position of manner adverbials, because we get inconsistent data with regard to the position of the direct object. Section 4 presents the account by Eckardt (2003), who argues for a base position of manner adverbials before the direct object. Section 5 presents the account by Frey and Pittner, who argue for the opposite order. In section 6, I will present my own account, which is essentially a stricter version of the Frey and Pittner account. In this section I also show that two further diagnostics, the position of w-elements and the theme-rheme test, confirm my analysis. Finally, section 7 contains some further supporting data but also discusses some data that is more difficult to account for.

Note that in many cases the example sentences in this chapter are given as embedded sentences. The reason for this is that the embedding forces them to occur in the SOV-order; this in turn makes it easier to investigate the positioning of the non-verbal elements of the respective sentences.

A note on relative vs fixed positions for adverbials

In the (generative) syntactic literature on adverbial placement, there is disagreement on a number of fundamental issues. As far as the syntax-semantics interface is concerned, the fundamental question is whether the ordering of adverbials is seen either as entirely syntax-driven (cf. Cinque 1999 for a highly influential proposal), or as based on semantic scope, cf. e.g. Ernst (2002). For illustration, consider the sentences in (1).

(1)   a.   Marie probably cleverly found a good solution.
      b.   *Marie cleverly probably found a good solution.

On Cinque's account, adverbials are realized as specifiers of a fixed set of functional phrases, where the type of functional phrase determines the semantic type of the adverbial. (2b) is ungrammatical, because the occurrence of *probably* and *cleverly* does not match the order proscribed by the hierarchy of functional phrases. On a scopal account, in contrast, (1b) is impossible because the semantic object over which *probably* takes scope is higher on a scale of semantic objects than the semantic object that *cleverly* scopes over.

I remain agnostic here as to which account is the theoretically better solution. The tests or conditions which are presented here are taken from Frey and Pittner and are geared to definitions in terms of base positions.

For a detailed overview covering the different syntactic approaches, cf. Ernst (2002: section 1.2.3) and Alexiadou (2004).

2. Establishing syntactic positions

Several diagnostics can be used to establish syntactic positions of adverbials, cf. e.g. the six syntactic criteria used in Frey and Pittner (1998), which are listed below along with a short description (for full descriptions of those criteria not discussed later in this chapter, the reader is referred to Frey and Pittner 1998):

1. *Focus projection*: Whether a sentence containing an adverbial can carry maximal focus or not can be linked to whether or not the adverbial appears in its base position.
2. *Theme-rheme condition*: Under certain conditions, an adverbial can only be part of the rheme when appearing in its base position.
3. *Principle-C effects*: The possibility of coindexing two constituents, one within a preposed complex constituent, one occuring as a pronoun in the middle field, is used in order to establish the base positions in accordance with the principle C of standard binding theory.
4. *Existentially interpreted w-phrases*: Taking the syntactic position of existentially interpreted w-phrases as fixed, the position of adverbials relative to that position can be used to indicate their base positions.
5. *Complex frontings*: The way that an adverbial can take part in complex frontings indicates its base position.
6. *Scope*: The scope of constituents containing quantifiers can be used to reconstruct their base position.

Most of the tests were originally introduced to account for the syntactic position of arguments in German sentences. Their adaption to adverbials is due to the work of Frey and Pittner.

For adverbial adjectives, the tests involving Principle C Effects and Quantifier Scope are irrelevant, as adjectival short-forms do not contain bound material or traces.[50] In addition, I will not use data involving complex frontings. For one thing, the judgments on data involving adverbial adjectives are often far from clear, and for another thing, the test is based on specific assumptions that seem somewhat ad hoc. This can be seen when looking at one example, cf. (2), (33) in Frey and Pittner (1998). According to Frey and Pittner (1998), (2a) is not acceptable, while (2b) is acceptable.

(2) a. **Einige Artikel gelesen hat Hans heute **sorgfältig**.*
         a.few   articles read   has Hans today careful
     b. ***Sorgfältig** gelesen hat Hans heute einige Artikel.*
         careful   read   has Hans today a.few   articles
         'Today, Hans carefully read a few articles.'

Frey and Pittner (1998) account for this pattern based on the assumption that traces in the surface structure produced by scrambling must be bound by their antecedent. Accordingly, the explanation for the unacceptability of (2a) is that it contains traces which are not bound in its surface structure, while (2b) does not contain such traces. If the base position of *sorgfältig* 'careful' in these sentences is between the direct object and the verb, then we find that (2a) and (2b) do differ in exactly this respect. A partial structural representation of (2a) with the trace of the adverbial included is given in (3), the representation of (2b) in (4).

(3)   *[Einige Artikel t_i gelesen]$_j$ hat Hans heute **sorgfältig**$_i$ t_j.*
      a.few   articles   read   has Hans today careful

(4)   *[**Sorgfältig** gelesen]$_i$ hat Hans heute einige Artikel t_i.*
      careful   read   has Hans today a.few   articles
      'Today, Hans read a few articles carefully.'

In (3), the trace of the adverbial *sorgfältig* 'careful' is included in the fronted complex, while its binder is in sentence-final position and therefore not able to bind its trace on the surface structure. In (4), on the other hand, the fronted complex contains no unbound traces. Clearly, the whole explanation only makes sense if one follows all of the assumptions about binding and topicalization implicit in this account. As these assumptions are not even shared by all authors in the generative tradition (Frey and Pittner 1998 mention Müller 1996 for a diverging opinion), I will not use this test as a diagnostic.

This leaves us with three diagnostics, two of which are connected to questions of information structure. We will therefore now turn to the rather intricate interrelationship between adverbials and information structure.

3. Adverbial modification and information structure

This section turns to the use of tests involving information structure and their application to sentences containing manner adverbials. I will start with tests involving focus projection, and then look at the theme-rheme condition. In both sections, I will first present the logic of the diagnostic, and then discuss the application of this diagnostic to adverbial modification.

3.1.   Focus projection

The concept of *Fokusprojektion* 'focus projection' was first introduced by Höhle (1982:98-99), who was interested in determining the unmarked or normal word order (*"Normalabfolge"*) of a given sentence. To understand the relation between Höhle's notion of normal word order and focus projection, it is necessary to introduce a few of the main concepts of Höhle's work.

To arrive at the standard word order of a sentence, Höhle (1982) makes use of the concept of *stilistisch normale Betonung* 'stylistically standard accentuation pattern', cf. (5), adapted from his (79).

(5)   [stylistically standard accentuation pattern]
      The intonation of a given sentence S_i is stylistically normal if S_i is, as far as its accentuation pattern is concerned, contextually relatively unmarked. The accentuation pattern is stylistically not normal if the accentuation pattern of S_1 is contextually marked.

The phrase *contextually relatively unmarked* is defined in (6), translating his (78).

(6)   [Contextually relatively unmarked]
      Given a set of sentences whose only distinguishing characteristic is the accentuation of their constituents, there will be sentences in this set that are *contextually relatively unmarked* as far as their intonation is concerned. These sentences can appear in the highest number of types of contexts. All other sentences in this set are contextually marked as far as their prosody is concerned.

Given these two notions, Höhle (1982) defines *Stilistisch normale Wortstellung* 'stylistically standard word order' as in (7), translating his (147).

(7)   [stylistically standard word order]
      Given be a set of sentences whose only distinguishing characteristic is the accentuation of their constituents and/or the linear order of those constituents. Among all sentences in this set, those sentences have *stylistically standard word order* that are members of a set of sentences differing only in their accentuation in which exists one sentence which can appear in the most types of contexts when compared to all sentences in the set of sentences differing in accentuation and/or linear order of their constituents.

The ability of a sentence to appear in different contexts is closely linked to its ability to project focus. Consider the sentence in (8), where UPPERCASE indicates the main accent.

(8)   *Karl hat dem   Kind das   BUCH geschenkt.*
Karl has the.DAT child the.ACC book   given
'Karl gave the child the book.'

Sentence (8) contains at least one accented element,[51] in this case the second element of the noun phrase *das Buch* 'the book'. The phrase itself forms a possible focus, the minimal focus (cf. (66) in Höhle 1982:98).[52]

If we model contexts for the sentence in (8) with the help of questions, cf. (9), Höhle's (49a-e), the question (9a) yields an appropriate context for the minimal focus, e.g. focus on the noun phrase *das Book* 'the book', cf. (9a). Sentence (8) fits other contexts, too. E.g., it can answer the questions in (9b) to (9e), resulting in the different foci for (8) given in (10), Höhle's (50). All these foci include the accented elements contained in the minimal focus and are the result of focus projections (for the exact definition of focus projection, cf. (70) in Höhle 1982:99).

(9)   a.   *Was hat Karl dem Kind geschenkt?*
what has Karl the child given.as.a.present
'What did Karl give to the child?'

b.   *Was hat Karl hinsichtlich   des Kindes getan?*
what has Karl with.regard.to the child   done
'What did Karl do with regard to the child?'

c.   *Was hat Karl getan?*
what has Karl done
'What did Karl do?'

d.   *Was hat das Kind erlebt?*
what has the child experienced
'What did the child experience?'

e.   *Was ist geschehen?*
what is happened
'What happened?'

(10)   a.   das Buch [minimal focus]
'the book'

b.   das Buch + geschenkt
'the book + given as a present'

c.   dem Kind + das Buch + geschenkt
'to the child + the book + given as a present'

  d.   Karl + das Buch + geschenkt
       'Karl + the book + given as a present'
  e.   Karl + dem Kind + das Buch + geschenkt [set of all constituents]
       'Karl + to the child + the book + given as a present'

The representation of focus projection up to this point exactly followed Höhle (1982). Frey and Pittner's usage of focus projection to establish base positions, however, is based on one further assumption: in cases where a nonverbal element is accented, focus projection is only possible if this non-verbal element is the element that is structurally closest to the verb (cf. Frey and Pittner 1998:492).[53] Frey and Pittner (1998) illustrate their usage of focus projection to determine base positions with the example (11), cf. their (6).

(11)   *Was ist geschehen?*
        what is happened
        'What happened?'

   a.   *Ein Kollege   hat einer Dame ein   GeDICHT vorgetragen*
        a   colleague has a.DAT lady a.ACC poem   recited
        'A colleague recited a poem to a lady.'
   b.   *#Ein Kollege   hat ein   Gedicht einer   DAme vorgetragen*
        a   colleague has a.ACC poem   a.DAT lady   recited

Only (11a) is a good answer to the question in (11). Apparently its focus exponent allows focus projection up to the whole sentence. Accordingly, (11a) represents the normal word order, and is taken to show that the base position of the direct object follows the base position of the indirect object.

    Note that the usage of data concerning focus projection to determine the syntactic position of constituents of a clause deviates from the intention of Höhle's paper. Höhle (1982) sees his *stylistically standard word order* ('stilistisch normale Wortstellung') as a pragmatic phenomenon and does not link it to syntactic base positions. He explicitly allows for two different linear orderings to function as stylistically standard word orders. Sentences (12a) and (12b), his (130), represent for Höhle (1982) such a case.

(12)   a.   *Karl hat dem   Kind das   Buch geschenkt.*
            Karl has the.DAT child the.ACC book given.as.a.present
            'Karl gave the child the book as a present.'
       b.   *Karl hat das   Buch dem   Kind geschenkt.*
            Karl has the.ACC book the.DAT child given.as.a.present
            'Karl gave the book to the child as a present.'

For Höhle (1982), both the order **indirect object > direct object** in (12a) and the order **direct object > indirect object** in (12b) allow focus on the whole sentence, as long as in both cases the accentuation is on the object closest to the verb, cf. Höhle (1982:120, (130-31)). Note also that this data is structurally parallel to Frey and Pittner's example (11), where Frey and Pittner (1998) assume that only (11a) may carry wide focus.

In this work, I will follow Frey & Pittner's implicit assumption that there is usually only one word order which is the stylistically standard word order, without denying that the judgements involved are sometimes rather subtle.

3.2. Adverbials and normal word order

As soon as we turn to adverbials and their place in the normal word order, we encounter a few complications. Consider the example in (13), corresponding to (63) in (Frey and Pittner 1998:508).

(13)   a.   *weil   Otto **absichtlich** den ZAUN zerstörte.* [wide focus]
            because Otto intentional the fence destroyed
       b.   *weil   Otto den Zaun **abSICHTlich** zerstörte.*[narrow focus]
            because Otto the fence intentional   destroyed
       c.   *weil   Otto den Zaun **abSICHTlich** zerSTÖRte.* [narrow f.]
            because Otto the fence intentional   destroyed
            'because Otto destroyed the fence intentionally'

Frey and Pittner's interpretation of this data is straightforward: Only in (13a) is the direct object able to project a wide focus, which indicates that there is no trace between direct object and verb, whereas in (13b) there is narrow focus on the adverbial, in (13c) on the adverbial plus verb. Note that one accent suffices for wide focus projection in (13a).

The complication that now occurs is that there are cases where the judgement on which word order allows for the projection of wide focus is much more difficult to make. Thus, Eckardt (2003:261) notes that all of the combinations in (14) and (15) are "equally well formed", regardless of whether the order is **adverbial > direct object > verb** or **direct object > adverbial > verb,** and regardless of whether the object is an indefinite noun phrase or a definite noun phrase.

(14)   a.   *(dass) Hans **vorsichtig** eine Nuss öffnete.*
            (that) Hans careful   a   nut opened
            '(that) Hans carefully opened a nut.'

      b.   *(dass) Hans eine Nuss **vorsichtig** öffnete.*
             (that) Hans a   nut   careful   opened
             '(that) Hans opened a nut carefully .'

(15)   a.   *(dass) Hans **vorsichtig** die Nuss öffnete.*
             (that) Hans careful   the nut   opened
             '(that) Hans carefully opened the nut.'
      b.   *(dass) Hans die Nuss **vorsichtig** öffnete.*
             (that) Hans the nut   careful   opened
             '(that) Hans opened the nut carefully.'

Importantly, and in contrast to the data in (13), it is not very clear whether any of the orders in these pairs dissallows wide focus projections.

The patterns in (15) and (14) and judgments on them will constitute the core issue to be discussed in this chapter. As far as word order is concerned, the main issue will be whether event-related adverbials and verb-related adverbials and their respective subclasses are preferably placed before or after the direct object, cf. (16).

(16)   a.   **subject > adverbial > direct object > verb** (=ADV DO)
      b.   **subject > direct object > adverbial > verb** (=DO ADV)

This question has been discussed controversially, especially as far as manner adverbials are concerned, where Frey and Pittner (1998) argue for the position after the direct object as the base position. In contrast, Eckardt (1998, 2003) favors a base position of manner adverbials (MA) before the direct object (DO).

For both accounts, the status of the direct object in these examples plays a very important role. Eckardt (2003) explains the data that does not fit her assumption as far as the surface order is concerned by arguing for object movement. Frey and Pittner (1998) explain the data by arguing for object integration. I will first present their accounts, and then present my account, which basically follows Frey and Pittner's position, but is more strict in that it does not make use of object integration.

4.   Eckardt's account: Scrambled indefinite direct objects

Eckardt (2003) presents a survey of the variation between ADV DO and DO ADV orders. She discusses in detail two different verb classes as well as the influence of the type of the direct object, that is, whether it is definite or indefinite, and in the latter case, whether it receives an existential, partitive, or generic reading.

4.1.   Restricted combinations: Implicit resultatives and verbs of creation

Eckardt starts out with the data given in (14) and (15), where we saw no obvious effect of the relative word order. Other adjective-verb pairings do not occur in all these combinations, compare (17) and (18), Eckardt's (3)-(5).

(17)   a.   *(dass) Hans **schwer** einen Wagen   belud*
           (that) Hans heavy   a   carriage loaded

       b.   *(dass) Hans einen Wagen   **schwer** belud*
           (that) Hans a   carriage heavy   loaded
           '(that) Hans loaded a carriage heavily.'

(18)   a.   *(dass) Hans **schwer** den Wagen   belud*
           (that) Hans heavy   the carriage loaded

       b.   *(dass) Hans den Wagen   **schwer** belud*
           (that) Hans the carriage heavily loaded
           '(that) Hans loaded the carriage heavily.'

In the terminology of chapter 3, *schwer* 'heavy' is used here as an implicit resultative: it is not the carriage that is heavy as a result of the loading-event, but the load itself (Eckardt 2003 refers to *schwer* as a *resultative adverb* or *result modifier*). In this usage, *schwer* 'heavy' can only occur after the direct object.

Eckardt (2003) introduces additional data where adjectives occur together with verbs of creation and verbs of coming into existence, here *schnitzen* 'carve' and *stricken* 'knit'. An adjective like *geschickt* 'skillful' allows the **adverbial > indefinite direct object** order only on a restricted number of readings of the indefinite direct object, cf. (19b) (here and in the following examples, the #-symbol marks this restriction in readings). In all other combinations, the readings of the indefinite are not restricted, cf. (19a) and (20).

(19)   a.   *(dass) Hans **geschickt** eine Flöte schnitzte*
           (that) Hans skillful   a   flute   carved
           '(that) Hans skillfully carved a flute'

       b.   #*(dass) Hans eine Flöte **geschickt** schnitzte*
           (that) Hans a   flute skillful   carved
           '(that) Hans carved a flute skillfully'

(20)   a.   *(dass) Hans **geschickt** die Flöte schnitzte*
           (that) Hans skillful   the flute carved
           '(that) Hans skillfully carved the flute'

b. *(dass) Hans die Flöte **geschickt** schnitzte*
(that) Hans the flute skillful carved
'(that) Hans carved the flute skillfully '

What is special about (19b)? As Eckardt points out, the possible readings of the indefinite are restricted: we do not get an existential reading, but only partitive or generic readings, which may be paraphrased as in (21a) and (22b), respectively.

(21) a. Usually, Hans carved flutes skillfully.
      b. Hans carved one of the flutes he carved skillfully.

Implicit resultatives show the same behavior, cf. (22) and (23).

(22) a. #*(dass) Hans einen Pullover **locker** strickte*
         (that) Hans a   pullover loose knitted
         '(that) Hans knitted a pullover loosely'
      b. **(dass) Hans **locker** einen Pullover strickte*
         (that) Hans loose a   pullover knitted

(23) a. *(dass) Hans den Pullover **locker** strickte*
         (that) Hans the pullover loose knitted
         '(that) Hans knitted the pullover loosely'
      b. **(dass) Hans **locker** den Pullover strickte*
         (that) Hans loose the pullover knitted

The adjective *locker* 'loose' is an implicit resultative, because it predicates over the stitches that result from the knitting, not over the manner of the knitting nor over the pullover as a whole. In (22a), the indefinite is again restricted to a generic or a partitive interpretation. Since the word order **implicit resultative > direct object** is impossible, too, this has the consequence that an indefinite object NP can never have an existential reading when combined with a verb of creation and an implicit resultative. Conceptually, this fits in well with an analysis of verbs of creation that Eckardt adopts from Stechow (2001) and discusses with the help of the sentence *Andrea baute eine Machine* 'Andrea built a machine'. Stechow's analysis, writes Eckardt, "will imply the existence of a machine of the appropriate kind *after* the event of creation has been completed, but without stating that any kind of machine-entity is existent *before* or *while* the event takes place. In particular, it is explicitly stated that *no machine-created-in-e* exists prior to the event in question" (Eckardt 2003:270, her emphasis).

4.2.   The readings of indefinites and topicality

Eckardt (2003), building on previous work, notably Jäger (1996), links the discussion of the reading of indefinites to the question of topicality, which, in turn, is linked to scrambling. In short, she claims that generic and partitive readings are only available for topical NPs, and that topical NPs have been scrambled out of their base position. On this view, the base position for implicit resultative is between the subject and the direct object, cf. (24).

(24)   implicit resultatives: base position
subject > adverbial$_{IMPL\_RES}$ > direct object > verb

However, if the direct object is an indefinite NP, then the implicit resultatives can never occur before the direct object, because the direct object would receive an existential reading, which is not available. Therefore, the indefinite direct objects have to be scrambled over the adverbial, leading to the surface order in (25).

(25)   implicit resultatives: surface position
subject > direct object > adverbial$_{IMPL\_RES}$ > verb

Assuming for the moment that this, though counterintuitive, is correct, then what about the examples with manner modification and indefinite noun phrases? Can we also find reading effects here, i.e., are there differences in the possible readings for the indefinite direct objects in the pair of sentences in (26), repeated from (14)?

(26)   a.   *(dass) Hans **vorsichtig** eine Nuss öffnete*
                (that) Hans careful   a   nut   opened
                '(that) Hans carefully opened a nut'
        b.   *(dass) Hans eine Nuss **vorsichtig** öffnete*
                (that) Hans a   nut   careful   opened
                '(that) Hans opened a nut carefully '

Eckardt argues that there is indeed a subtle difference, and that (26b) does not receive an existential reading, but an in-group reading.

4.3.   In-group readings

What are in-group readings? Basically, this term is used by Eckardt to indicate that the referent of a noun phrase is taken from a known set of individuals. According to Eckardt, the contextual restrictions for these readings are minimal, as she illustrates with the help of (27), her (68).

(27)   *Alicia hat ein Huhn   **vorsichtig** gestreichelt.*
         Alicia has a   chicken careful   stroked
         'Alicia carefully stroked a chicken.'

According to Eckardt, the indefinite direct object can receive three readings, a generic, a partitive, and an in-group reading. The readings available for DO in pre-adverbial position are associated with different intonation patterns, cf. (28), her (70).

(28)   *Alicia hat ein Huhn   **vorsichtig** gestreichelt.*
         Alicia has a   chicken carefully   stroked.
         a.   Generic: Alicia hat ein Huhn VORSICHTIG GESTREICHELT
              /VORSICHTIG gestreichelt/vorsichtig GESTREICHELT.
         b.   Partitive: Alicia hat EIN Huhn VORSICHTIG gestreichelt.
         c.   In-Group: Alicia hat ein HUHN VORSICHTIG GESTREICH-
              ELT.

In-group readings of the indefinite direct objects in (28) are minimal in the sense that they require almost no contextual support: "They require the hearer to accommodate an interest in the question *What did Alicia do in the situation that the speaker wants to describe?* This minimal interest will be supplied at least by politeness and hence has never been diagnosed as a "presupposition" of the respective sentences" (Eckardt 2003:284).[54]

An example where the minimal requirements are explicitly met is given in (29), Eckardt's (71), where the mention of animals in the first sentence provides the group that contains the referents of the following indefinite objects as its members.

(29)   Alicia ging in den Stall und hat alle Tiere begrüßt.
         'Alicia went to the stable and greeted all animals.'

                  Sie hat ein HUHN VORSICHTIG GESTREICHELT, (... sie
                  she has a   chicken careful   stroked   (... she
                  hat eine KUH ZÄRTLICH GESTUPST, und sie hat ein
                  has a   cow tender   pushed   and she has a
                  PFERD LIEBEVOLL GEFÜTTERT.)
                  horse   affectionate fed)
                  'She carefully stroked a chicken, (she tenderly gave a little push
                  to a cow, and she affectionately fed a horse).'

If the group that contains the in-group referents is not explicitly given, it needs to be accommodated, and the standard way to accommodate is to equate this group with the visible things around the agent. The restriction on visible things is used by Eckardt (2003) to account for the fact that (30), her (74), does not allow an in-group reading, but only a partitive reading:

(30)   *Alicia hat eine Taschenlampe vorsichtig konstruiert.*
        Alicia has a   torch   careful   constructed
        'Alicia carefully constructed a torch.'

Because the torch is not among the visible things around Alicia before the constructing-event is finished, Eckardt argues, it is not available for accommodation.

Assuming that in-group readings are again bound to a topical position of the indefinite direct object, Eckardt concludes that the base position that holds for implicit resultatives also holds for manner adverbials, so that we can generalize over the two classes, resulting in the base order in (31) and the surface order in (32).

(31)   implicit resultatives and manner adverbials: base position
        subject > adverbial$_{IMPL\_RESandMANNER}$ > direct object > verb

(32)   implicit resultatives and manner adverbials: surface position
        subject > direct object > adverbial$_{IMPL\_RESandMANNER}$ > verb

4.4.   Problems for Eckardt's account

In this section, I discuss two issues that are problematic for Eckardt's account: strong readings of indefinites and the combination of manner adverbials with verbs of creation. The main argument against her account is that she does not distinguish between event-external and verb-related adverbials, a shortcoming that will become clearer from the discussion of my account in section 6.

4.4.1.   *Frey vs Eckardt: The strong reading of indefinites*

Eckardt's argumentation relies on the assumption that the existential reading of indefinite direct objects is their unmarked reading, and that, consequently, the absence of this reading serves as an indicator of the topical status of these readings. This assumption is called into question by Frey 2001, 2003. In particular, Frey (2003) points out that a strong reading (= a partitive or generic reading) of an indefinite does not mean that that indefinite is in the position of a designated middle field topic. This point is not immediately relevant for the discussion of base positions, because we would have to sort out the notions of topic and topicality as used by the different authors in more detail first. A second point Frey makes, cf. Frey (2003: footnote 14), is of more immediate relevance: Eckardt's interpretation of in-group readings as topical readings means that we do not have any testable means of distinguishing between in-group and existential readings anymore, since her notion of in-group readings is simply too vague.

Frey (2001:151) acknowledges that we find reading effects in connection with verbs of creation, but offers an alternative explanation, which will be discussed in section 5.

4.4.2.   *Manner adverbials and verbs of creation*

Eckardt argues that the word order of the sentence in (33), repeated from (19a), with the indefinite NP following the adverbial, corresponds to the base word order. Accordingly, the indefinite noun phrase *eine Flöte* 'a flute' should receive an existential interpretation.

(33)   *(dass) Hans **geschickt** eine Flöte schnitzte.*
         (that) Hans skillful   a   flute carved
         '(that) Hans carved a flute skillfully.'

This is at odds with her claim, stated in section 4.1, that the objects created in the activities referred to by verbs of creation only come into existence after the event is completed. Even worse, if the indefinite direct object in (33) receives an existential interpretation, then it is unclear why the implicit resultatives discussed in section 4.1 cannot occur before the direct object.

5.   **Frey and Pittner: Object integration**

Frey and Pittner (1998:502-505) argue that variation in word order between **manner adverbial > direct object** and **direct object > manner adverbial** can be explained by taking recourse to integration in the sense of Jacobs (1993). They hold that the base linear order is **direct object > manner adverbial**, and that the deviant **manner adverbial > direct object** word order results from the direct objects in question being integrated into the verb, forming a structurally complex predicate.[55] In order to do justice to this explanation it is necessary to introduce the idea of *integration* in some detail. The basic intuition behind integration is best illustrated by the original introductory examples in Jacobs (1993), cf. (34), and Jacobs' own comments on them, reproduced below the examples.

(34)   a.   [Flüssig$_1$treibstoff$_2$]
               liquid.fuel
               'liquid fuel'

    b.   [[Ein Gewitter]$_1$[zieht auf]$_2$]
               a thunderstorm draws up
               'A thunderstorm is brewing up.'

    c.   [[Eine Türe]$_1$öffnen$_2$]
               a door open
               'to open a door'

    d.   [auf$_2$[dem Auto]$_1$]
               on the car
               'on the car'

> Die für Integration konstitutive gemeinsame Eigenschaft von (1)-(4) [(34)[a]-(34)[d]] ist die holistische Weise, in der der außersprachliche Bezug dieser Ausdrücke hergestellt wird: Obwohl sich ihre Bedeutung aus den Bedeutungen der beiden Tochterkonstituenten zusammensetzt, ist mit den Ausdrücken (1)-(4) [(34)[a]-(34)[d]] nicht ein zweifacher Zugriff auf Außersprachliches verbunden. Vielmehr entspricht jeweils mindestens einer Teilkonstituente kein eigener semantischer Verarbeitungsschritt. (Jacobs 1993:64)
> [The constitutive property of integration that is shared by (33a-d) is the holistic manner in which these expressions establish language-external reference. Although their meaning is composed out of the meaning of two sister constituents each, this does not correspond to a double reference to language external entities. Rather, no extra semantic processing is required for at least one of the sister constituents.] (my translation)

In my view, these opening examples from Jacobs in combination with his comments already expose the weakest point of the concept of integration: it is so informal and vague, that it is not clear when something is integrated or not. Intuitively, I can follow Jacobs's comments especially in view of the examples (33a) and (33b). However, why (33c) and (33d) should fall into the same category is hard to understand.

Formally, integration is a relationship that holds between two constituents if the conditions in (35), a translation of Jacobs's *BedI*, are fulfilled.

(35)   Constituent X_1 is integrated into constituent X_2, iff the following holds:

a. X_1 and X_2 are daughters of the same constituent Y, and X_2 is the head of Y

b.   (i) X_1 is an argument of X_2, or
       (ii)   Y is a word and X_1 is a specification ('eine nähere Bestimmung zu') of X_2

c.   if X_1 is assigned a theta-role through X_2, the following holds:
       (i) X_2 does not assign a property to X_1 which is unlimited in time
       (ii) X_1 has prototypical semantical object properties

d. X_2 contains no more constituents than the following:
       (i)   a non-complex core-constituent L
       (ii)   (optionally) functional elements, that extend L

Frey and Pittner (1998) now adduce the example in (36) and (37), their (36a) and (36b).

(36)   a.   *Ich habe den   Mann **abgrundtief** verachtet.*
               I   have the.ACC man   profound   despised
               'I profoundly despised the man.'

b.   **Ich habe **abgrundtief** den   Mann verachtet.*
               I   have profound   the.ACC man   despised

(37)   a.   *Sie hat jedes Hemd **sorgfältig** gebügelt.*
               she has every shirt   careful   ironed
               'She ironed every shirt carefully.'

b.   **Sie hat **sorgfältig** jedes Hemd gebügelt.*[56]
               she has careful   every shirt   ironed

According to Frey and Pittner, there is no integration in the above examples because in (36) the direct object is the stimulus, that is, the direct object is not a proto-patient a la Dowty (1989), and in (37) the direct object contains *jeder*-quantification, and quantifiers with distributive readings block integration (as Frey and Pittner argue).[57]

Note that the adverbial *abgrundtief* 'profoundly' is, within the terminology of this work, not a manner but a degree adverbial. Additionally, the data in (37) and (36) is fully compatible with the hypothesis that the event-related adverbials are placed before the direct object, and the verb-related adverbials are placed after the direct object.

In general, Frey and Pittner assume that if the surface order does not correspond to the order **direct object > manner adverbial**, then the direct object is integrated.

5.1.   Resultatives and integration

Eckardt (2003) argues that the integration hypothesis will lead to problems when we do not only look at manner adverbials, but again take resultatives and verbs of creation into consideration. Under the assumption that the very same direct object-verb combination should lead to object integration regardless of whether an implicit resultative or a manner adverbial is added, her data raises questions that cannot be dealt with in Frey and Pittner's account as it stands. She demonstrates this with the help of the sentence (38).

(38)   *Berenike hat den Baum dekoriert.*
       Berenike has the tree   decorated
       'Berenike decorated the tree.'

As shown in section 4.1, if an implicit resultative is added, the word order **manner adverbial > direct object** is ungrammatical, cf. (39a), while the order **direct object > manner adverbial** is OK, cf. (39b), her (97).

(39)   a.   **Berenike hat **üppig** den Baum dekoriert.*
            Berenike has lavish the tree   decorated
       b.   *Berenike hat den Baum **üppig** dekoriert.*
            Berenike has the tree   lavish decorated
            'Berenike lavishly decorated the tree.'

If, in contrast, a manner adverbial is added, the order **manner adverbial > direct object** is perfectly acceptable, cf. (40), her (98) (The order DO MA is also OK, incidentally).

(40)   *Berenike hat **vorsichtig** den Baum dekoriert.*
       Berenike has careful   the tree   decorated
       'Berenike carefully decorated the tree.'

The unacceptability of (39a) could be taken to indicate that the direct object *der Baum* 'the tree' cannot integrate with the verb. Example (40) seems to show the exact opposite.

Eckardt speculates that in order to defend integration in these cases, one might claim that the resultatives change the overall thematic structure of the verb, which is another licenser of integration. In other words, the resultative adverbial is also integrated, and it stands in a closer relation to the verb than the direct object.[58] This corresponds to the position defended by Frey (2003:footnote 14), where Frey says that resultatives are part of the complex predicate in German. In addition, Frey argues that the very fact that the direct object that comes along with verbs of creation is "just part of the intentions or plans which are denoted by the verb" shows that the direct object is integrated. Frey assumes here that more than one element can participate in complex predicate formation.[59]

Frey's assumption that resultatives take part in the process of predicate formation, and therefore are integrated, appears plausible. However, for this to work formally, the conditions on integration would have to be changed. As we will see, though, we can explain the data without resorting to integration.[60]

6. An alternative account: It's the adverbial's reading that is decisive

In this section, I argue that event-related adverbials are located before the direct object and verb-related adverbials are positioned between the direct object and the verb, yielding the scheme in (41).

(41)   event-related adverbials and verb-related adverbials: base positions
         **subject > adverbial$_{EVENT-RELATED}$ > direct object >
         adverbial$_{VERB-RELATED}$ > verb**

Thus, my account follows Frey and Pittner's analysis, but differs in that it does not make use of object integration. To start with, we will take a closer look at event-related and verb-related adverbials and the question of focus and focus projection, touching also on some issues regarding the topic-comment structures involved.

6.1.   Adverbials out of the blue

In the discussion of focus projection, especially when used as a test case for base positions, the possibility of wide focus projection plays an important role. Wide focus projection refers to the phenomenon that the focus is not restricted to the focus exponent, i.e., the element that carries the focus accent, but that more material is included in the focus. In the extreme case, wide scopus means that the entire sentence is in the focus. A sentence which contains only focused material can be uttered out-of-the-blue; since everything is new information, no contextual restrictions apply. Eckardt (2003) makes use of out-of-the-blue contexts in her discussion of the correct base position for manner adverbials.[61] In particular, she argues that the behavior of sentences containing manner adverbials in out-of-the-blue contexts can be counted as evidence for the correct assignment of the base position of manner adverbials. A standard way to model out-of-the-blue contexts is to use questions such as *What happened?*[62]

Eckardt (2003:294) argues that definite NPs in categorical judgments cannot be used to reliably establish wide focus, because they must be topical. And if they are topical, then, according to her, if the subject and the object of a sentence refer to a known object in the common discourse universe, the question *What happened then?* is interchangeable with the question *What did the subject do to the object?* Therefore, only indefinite NPs should be used for categorical judgments in out-of-the-blue-contexts.

Note that Eckardt's understanding of focus thus clearly and significantly differs from that of Höhle (1982), cf. the endnote 52 in section 3, where Höhle makes it clear that for him known material can be in the focus whenever its function is new.

In the following, I argue that focus tests that rely on indefinite direct objects cannot be used to determine the base position of manner adverbials, because verb-related adverbials principally do not go together with new direct objects in out-of-the-blue contexts. This will be demonstrated with the help of the following example involving *laut* 'loud', *ein Lied* 'a song', and the verb *singen* 'sing'.

(42)   Was ist passiert?
       'What happened?'

       a. ??*Ein Mann hat ein Lied **laut** gesungen.*
           a   man   has a   song loud sung
       b. *Ein Mann hat **laut** ein Lied gesungen.*
           a   man   has loud a   song sung
           'A man loudly sang a song.'

The judgment on (42) is clear: (42a) is not an appropriate answer to the question, whereas (42b) constitutes an appropriate answer. Crucially, though, it is not the optimal utterance in an out-of-the-blue context. This can be seen by comparing (42) to (43).

(43) Was ist passiert?
'What happened?'

    a. *Ein Mann hat ein Lied gesungen.*
       a   man has a   song sung
       'A man sang a song.'

    b. *Ein Mann hat laut gesungen.*
       a   man has loud sung
       'A man sang loudly.'

    c. *Ein Mann hat gesungen.*
       a   man has sung
       'A man sang.'

All sentences in (43) are appropriate answers to the question, so that we can compare which of the four appropriate answers in (43) and (42) are the best or optimal utterances in an out-of-the-blue context. According to my intuitions, it is very clear that the best utterances in all of (43) and (42) are (43a) and (43b).

This preference can already be explained with the help of the Gricean maxims, in particular with the maxims regarding quantity. Grice (1975) distinguishes two maxims that fall into the category of quantity, cf. (44).

(44)   a.   Make your contribution as informative as is required (for the current purposes of exchange).

      b.   Do not make your contribution more informative than is required.

For our discussion, a point that Grice raises with respect to (44b) is of interest: "[...] overinformativeness may be confusing in that it is liable to raise side issues; and there may also be an indirect effect, in that the hearers may be misled as a result of thinking that there is some particular *point* in the provision of the excess of information." (Grice 1975:152)

For (42), the answer in (42a) suffers exactly from this kind of overinformativeness that Grice is describing, and it is clearly not good in an out-of-the-blue context. But it is not enough to explain this kind of overinformativeness by just pointing to the fact that it is more informative than the three answers in (44), because that leaves the appropriateness of the answer in (42b) unexplained, which clearly is also more informative than the three answers in (44). The characteristic of utterances containing verb-related adverbials that makes them inappropriate for out of the blue contexts lies rather in their internal structure than in a simple count of the constituents that present new information.

Before looking at a few other instances that lend support to this point, it is helpful to have a short look at those sentences that are widely agreed to be able to occur in out-of-the-blue contexts, the so called thetic sentences.

6.1.1. Thetic sentences

In a tradition going back to Brentano (1874), judgements are classified into two basic types, thetic judgements, and categoric judgements (cf. e.g. Marty 1940, Kuroda 1972, Sasse 1987, Ladusaw 1984, Eckardt 1996). Simply put, categoric judgements involve two steps: first, an object is selected, and second, a predication is made over this object. In contrast, thetic judgement don't involve two separate steps. Correspondingly, sentences can be classified into thetic and categorical sentences, depending on their prototypical usage. Standard examples of thetic sentences are given in (45), all taken from Eckardt (1996).

(45)   a.   *Die Sonne scheint.*
                the sun   shines
                'The sun is shining.'
          b.   *Es schneit.*
                it snows
                'It is snowing.'
          c.   *Es schneit nicht.*
                it snows not
                'It is not snowing.'
          d.   *Friedrichs ist gestorben.*
                Friedrichs is died
                'Friedrichs has died.'

Thetic sentences are special in that in "making a thetic judgment, the speaker has in his mind a state of affairs as a whole, something which can not be separated any further into a property and an object [...]" Eckardt (1996:23). Categorical sentences, on the other hand, are always about an object, and state whether or not that object has a certain property (Eckardt 1996:22).

While I will not go further in the discussion of thetic and non-thetic sentences, the important point for the further discussion is that in thetic sentences, a situation is presented holistically, allowing no further division into individual parts. Returning to the issue of verb-related and event-related adverbials, I will argue that verb-related adverbials are always specific in the sense that they force us to break up any holistic view on a situation and look at some aspects in detail, whereas event-related adverbials do not force us to do so. With this in mind, let's take another look at the minimal pair introduced in (42) above, repeated here as (46).

(46)   a. ??*Ein Mann hat ein Lied **laut** gesungen.*
         a   man has a   song loud sung
    b. *Ein Mann hat **laut** ein Lied gesungen.*
         a   man has loud a   song sung
         'A man loudly sang a song.'

(46b) allows a holistic interpretation, because subject, object, adverbial and verb can be directly linked in one step to the event described by the sentence: The subject and the object provide the agent and the patient, the adverbial says that it was a loud event, and the verb informs us that it was a singing event. This is not possible for (46a), where *laut* 'loud' needs, due to its position, to be interpreted as a verb-related adverbials. It therefore needs to access the internal dimensions of the singing event, and does not apply to the event as a whole.[63]

Two pieces of evidence support this view. Firstly, if an adjective allows a manner reading and and event-related reading, then the event-related reading is bound to the pre-object position. Secondly, adjectives that only allow verb-related readings cannot occur in the pre-object position.

Thus, (46b) allows the *wobei*-paraphrase, cf. (47).

(47)   a. *Ein Mann hat **laut**   ein Lied gesungen.*
         a   man has loudly a   song sung
         'A man loudly sang a song.'
    b. *Ein Mann hat ein Lied gesungen, wobei   er laut war.*
         a   man has a   song sung,   in.doing.so he loud was
         'A man sang a song. In doing so, he was loud.'

With definite direct objects, where both orders are acceptable, we get corresponding reading preferences, cf. (48), where the appropriateness of the *wobei*-paraphrase is compared to that of the *Wie-das-ist*-paraphrase.

(48)　　a.　*Peter hat das Lied **laut** gesungen.*
　　　　　　Peter has the song loud sung
　　　　　　'Peter sang the song loudly.'

　　　　　　(i)　??*Peter hat das Lied gesungen, wobei　　er laut war.*
　　　　　　　　Peter has the song sung,　　in.doing.so he loud was
　　　　　　　　'Peter sang the song. In doing so, he was loud.'

　　　　　　(ii)　*Wie Peter das Lied gesungen hat, das war laut.*
　　　　　　　　how Peter the song sung　　has, that was loud
　　　　　　　　'The way Peter sang the song was loud.'

　　　　b.　*Peter hat **laut** das Lied gesungen.*
　　　　　　Peter has loud the song sung
　　　　　　'Peter loudly sang the song.'

　　　　　　(i)　*Peter hat das Lied gesungen, wobei　　er laut war.*
　　　　　　　　Peter has the song sung,　　in.doing.so he loud was
　　　　　　　　'Peter sang the song. In doing so, he was loud.'

　　　　　　(ii)　??*Wie Peter das Lied gesungen hat, das war laut.*
　　　　　　　　How Peter sang the song,　　that was loud
　　　　　　　　'The way Peter sang the song was loud.'

If the adverbial precedes the direct object, the *wobei*-paraphrase is better than the *Wie-das-ist*-paraphrase. The other way around, with the direct object preceding the adverbial, the *Wie-das-ist*-paraphrase delivers a good paraphrase, while the *wobei*-paraphrase is not appropriate.

The second piece of evidence comes from adjectives that can serve as a verb-related adverbial but do not allow usages as event-related adverbials. One such case is the adjective *forte* 'forte', the musical term contrasting with *piano* 'piano' expressing the two opposed musical dynamics roughly corresponding to a loud vs. quiet distinction. In (49), *laut* 'loud' is replaced by *forte* 'forte'.

(49)　　Was ist passiert?
　　　　'What happened?'

　　　　a.　??*Ein Mann hat ein Lied **forte** gesungen.*
　　　　　　a　man　has a　song forte sung

　　　　b.　**Ein Mann hat **forte** ein Lied gesungen.*
　　　　　　a　man　has forte a　song sung

What we get here shares the pattern with Eckardt's examples of implicit resultatives in combination with verbs of creation, although *forte* clearly constitutes a manner modification, and *sing* clearly is not a verb of creation. What these data show are two things: Firstly, verb-related adverbials are always placed after the direct object.[64] Secondly, since they always specify an internal aspect of the event and not the whole event globally, they are never good in out-of-the-blue contexts. As a consequence, the indefinite direct object in (49a) cannot receive an existential reading, and the sentence is inappropriate in that context.

All this is very much in conformity with another well-known finding from the literature, namely that the sentences with the order adverbial-direct object show a neutral stress pattern with only a single accent, whereas in the other order, multiple accents are required. The data in this respect are quite clear; consider e.g. Eckardt's own example in (50), her (68a) and (69) (cf. also the discussion in section 4.3).[65]

(50)   a.   *Alicia hat ein HUHN VORSICHTIG GESTREICHELT.*
            Alicia has a   chicken careful   stroked
            'Alicia stroked a chicken carefully.'
    b.   *Alicia hat vorsichtig ein HUHN gestreichelt.*
            Alicia has careful   a   chicken stroked
            'Alicia carefully stroked a chicken.'

Sentence (50a) is the only possible accentuation pattern which avoids narrow focus on any of the three constituents following the finite verb, whereas (50b) allows wide focus with the help of a single accent on the DO.

Frey and Pittner (1998) also agree that the word order **direct object > manner adverbial** needs multiple accents, resulting in the pattern in (51), their (43b) for the manner reading of *langsam* 'slowly'.

(51)   *Du könntest das Essen LANGsam KOchen.*
        You could   the food slowly   cook
        'You could cook the food slowly.'

How does this data link to the idea that manner adverbials always specify an internal aspect of the event? I believe that the crucial link is the observation that true out-of-the-blue focus is indeed impossible for these sentences and that the two accents indicate the close conceptual connection of the adverbial and the verb.

6.2.   Re-interpreting the controversial examples

This section will show that we can fruitfully reanalyze all of the examples controversially discussed in the previous section and in the previous literature when we pay close attention to the differences between event-related and verb-related readings. In the first two sections, we investigate how the two remaining diagnostics for base position fare in this respect, the existentially interpreted w-phrases and the theme-rheme condition.

6.2.1.   *Existentially interpreted w-phrases*

Properties of German w-phrases, that is, phrases that are headed by elements from the wordclass of interrogative pronouns or interrogative determiners like *wer, was* 'who, what' or *welcher, welches* 'which', have been employed by Frey and Pittner (1998) in establishing the base positions of adverbials.[66] They note that when w-phrases are existentially interpreted, they are restricted in the number of positions available to them. This restriction can be seen in the examples (52), (12a-b) of Frey and Pittner (1998).

(52)   a.   *weil   ein Professor wen   beleidigt hat.*
              because a   professor someone.ACC insulted has
              'because a professor insulted someone.'
       b.   **weil   wen   ein Professor beleidigt hat.*
              because someone.ACC a   professor insulted has

If, as in (52), an existentially interpreted w-phrase serves as the direct object, only the word order **subject > direct object** is possible. The word order **direct object > subject** is not possible.

Frey and Pittner (1998:495) argue that the most plausible explanation for this behavior is the assumption that existentially interpreted w-phrases cannot move out of their base position. Assuming this, their placement can be used to establish base positions for other constituents of a sentence relative to the position of the existentially interpreted w-phrases.

Frey and Pittner (1998) adduce data that aims to show that manner adverbials are positioned between the lowest-ranked argument *was* 'something', per assumption in its base position, and the minimal verb domain, cf. (53), corresponding to their (34),[67] and an additional example in (54), corresponding to (61) in Frey (2003).

(53)   *weil   Maria heute was   **sorgfältig** durchgearbeitet hat.*
      because Maria today something carefully   studied   has
      'because today Maria carefully studied something.'

(54)   *Peter will   jetzt was   **konzentriert** lesen.*
      Peter wants now something carefully   read
      'Peter wants to read something carefully now.'

If *was* 'something' appears in its base position in these sentences, then, according to Frey and Pittner's assumption, the base position of manner adverbials is to the right of the direct object.

Eckardt (2003) does not dispute the test itself, but notes that for other sentences, we get a clear preference for the order adverbial before direct object.

(55)   a.   *Alicia hat dann **gierig**   was   gegessen.*
           Alicia has then greedily something eaten
           'Alicia then greedily ate something.'
      b.   *Peter hat dann **vorsichtig** wen   gefragt.*
           Peter has then carefully   someone asked
           'Peter then carefully asked someone.'
      c.   *Claudia hat **demonstrativ** was   gelesen.*
           Claudia has ostentatiously something read
           'Claudia ostentatiously read something.'
      d.   *Eberhard zog **schüchtern** was   aus.*
           Eberhard took shyly   something off
           'Eberhard shyly took something off.'

As far as Eckardt is concerned, in all four sentences, the manner adverbial is positioned before the existentially interpreted w-phrase. Eckardt (2003:293) concludes drily that "[t]he result of these findings is (somewhat disappointingly) that either test (I) cannot be trusted or that there are in fact two base positions for manner adverbs."

6.2.1.1.   W-phrases and integration

Frey (2003:206, footnote 14) claims that w-phrases can participate in the formation of a complex predicate. If one allows for this possibility, then the order adverbial-w-phrase could be analysed as the result of complex predicate formation. If we look at the conditions on integration given in (35), then the w-phrases in Eckardt's example (91), repeated here as (56), all meet them:

the verb and the w-phrase are daughters, cf. (35a); the w-phrases are arguments of the verb, cf. (35bi), they are not assigned properties unlimited in
time (35ci) and their theta-roles are prototypical (35cii).[68]

Thus, Frey and Pittner can simply argue that in all of Eckardt's examples,
the direct object is integrated and therefore they do not constitute counterexamples to their own data. However, this account fundamentally undermines
the usefulness of this test, at least as far as event-related and verb-related adverbials are concerned, because we will now have many cases that cannot be
used for testing anymore because the object might be integrated.

6.2.2.   W-phrases: Re-interpreting the data

On the view advanced here, and assuming that w-phrases appear in their base
position, we expect the distribution in (56).

(56)   event-related adverbial > existentially interpreted w-phrase > verb-
         related adverbials

Note that, following the argumentation in section 6.1, existentially interpreted
w-phrases are predicted not to co-occur with verb-related adverbials in out-
of-the-blue contexts. In the following two sections, I will show that all the
data by Frey and Pittner as well as Eckardt can be explained without making
use of object integration. Instead, I will show that the distinction between
event-related and verb-related usages is sufficient to account for the data.

In (57), and (58), I formed minimal pairs on the basis of the example sentence discussed in section 6.2.1, (where (57a) repeats (53) and (58a) repeats
(54)).

(57)   a.   *weil   Maria heute was   sorgfältig durchgearbeitet*
                because Maria today something careful   studied
                hat.
                has
                'because today Maria carefully has studied something.'
        b.   *weil   Maria heute sorgfältig was   durchgearbeitet*
                because Maria today careful   something studied
                hat.
                has
                'because today Maria carefully studied something.'

(58)   a.   *Peter will   jetzt was   **konzentriert** lesen.*
           Peter wants.to now something careful   read
           'Peter now wants to read something carefully.'
       b.   *Peter will   jetzt **konzentriert** was   lesen.*
           Peter wants.to now careful   something read
           'Peter now wants to read something carefully .'

What this data shows is that in both cases both linear orderings are fine, which, on the face of it, seems to support Eckardt's pessimistic conclusions with regard to the test under discussion (cf. section 6.2.1).

However, there are two other possible explanations for the data. One explanation would argue that only the *was* in the b-sentences receives an existential reading. In contrast, the indefinite noun phrases in the a-sentences receive a specific reading ('a certain'). Assuming that specific readings of indefinites are at least a subclass of either partitive or in-group readings, this rules out (57a) as evidence supporting any assumption regarding base positions.[69] This explanation is problematic, because native speaker judgements on whether or not the *was* 'something' in the b-sentence needs to be interpreted with a specific reading are unclear (for one, this judgement would diverge from the interpretation of the reading of (57a) given in Frey and Pittner 1998).

The second explanation is that the adverbial usages in the two sentences are actually different: Only in the a-sentences are *sorgfältig/konzentriert* 'careful' used as manner adverbials. In the b-sentences, they are used as event-related adverbials. That this is the correct explanation can be seen by applying the different paraphrases. In both cases, the order adverbial-direct object calls for the *wobei*-paraphrase, whereas the other order needs the *Wie-das-ist*-paraphrase, although this cannot be shown for (58) directly, due to the modal *will* in the sentence. The tricky part is that these two readings are in both cases hard to tell apart. We will come back to this problem in section 7.2.

If we now take a closer look at Eckardt's data, we see that they also do not contain manner adverbials in pre-object position. Thus, Eckardt's interpretation of her data is correct insofar as we have here existentially interpreted indefinite direct objects, and the adverbials appear in their base position. However, in no instance are these adverbials verb-related adverbials. Instead, they serve as event-related or even higher adverbials. A closer look at her four sentences from (55), repeated her as (59), supports this view.

(59)   a.   *Alicia hat dann **gierig** was   gegessen.*
            Alicia has then greedy something eaten
            'Alicia then greedily ate something.'
       b.   *Peter hat dann **vorsichtig** wen   gefragt.*
            Peter has then careful   someone asked
            'Peter then carefully asked someone.'
       c.   *Claudia hat **demonstrativ** was   gelesen.*
            Claudia has ostentatious   something read
            'Claudia ostentatiously read something.'
       d.   *Eberhard zog **schüchtern** was   aus.*
            Eberhard took shy   something off
            'Eberhard shyly took something off.'

Gierig 'greedy' in (59a) is clearly a mental-attitude adverbial, apart from its semantics this is also obvious from its behavior with regard to negation, cf. (60).

(60)   a.   *Roland hat gierig nicht aufgehört zu essen.*
            Roland has greedy not   stopped   to eat
            'Roland greedily didn't stop eating.'
       b.   *Roland hat gierig kein Trinkgeld gegeben.*
            Roland has greedy no   tip   given
            'Roland greedily didn't leave a tip.'

Vorsichtig 'cautious' in (59b) displays the by now familiar pattern: a *wobei*-paraphrase is required, a clear sign of event-related adverbials.

   Demonstrativ 'ostentatious' in (59c) can also be shown not to be an instance of verb-related modification. The sentence in (61) will make this point clearer.

(61)   *Während alle   mit glänzenden Augen auf ihren Freund*
        while   everybody with bright   eyes on her   friend
        *starrten, hat Claudia **demonstrativ** was   gelesen.*
        stare,   has Claudia ostentatiously something read
        'While everybody glared with bright eyes at her boyfriend, Claudia read ostentatiously.'

Clearly, in this example, *demonstrativ* 'ostentatiously' does not modify the manner in which Claudia reads, but characterizes the fact (or event) that she reads as *demonstrativ*. Consequently, (62a) but not (62b) can be uttered in commenting on the situation described in (61).

(62)   a.   *Dass Claudia etwas   gelesen hat, das war demonstrativ.*
             that   Claudia something read   has, that was ostentatious
             'That Claudia read was ostentatious.'
       b.   *Wie Claudia etwas   gelesen hat, das war demonstrativ.*
             how Claudia something read   has, that was ostentatious
             'The way Claudia read was ostentatious.'

The upshot of this is that *demonstrativ* does not have a manner reading, but is used here as a subject oriented adverbial. Unsurprisingly, *demonstrativ* 'ostentatious' can have scope over negation, cf. (63).

(63)   *Claudia ist **demonstrativ** nicht zur Schule gegangen.*
        Claudia is ostentatious   not   to   school gone
        'Ostentatiously, Claudia did not go to school.'

Schüchtern 'shy' in (59d) is a psychological adjective, here used as a transparent adverbial. Again, evidence comes from looking at the negated counterpart, cf. (64).

(64)   *Eberhard zog **schüchtern** nichts   aus.*
        Eberhard took shy   nothing off
        'Eberhard took nothing off, because he was shy.'

All in all, Eckardt's data thus clearly confirms the claim that event-related adverbials are always positioned before the direct object.

6.3.   Theme-rheme condition

The *theme-rheme condition* proposed by Lenerz (1977) and reproduced in (65), corresponding to his (14), is another test for argument serialization:[70]

(65)   Whenever two satzglieder[71] A and B can occur in the order AB as well as BA, and if BA occurs only under certain, testable conditions, which do not hold for AB, then AB represents the unmarked order and BA the marked order.

Frey and Pittner (1998) illustrate this principle with the data in (66) and (67), their (7) and (8), where the two different constituent questions used are to be understood as one of the 'certain, testable conditions' referenced in the definition (65).

(66)   *Wem   hat Otto heute ein Gedicht vorgetragen?*
          whom has Otto today a   poem   recited
          'To whom did Otto recite a poem today?'

   a.   *Otto hat heute [einer KolLEGin]_A   [ein Gedicht]_B*
          Otto has today a   colleague.DAT a   poem.ACC
          vorgetragen.
          recited

                            rheme   >   theme
          'Today, Otto recited a poem to a lady colleague.'

   b.   *Otto hat heute [ein Gedicht]_B [einer KolLEGin]_A*
          Otto has today a poem.DAT   a colleague.DAT
          vorgetragen.
          recited

                            theme   >   rheme
          'Today, Otto recited a poem to a lady colleague.'

(67)   Was hat Otto heute einer Kollegin vorgetragen?
          'What did Otto recite to a colleague today?'

   a.   *Otto hat heute [einer Kollegin]_A [ein GeDICHT]_B*
          Otto has today a colleague.DAT a poem.ACC
          vorgetragen.
          recited

                            theme   >   rheme
          'Today, Otto recited a poem to a lady.'

   b. ??*Otto hat heute [ein GeDICHT]_B [einer Kollegin]_A*
          Otto has today a poem.DAT   a colleague.DAT
          vorgetragen.
          recited

                            rheme   >   theme

In (66), the question, serving as the context, asks for the recipient of the recital of the poem, making the noun phrase *einer Kollegin* 'a colleague', indexed as satzglied A, the rheme in (66a) and (66b). In contrast, the satzglied indexed B, *ein Gedicht* 'a poem', is part of the theme, or thematic, as it is already given in the context (since it appears in the question). As an answer to the question, both orders *einer Kollegin ein Gedicht* ($A_{rheme}B_{theme}$) and *ein Gedicht einer Kollegin* ($B_{theme}A_{rheme}$) are acceptable. In contrast, in (67) the patient (= the colleague, satzglied A) is thematic and satzglied B, *ein Gedicht* 'a poem' serves as the rheme. Here, only the order *einer Kollegin ein Gedicht* ($A_{theme}B_{rheme}$) is acceptable as an answer to the question, but not *ein Gedicht einer Kollegin* ($B_{rheme}A_{theme}$). Therefore, the order indirect object > direct object is the unmarked order for the sentence. As Frey and Pittner (1998:494) write, this observation is often reconstructed as illustrating that focussed material cannot be moved out of its base position. Assuming this, the results from the application of the theme-rheme condition support the hypothesis that the base position of verb-related adverbials, in this case again manner adverbials, is between direct object and verb, cf. (68).

(68)   Wie hat Otto das Lied vorgesungen?
         'How did Otto sing the song?'

     a.   *Otto hat [laut]$_A$ [das Lied]$_B$ vorgesungen.*
         Otto has loudly   the   song   sung
                 rheme > theme

     b.   *Otto hat [das Lied]$_B$ [laut]$_A$ vorgesungen.*
         Otto has the   song   loudly sung
              theme   > rheme
         'Otto sang the song loudly.'

In the context of a *Wie?* 'How?' question, only the word order DO MA is acceptable.[72]

If we now contrast the behavior of the material used in (68) to the same material in the context of a *Was?* 'What?' question, we see a different pattern, cf. (69).

(69)   Was hat Otto laut vorgesungen?
         'What did Otto sing loudly?'

     a.   *Otto hat [laut]$_A$ [ein Lied]$_B$ vorgesungen.*
         Otto has loudly   a   song   sung
               theme > rheme

     b.   *Otto hat [ein Lied]$_B$ [laut]$_A$ vorgesungen.*
         Otto has a   song   loudly sung
               rheme > theme
         'Otto loudly sang a song.'

The order **direct object > adverbial** is less restricted than the opposite order. The result of the application of the Lenerz test is therefore that this is the unmarked word order for the material in this sentence.[73]

Note that the theme-rheme condition only works as a diagnostic for the base position of manner adverbials on the assumption that the *Wie*-question picks out the verb-related reading, and not the event-related reading. As far as I can see, this is indeed the typical target in the context of the question in (68), but I do not see a way in which this could be controlled in a principled way. Therefore, this test needs to be used with great caution.

At least for those cases where only an interpretation as a verb-related adverbial is possible, the diagnostic gives strong support to the view that the base position is between direct object and verb, cf. e.g. (70).

(70)   Wie hat Otto die Frage beantwortet?
      'How did Otto answer the question?'

    a.   *Otto hat die Frage   intelligent beantwortet.*
          Otto has the question intelligent answered
          'Otto answered the question intelligently.'

    b.   **Otto hat intelligent die Frage   beantwortet.*
          Otto has intelligent the question answered

(71)   Was hat Otto intelligent beantwortet?
      'What answered Otto intelligently?'

    a.   *Otto hat eine Frage   intelligent beantwortet.*
          Otto has a   question intelligent answered
          'Otto answered a question intelligently.'

    b.   *?Otto hat intelligent eine Frage   beantwortet.*
          Otto has intelligent a   question answered

The pattern for *intelligent* deviates from the patterns exhibited by the sentence pair containing *laut* 'loudly' in that the pattern in (71b) is not very good, which could be explained by assuming that (71b) suggests an event-related reading, which is not available.

7.   More evidence and some subtleties

7.1.   Clear minimal pairs

In cases where the *wobei*-paraphrase is inappropriate, the pre-object position is not available, cf. (72) for an example with *wunderbar* used as a pure manner adverbial.

(72)   a.   **Robert hat **wunderbar** Stella geführt.*
          Robert has wonderful Stella led

b. *Robert hat Stella **wunderbar** geführt.*
Robert has Stella wonderful led
'Robert led Stella wonderfully.'

(i) *Robert hat Stella geführt, wobei   er wunderbar*
Robert has Stella led,   in.doing.so he wonderful
war. (≠ b)
was
'Robert led Stella, in doing so, he was wonderful.'

(ii) *Wie Robert Stella geführt hat, das war wunderbar. (≈b)*
how Robert Stella led   has, that was wonderful
'The way Robert led Stella was wonderful'

The best minimal pairs are cases where the event-related reading is clearly different from the verb-related reading. The adjective *laut* was contrasted in section 6.1.1 against *forte*, using the opposite, *leise* and *piano* yields even clearer distinctions, cf. the data in (73) and (74).

(73)   a. **Fritz hat **piano** die Einleitung   gesungen.*
Fritz has piano the introduction sung

b. *Fritz hat die Einleitung   **piano** gesungen.*
Fritz has the introduction piano sung
'Fritz sang the introduction piano.'

(74)   a. *Fritz hat **leise** die Einleitung   gesungen.*
Fritz has quiet the introduction sang
'Fritz sang the introduction quietly.'

b. *Fritz hat die Einleitung   **leise** gesungen.*
Fritz has the introduction quiet sung
'Fritz sang the introduction quietly.'

While both (73b) and (74b) can be used to describe the very same situation, only *leise* 'quiet' can be positioned before the direct object. However, when *leise* is positioned before the direct object, it is interpreted as an event-related adverbial and requires the *wobei*-paraphrase. *Piano* does not even allow such a paraphrase, because it cannot be used to predicate of persons.[74] In addition, *leise* 'quiet' in (74a) suggests that the agent in the event tried to act unobtrusively or was in a reclusive state of mind when singing, functioning thus quite similarly to a transparent adverbial.

Other minimal pairs involve adjectives like *schön* 'beautiful' and *schwer* 'heavy' in verb-related as opposed to event-related usages, cf. the minimal pair in (75), (122) in Pittner (1999:107).

(75)   a.   *Sie hat **schön**   das Bild   gemalt.*
            She has beautifully the picture painted
            'Luckily, she quietly painted the picture.'
       b.   *Sie hat das Bild   **schön**   gemalt.*
            She has the picture beautifully painted
            'She painted the picture beautifully'

In (75a), the activity as a whole is characterized as beautiful (for more on the exact meaning of this reading, cf. the discussion in section 2.2.1 of chapter 4; in the free translation, I tried to mimic the effect by using *luckily* in combination with *quietly*), whereas in (75b) *schön* yields a blend between manner and resultative reading (Pittner (1999:107) speaks of a *resultatsbezogenes Adverbial der Art und Weise* 'result-oriented manner adverbial'). A further example of the event-related usage of *schön* is given in (76).

(76)   *Der Vater hat **schön**   die Wasserkisten hochgeschleppt.*
       The father has beautifully the water.crates   carry.upstairs
       'Luckily, the father has nicely carried the water crates upstairs'

For *schwer* 'heavy' we also get minimal pairs if we take the event-related reading into account, cf. (77), the repeated start example (18) from section 4.1.

(77)   a.   *(dass) Hans **schwer** den Wagen   belud*
            (that) Hans heavily the carriage loaded
            '(that) Hans heavily loaded the carriage'
       b.   *(dass) Hans den Wagen   **schwer** belud*
            (that) Hans the carriage heavily loaded
            '(that) Hans loaded the carriage heavily'

(77a) cannot be understood as an implicit resultative (and was therefore starred in the original example), but it can be used as an event-related adverbial, yielding a sentence meaning roughly paraphrasable by *Hans loaded the carriage, and he really worked hard doing so.*

Maienborn (2003a:94) also discusses an asymmetry between *schnell* and *langsam* that fits right into the picture presented here: since the latter cannot be used with a holistic reading, it cannot occur before the direct object, cf. (78), her (83).

(78)   a.   **Jochen schmückte **langsam** den Weihnachtsbaum.*
           Jochen decorated slowly   the Christmas.tree

       b.   *Jochen schmückte den Weihnachtsbaum **langsam**.*
           Jochen decorated the christmas.tree   slowly

In contrast, as already shown with the help of the minimal pair (22) discussed in chapter 4, *schnell* allows a holistic reading and is therefore acceptable in pre-object position.

7.2.   Lexical semantics and verb-adverbial combinatorics

In some instances, variation in the order of the elements seems to yield little meaning differences. On the one hand, this holds for adjectives like *sorgfältig* where the lexical meaning of the adjective prevents clear differentiation.

(79)   a.   *Peter hat **sorgfältig** das Buch durchgearbeitet.*
           Peter has careful   the book studied
           'Peter carefully studied the book.'

       (i)   *Peter hat das Buch durchgearbeitet, wobei   er*
             Peter has the book studied,   in.doing.so he
             sorgfältig war. (≈ a)
             careful   was
             'Peter studied the book. In doing so, he was careful.'

       (ii) *Wie Peter das Buch durchgearbeitet hat, das war*
             how Peter the book studied   has, that was
             sorgfältig. (?≈ a)
             careful
             'The way in which Peter studied the book was careful.'

   b.   *Peter hat das Buch **sorgfältig** durchgearbeitet.*
        Peter has the book careful   studied
        'Peter studied the book carefully.'

       (i)   *Peter hat das Buch durchgearbeitet, wobei   er*
             Peter has the book studied,   in.doing.so he
             sorgfältig war. (?≈ b)
             careful   was
             'Peter studied the book. In doing so, he was careful.'

       (ii) *Wie Peter das Buch durchgearbeitet hat, das war*
             how Peter the book studied   has, that was
             sorgfältig. (≈ b)
             careful
             'The way in which Peter studied the book was careful.'

While I consider the *wobei*-paraphrase a better paraphrase for (79a) and the *Wie-das-ist*-paraphrase a better paraphrase for (79b), the differences are slight. The reason is that an adjective like *sorgfältig* 'careful' makes it all but impossible to disentangle clearly a manner of doing something from simply being careful while doing something: if you do something in a careful manner you are necessarily careful while doing it and vice versa. Thus, the wrong position can in these cases effortlessly be accomodated.

When the event-related and the verb-related usage are closely related, as in the case of *sorgfältig* 'carefully' in the sentences just discussed, it is usually impossible to form sentences with antonymic adjectives occupying the event-related and the verb-related position, cf. (80) (see also the discussion in section 3.2.3 of chapter 4).

(80)   a. ??*Er hat **laut** das Kind **leise** gerufen.*
           he has loud the child quiet called
           'He loudly called the child quietly.'
        b. ??*Er hat **sorgfältig** das Buch **oberflächlich** durchgearbeitet.*
           he has careful   the book superficial   worked.through
           'He carefully worked through the book superficially.'

Only in very elaborate contexts are sentences like (81) acceptable.

(81)   *Sie   haben sorgfältig   das Zimmer schlampig   geputzt.*
        They have   painstakingly the room   half-assedly cleaned
        'They painstakingly cleaned the room half-assedly.'

A context where (81) could be an adequate description would be the description of a film-crew that aims to set up a room as looking half-assedly cleaned.

7.3.   Scrambling

Finally, it should be clear that in many instances, the surface order might simply be the result of scrambling. Thus, if we have a case involving modification of complex events as discussed in chapter 4, we can easily form pairs like in (82), where (82a) is repeated from (46) in chapter 4.

(82)   a. *Hans hat **geschickt** die Frage   **dumm** beantwortet.*
           Hans has skillful   the question stupid answered
           'Hans skillfully answered the question stupidly.'
        b. *Hans hat die Frage   **geschickt dumm** beantwortet.*
           Hans has the question skillful   stupid answered
           'Hans skillfully answered the question stupidly.'

Here, the best explanation for the semantic equivalence of the adverbials in these two sentences is that in (82b) the direct object was scrambled over the event-related adverbial.

Similarly, for all those cases where no clear verb-related reading is available due to the lexical semantics of the verb, scrambling is the best explanation for surface orders with an event-related adverbial following the direct object. One such case concerns (54), the example for associated readings given in section 3.2.3 of chapter 4, repeated here as (83), along with the varying order in (83b).

(83)   a.   Fritz hat Isolde **laut** verfolgt.
                 'Fritz loudly followed Isolde.'
        b.   Fritz hat **laut** Isolde verfolgt.
                 'Fritz loudly followed Isolde.'

(84)   Fritz hat Isolde verfolgt, wobei er laut war.
         'Fritz followed Isolde. In doing so, he was loud.'

Since only an associated reading is available in the first place, there can be no contrasting verb-related reading, and the paraphrase in (84) is appropriate for both sentences of (83). The order in (83a) results from scrambling.

8. Summary

This chapter discussed the syntactic position of manner adverbials, which have been claimed to have their base position either before or after the direct object. I discussed in detail the accounts of Eckardt and Frey & Pittner, showing that Eckardt's account cannot explain all the data. Instead, I adopted the main finding of Frey & Pittner's account, namely that the base position of manner adverbials is after the direct object. I departed from their account only in that I assume that there is no object integration. Event-related adverbials have to be positioned before the direct object, and verb-related adverbials have to be positioned after the direct object in all cases.

Chapter 6
Adverbials in formal semantics: The classical analyses

The analysis of adverbials is one of the most challenging areas of formal semantics. On the one hand, as has been shown in chapters 2 to 4, they cover a wide variety of different meanings. On the other hand, and this comment is more technical in nature, they fall squarely outside any simple predicate-argument structure. This chapter describes the most influential formal semantic accounts that target those adverbials classified in this work as verb- and event-related adverbials.

Section 1 discusses the operator approach most prominently advocated by Thomason and Stalnaker (1973). Section 2 deals with the argument approach by McConnell-Ginet (1982). Section 3 introduces the predicate approach, whose breakthrough came with the spread of Davidsonian event semantics, trailing the publication of the original proposal, Davidson (1967), by decades. The order does therefore not so much reflect the original publication history, but rather the influence of the various approaches on the linguistic community.

Reichenbach (1966) offers a formal analysis that preceded all three approaches but never reached a larger audience, see Piñón (2008) for a comprehensive reassessment.

Besides forming a helpful background for my own proposal presented in chapter 7, this discussion aims to sharpen the awareness that there exists no single perfect formal representation that intuitively covers all the different types of adverbials discussed so far, nor are there any agreed criteria that would lead to the complete dismissal of any of the three treatments presented below. Rather, all three approaches have their own merits, and perhaps a combination of elements from all three theories will one day be seen as the most adequate approach to adverbial semantics.

1. The operator approach

The operator approach was developed in the late sixties and early seventies of the last century, when Romane Clark, Hans Kamp, Richard Montague, and Terence Parsons independently (cf. Parsons 1972:127) proposed this kind of approach (their results can be found in the publications that eventually followed: Clark 1970, Parsons 1972, Montague 1970, and Kamp 1975). Thomason and Stalnaker (1973) is perhaps the most influential article endorsing this approach.

The operator approach is based on the standard assumption that verbs denote sets of individuals or sets of pairs of individuals. According to the most basic variant of the predicate modifier theory, an adverb like *quickly* is represented as a function that applies to predicates and yields new predicates. A representation of (1) within this framework is given in (2).

(1)   Fritz runs **quickly**.

(2)   (QUICKLY(RUN))(fritz)

That is, the function representing the adverb *quickly* takes the set of individuals that run as an argument and yields the set of individuals that run quickly.

To derive this sentence, we must assume the lexical entries for *quickly* and *run* given in (3) and (4), respectively.

(3) $\lambda P \, \lambda x \, [QUICKLY(P(x))]$

(4) $\lambda x \, [RUN(x)]$

Given these entries, the derivation is straightforward, cf. (5).

(5)   [1] $\lambda P \, \lambda x \, [QUICKLY(P(x))]$ $(\lambda x \, [RUN(x)])$
       [2] $\lambda x \, [QUICKLY((\lambda x \, [RUN(x)]) \, (x))]$
       [3] $\lambda x \, [QUICKLY(RUN(x))]$
       [4] $\lambda x \, [QUICKLY(RUN(x))](fritz)$
       [5] $QUICKLY(RUN(fritz))$

So far, this approach is purely extensional. This leads to unwanted results (cf. e.g. McConnell-Ginet 1982:162, Cresswell 1985:42 or Eckardt 1998:4). To see this, consider a model where the extension of the verb *run* is the same as the extension of the verb *talk*, e.g. both denote the set consisting of the individual *Anna*. Furthermore, we assume that in this model, the sentence (6) is true.

(6)   Anna runs **quickly**.

If (6) is true, then, due to Leibniz' Law, (7) will also be true. *Talk* and *run* have the same extensions and can therefore be substituted for each other.

(7)   Anna talks **quickly**.

One move that circumvents this consequence is to have the adverbials denote functors on intensions. In the following, I will present the intensional analysis given by Thomason and Stalnaker (1973) in some more detail, followed by some pros and cons of the analysis.

1.1.   Thomason and Stalnaker

Thomason and Stalnaker (1973) intend to account for the differences between adverbials like *slowly* and *intentionally* on the one hand and *necessarily* on the other. They analyze the former as predicate modifiers and the latter as a sentence modifier. One important difference between the two types of modifiers lies in their behavior with regard to opaque contexts. The epistemic adverbial *necessarily* gives rise to opaque contexts everywhere in a sentence, whereas *intentionally* only creates opaque contexts for the object position (for details, cf. the discussion in section 3.2 of chapter 2 and section 1 of chapter 4, respectively). Thomason and Stalnaker (1973) account for this difference by analyzing sentence modifiers as functions from sentence intensions to sentence intensions, that is, *necessarily* is of type $<<s,t>,<s,t>>$, and sentence (8a) can be represented as (8b), where the caret is used to indicate the intension.

(8)   a.   Necessarily, nine is odd.
        b.   NECESSARILY $^\cap$[ODD (nine)]

Under this analysis the opaqueness effects are accounted for, because sentence modifiers apply to sentence intensions. In contrast, predicate modifiers map the intensions of one-place predicates to intensions of one-place predicates. The restriction to one-place predicates means that, in the case of transitive verbs, predicate modifiers are applied after the direct object has combined with the verb, but before the verb combines with the subject, cf. (9).

(9)   a.   Oedipus **intentionally** married Jocasta.
        b.   INTENTIONALLY $^\cap$[λx [MARRY (x, jocasta)]](oedipus)

This account correctly predicts that opacity arises with regard to the object position but not with regard to the subject position (note that λ-conversion into an intension is not possible here). The opacity pattern exhibited by *intentionally* is thus elegantly accounted for. Other adverbs like, e.g., *slowly* are treated in a similar way as *intentionally*, although there exist no parallel opacity effects, cf. (10).

(10)   a.   Renate **slowly** repaired the broken toy.
       b.   Renate is the director of the German Department.
            → The director of the German Department slowly repaired the broken toy.
       c.   The broken toy is my puppet.
            → Renate slowly repaired my puppet.

Clearly, the inferences in (10b) and (10c) are logically valid. No theory-internal explanation is available for these patterns. Eckardt (1998:8-9) points out that within this theory, one could capitalize on the difference between *intentionally* and *slowly* with regard to the opacity of the direct objects by assuming that those adverbials that do not give rise to opacity-effects must be applied to the verb before any nominal arguments, and adverbials that give rise to these effects are applied after the respective nominal arguments. Whether this strategy is feasible depends on the exact position of the adverbials involved.

1.2.   The operator approach and scope

One of the main motivations for the operator approach was to be able to account for scope effects. Parsons (1972) in particular argues that only this approach handles data where one adverbial takes scope over another adverbial, cf. his example in (11) (cf. also the examples in section 2.2.3 of chapter 4, where I discuss the modification of complex events).

(11)   John **painstakingly** wrote **illegibly**.

As Parsons argues, the correct interpretation of (11) requires that "the illegibility of the writing was at least one of the things John was taking pains to do" (Parsons 1972:131).

   This means that (11) does not correspond in meaning to (12), nor does it entail (13).

(12)   John wrote painstakingly and illegibly.

(13)   John wrote painstakingly.

In the operator approach, the correct semantic scope is directly reflected in the formal representation, cf. (14), taken from Parsons (1972:133).

(14)   PAINSTAKING[ILLEGIBLE$^\cap$[λx [WRITE(x)]]](john)

Interestingly, Parsons later criticized this feature of the operator approach. Parsons (1990:54-58) argues that the ability to express scope relations if more than one adverbial is present is not an advantage but a disadvantage. According to him, this account predicts ambiguity for sentences like (15), since they can be represented as either (16) or (17).

(15)   Brutus stabbed Caesar **violently with a knife**.

(16)   VIOLENTLY(WITH_A_KNIFE(STAB)) (brutus ,caesar)

(17)   WITH_A_KNIFE(VIOLENTLY(STAB)) (brutus, caesar)

The strength of this argument is tied to the role of syntax in the placement and interpretation of adverbial modifiers. On the assumption that the build-up of the semantic representation is guided by syntax and, additionally, that the adverbials are ordered relative to each other, there is no possibility of ambiguity here.

The second classical scope problem is discussed by Thomason and Stalnaker (1973) and concerns the different readings available for the two sentences given in (18).

(18)   a.   Sam **carefully** sliced all the bagels.
        b.   Sam sliced all the bagels **carefully**.

While the exact reading differences for (18a-b) are somewhat subtle (cf. the extensive discussion in 2.2.2 in chapter 4), they become more obvious if *carefully* is replaced, e.g., with *quickly*, where *quickly sliced all the bagels* is preferably interpreted as meaning that the overall time it took Sam to slice all the bagels was short, while *sliced all the bagels quickly* does not tell us anything about the overall amount of time, but only gives the time span for each individual slicing. Thomason and Stalnaker (1973) formalize this difference by having the quantifier within the complex predicate for (18a), but letting it have widest scope for (18b), see the formalizations in (19), where x is taken to range over bagels.

(19)   a.   CAREFULLY $^\cap$[λy ∀x [SLICE (y, x)]](sam)
        b.   ∀x [CAREFULLY $^\cap$[λy SLICE (y, x)](sam)]

Again, the features of the operator approach that allow us to capture the scope effects are its endocentricity and the stacked complex predicates that result from the application of the operators.

1.3.   The operator approach as a general analysis of modification structures

The operator approach has been used not only for modification in the verbal domain, but also for the analysis of adjectives in attributive modification.

Recall from the discussion in section 3.2 in chapter 1 that adjectives are commonly classified into intersective, subsective, and non-intersective, and subsective adjectives, cf. some examples of intersective adjectives in (20), and examples of non-intersective, non-subsective adjectives in (21).

(20)   four-legged, radioactive, sick, red

(21)   former, allegedly

As far as the formal semantic analysis of attributive modification is concerned, it is clear that intersective adjectives can be given an extensional analysis. This also accounts for the fact that inferences like the one in (22), repeated from (73) in chapter 1, are possible.

(22)   Max ist ein kranker Mann.   'Max is a sick man.'
         Max ist ein Linguist.   'Max is a linguist.'

         $\rightarrow$ Max ist ein kranker Linguist.   'Max is a sick linguist.'

Non-intersective adjectives, in contrast, do not show this behavior. An example is *alleged* in e.g. the phrase *alleged murderer*, where intersectivity is not given, cf. (23), and corresponding inference patterns to not hold, cf. (24) (see also the parallel example with *former* in chapter 1).

(23)   *alleged murderer*
         [[alleged murderer]] $\neq$ [[alleged]] $\cap$ [[murderer]]

(24)   Max is an alleged murderer.
         Max is a senator.

         $\nrightarrow$ Max is an alleged senator.

Since the operator approach is an intensional approach, it can be used to formalize non-intersective adjectives, cf. (25).

(25)   ALLEGED$^\cap$[λx [MURDERER(x)]]

It is thus a more general approach than the other two approaches to be discussed below. However, the price to be paid for the generality is that one has no explanation for the differences in behavior of the several different classes of adjectives in attributive modification, and a solution along the lines hinted at in the discussion of the differences between *intentionally* and *slowly* seems unlikely.

Note, too, that non-intersective adjectives, if used adverbially, cf. (26), are used as sentence adverbials.

(26)   *Fritz hat das Gedicht* **angeblich** *gesungen.*
        Fritz has the poem   alleged   sung
        'Fritz allegedly sang the poem.'

They therefore do not fall in the scope of the following two formal approaches.

1.4.   Criticism of the operator approach

Criticism of the operator approach often calls two specific aspects of this approach into question. One line of criticism takes issue with the cognitive plausibility of the account as an analysis of manner adverbials. The other line of criticism homes in on the limits of the approach that derive from specific aspects of its formalization. We will discuss both points in turn.

1.4.1.   *The cognitive inappropriateness of the intensional solution*

Above, I have shown that adverbials in the predicate modifier theory must be treated as being applied to intensions of verbal predicates. This is criticized in McConnell-Ginet (1982) and, following McConnell-Ginet, Larson (1998).

Following the representation in Larson (1998), the critique can be separated into two parts: (a) substitution failure does not entail intensionality and (b) the intensional account does not correspond to our intuitions about the data.

To demonstrate (a), both authors use the example of *cook* vs. *eat*. If we assume a model where all the people who eat are also the people who cook, then we can substitute $COOK(x)$ for $EAT(x)$ and vice versa. However, we do not need to use the intension of the intransitive verbs to circumvent the substitution, but can simply look for further details that distinguish between the two situations. As demonstrated by McConnell-Ginet (1982) and Larson

(1998), this further detail can be the hidden relationality of eating and cook-ing. That is, although in our model those who eat and those who cook are co-extensional, what is being eaten and what is being cooked can be differ-ent. If this is the case, then we simply reanalyze the intransitive variants of *eat* and *cook* as transitives with a hidden object argument.

The second point, (b), is very clearly stated in Larson (1998). He compares the reasons for entailment failure in two different cases, starting with the data in (27), his (8).

(27) Suppose: {x:x dances} = {x:x sings}
      Then: Olga dances. ↔ Olga sings.
      But: Max thinks Olga dances. ↮
                Max thinks Olga sings.
      Analysis: THINK(max,ˆDANCE(olga)) ↮
                THINK(max,ˆSING(olga))

Following Larson (1998), the entailment failure from *Max thinks Olga dances* to *Max thinks Olga sings* can be informally explained by arguing that al-though in the actual world the dancers and the singers are co-extensional, they do not have to be co-extensional in the world of Max's thoughts. This intuition about why the inference fails reappears in the formal analysis, where *think* is analyzed as a two place predicate that takes as its object the intension of a proposition.

The second case that Larson looks at is reproduced in (28), his (9).

(28) Suppose: {x:x eats} = {x:x cooks}
      Then: Olga eats. ↔ Olga cooks.
      But: Olga eats fish. ↮ Olga cooks fish.
      Analysis: EAT(olga,fish) ↮ COOK(olga,fish))

In contrast to (27), (28) shows that the entailment failure from *Olga eats fish* to *Olga cooks fish* can be explained without taking recourse to intensions, even though we assume that eaters and cooks are co-extensional.

Given these two possibilities to explain entailment failure, the question is which possibility is more intuitively plausible for the analysis of the data in the cases of adverbial modification. That is, how the pattern in (29) is best explained.

(29)   Suppose: {x:x talks} = {x:x walks}
        Then: Olga talks. ↔ Olga walks.
        But: Olga talks quickly. ↮ Olga walks quickly.

According to both McConnell-Ginet (1982:162-163) and Larson (1998), to account for the entailment failure with the help of intensions is counter-intuitive. We do not reason that although in this world walkers and talkers are co-extensional, there might be alternative worlds in which they are not co-extensional, and therefore, those who talk quickly and those who walk quickly must not refer to the same set of people. Rather, we argue along the following lines: "[...] whenever there is dancing and singing there is a performance. And even if the same people dance and sing, the performances are still different. And one might be beautiful, and the other not. Hence the conclusion doesn't follow" (Larson 1998:6).

1.4.2. Entailments in the operator approach

Entailments like the one in (30) do not follow logically from the respective representations, cf. (31).

(30)   Anna runs quickly. $\rightarrow_{entails}$ Anna runs.

(31)   a.   Anna runs quickly.
              QUICKLY(RUN)(anna)
        b.   Anna runs
              RUN(anna)

However, this entailment can be insured with the help of a meaning postulate like the one in (32), corresponding to the meaning postulate for manner adverbs in Eckardt (1998:4), her (3).

(32)   For all adverbials α the semantic representation [[α]] has the subset property: If [[α]] = F in $D_{<<e,t>,<e,t>>}$, then for all A in $D_{<e,t>}$: F(A) is a subset of A.

In prose: since the set denoted by *run quickly* is a subset of the set denoted by *run*, (31b) follows from (31a).

The situation becomes more difficult in the case of multiple adverbial modification, demonstrated here with the help of the sentence in (33), which will be discussed further in section 3 on the predicate approch and event-based semantic analyses.

(33)   Brutus stabbed Caesar in the back with a knife.

If we assume the representation in (34) for this sentence, then the postulate (32), modified to be used on transitive verbs, allows us to derive the entailments in (35).

(34)   IN_THE_BACK(WITH_A_KNIFE(STAB))(caesar,brutus)

(35)   a.   Brutus stabbed Caesar with a knife.
        b.   Brutus stabbed Caesar.

We cannot, however, derive the entailment in (36).

(36)   Brutus stabbed Caesar in the back.

To derive this entailment, we can adopt the principle of monotonicity introduced in Landman (2000:5-6), cf. (37).[75]

(37)   If A(N)(x) and N entails M then A(M)(x)

If we now let N be the complex predicate WITH_A_KNIFE(STAB)(x,y), M the predicate STAB(x,y) and A the functor IN_THE_BACK, then it follows from (37) that (36) is entailed by (33).

2.   The argument approach: McConnell-Ginet

An alternative to the operator approach is presented in McConnell-Ginet (1982). She also distinguishes between two classes of adverbials, sentence adverbials and ad-verbs. Her ad-verbs roughly correspond to the verb-related adverbials in this work, and I will focus on her treatment of these adverbials. For a useful critique of her treatment of sentence adverbials cf. Geuder (2000:123). Starting with the observation that some manner adverbials are obligatory in a similar way as direct objects (cf. the discussion in section 2.1.2), she argues that manner adverbials in general should be treated as verbal arguments. A representation of (38) is given in (39).

(38)   Fritz runs quickly.

(39)   RUN(fritz, quickly)

To be able to derive this representation, McConnell-Ginet (1982) first defines the operation of verb-augmentation, given in (40), cf. her (57).[76]

(40) Let α be a verb in category X that translates into an n-order predi-
cate denoting an n-ary relation $\mathfrak{R}$. Then α^+ is an ADMISSIBLE AUG-
MENTATION OF α IN CATEGORIES X AND X/Y only if α^+ trans-
lates into an $n/n+1$-order predicate denoting $\mathfrak{R}^+ = \mathfrak{R} \cup S$, where
$S \subset \mathfrak{R} \times$ Type Y. The augmented verb α^+ is ADMISSIBLE RELA-
TIVE TO $\xi \in$ Y only if $S \cap \mathfrak{R} \times \text{Den}(\xi) \neq \emptyset$.

This definition becomes clearer when explained with the help of an example, e.g. the augmentation of the verb *run* to include an argument place for
manner adverbials. The verb is intransitive and therefore denotes a one-place
predicate, cf. (41).

(41) $\lambda x [\text{RUN}(x)] <e,t>$

The augmentation of run to run$^+$, belonging to the category of intransitive
verbs and intransitive verbs/manner_adverbials, is admissible iff the following
is given:

1. run$^+$ translates into either a predicate of the type $<e,t>$ or a predicate
   of the type $<e,<e,t>>$.
2. run$^+$ denotes the unification set of the set denoted by RUN and the set
   S. The set S is a subset of the Cartesian product of the set denoted by
   RUN and the set of all relevant adverbials.
3. run$^+$ is admissible relative to a manner adverbial (e.g. *quickly*) only if
   the intersection of the set S and the Cartesian product of the set denoted
   by RUN and the singleton set QUICKLY is not the empty set.

In a second step, McConnell-Ginet (1982) defines verb-phrase-internal adverbial modification, cf. (42), her (58). In her terminology, adverbials that
can be used for verb phrase internal adverbial modification are categorized as
AD-Vs.

(42) a. Let α be a lexical verb belonging to Y/AD-V and ξ be an ex-
          pression belonging to AD-V. Then expression $\alpha\xi$ will belong
          to category Y. The translation of $\alpha\xi$ is specified by the rule of
          functional application:
          tr($\alpha\xi$)=tr(α)(tr(ξ))

      b. Let α be a lexical verb belonging to category X where X$\neq$
          Y/AD-V and ξ be an expression belonging to category AD-V.
          Then expression $\alpha\xi$ belongs to category X. A translation of $\alpha\xi$
          is defined if $\exists\alpha^+$, an admissible augmentation of α relative to ξ
          in categories X and X/AD-V. Then tr($\alpha\xi$)=tr(α^+)(tr(ξ))

The clause (42a) defines the procedure when the verb already subcategorizes for AD-Vs, the clause (42b) defines the procedure in the cases where verb-augmentation is needed.

2.1.   Entailments in McConnell-Ginet's approach

A simple entailment, like the one from (43a) to (43b), can be explained with the help of the general schema given in (44).

(43)   a.   Anna runs quickly.
        b.   Anna runs

(44)   For any augmented verb α^+: $\alpha^+(x,y)$ entails $\alpha(x)$

This schema does not need to be postulated, since it follows from McConnell-Ginet's definition of verb augmentation, cf. (40): The denotation of the augmented verb always contains the denotation of the un-augmented verb. Therefore, more complex entailments, e.g. from (45a) to (45b), are also unproblematic.

(45)   a.   Anna runs quickly on her crutches to the store.
        b.   Anna runs on her crutches.

Landman (2000:88-95) provides a reformulation of McConnell-Ginet's approach which also yields the correct entailments as well as free permutation of the adverbial modifiers.

3.   The predicate approach: Event-based semantics

Event-based semantics as introduced in Davidson (1967) assumes that the representation of a simple sentence like *Peter runs* contains a variable for events. This event variable is introduced by the verbal predicate. Disregarding tense, a simple sentence like *Brutus stabbed Caesar* is represented as in (46).

(46)   Brutus stabbed Caesar.
        $\exists e$ [STAB(brutus, caesar, e)]

Adverbials are treated as predicates over the event variable, forming a separate conjunct in the formal representation, cf. (47).

(47)   Brutus stabbed Caesar in the back.
        $\exists e$ [STAB(brutus, caesar, e) & IN(e, back)]

Davidson's main motivation for this approach is that it is able to account for typical entailment patterns of sentences containing adverbial modifiers. The sentence (48), taken from Parsons (1990:13), for example, entails all the sentences in (49).

(48)   Brutus stabbed Caesar in the back with a knife.

(49)   a.   Brutus stabbed Caesar in the back and Brutus stabbed Caesar with a knife.
         b.   Brutus stabbed Caesar in the back.
         c.   Brutus stabbed Caesar with a knife.
         d.   Brutus stabbed Caesar.

Within the entailed sentences in (49), (49a-c) entail (49d). This pattern can be conveniently represented with the help of a so-called *entailment diamond* (for this term, cf. e.g. Chierchia and McConnell-Ginet 2000:468), cf. figure 1.

Brutus stabbed Caesar in the back with a knife.

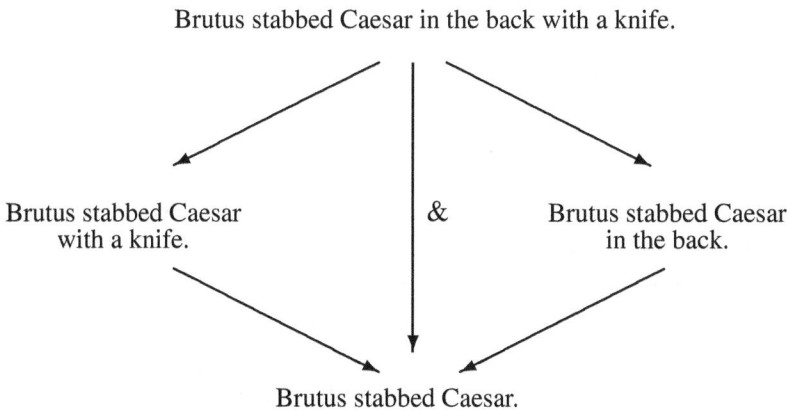

| Brutus stabbed Caesar with a knife. | & | Brutus stabbed Caesar in the back. |

Brutus stabbed Caesar.

Figure 1. The natural language version of the entailment diamont

In the event-based approach, these entailment relations follow via simplification from the semantic forms of the respective sentences, cf. figure 2.

∃e [STAB(brutus, caesar, e) & IN(e, back) & WITH(e, knife)]

∃e [STAB(brutus, caesar, e) &   &   ∃e [STAB(brutus, caesar, e) &
        WITH(e, knife)]   IN(e, back)]

∃e [STAB(brutus, caesar, e)]

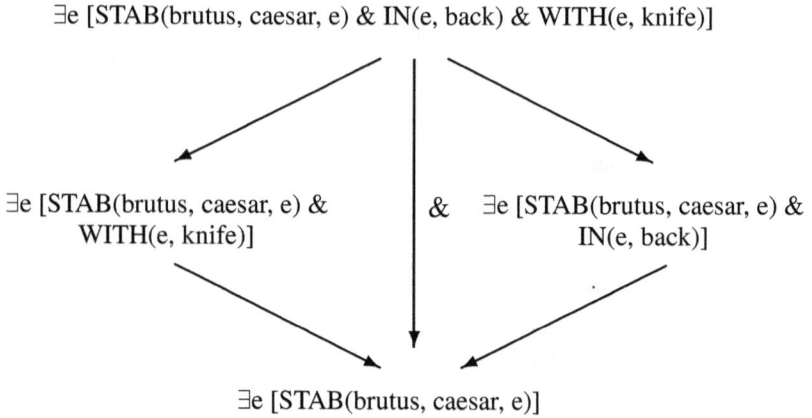

Figure 2. The entailment diamond, with semantic forms

Similar entailment patterns that arise if the number of adverbial modifiers is greater than two, cf. (50), can be derived in the same way.

(50)   Brutus stabbed Caesar with a knife in the back at midnight under the cover of darkness.

All of the modifiers can be dropped independently, since all are realized as autonomous conjuncts.

While Davidson explicitly restricted himself to participant adverbials (cf. section 3 in chapter 1), the approach was extended to manner adverbials in Parsons (1990). The reason why Davidson did not include adverbs like *quickly* in his approach was their context-sensitivity, a characteristic they inherit from being predominantly based on subsective adjectives (cf. the discussion in section 3.2 in chapter 1). Thus, both sentences in (51) may be true for the same situation, if the relevant comparison classes are changed (e.g. from crossing the channel by boat to crossing the channel by swimming).

(51)   a.   Barbara crossed the channel slowly.
        b.   Barbara crossed the channel quickly.

Parsons (1990:43–45) captured this context-sensitivity through the addition of a contextual parameter F that captures exactly this context sensitivity. A sentence like (51a) can then be represented as (52), where the SLOW(e, F) conjunct needs to be interpreted as *the event was slow in comparison to F*, with F being specified from the context.

(52)   Barbara crossed the channel slowly.
       $\exists$e [CROSS_THE_CHANNEL(Barbara ,e) & SLOW(e, F)]

Since this context-sensitivity is a problem of subsective adjectives in general, it cannot be used to distinguish between the three approaches to adverbial modification presented here. We will assume that some solution built on the introduction of a contextual parameter can be used, and will not consider this issue any further.

3.1.   Event-based semantics and intuitive plausibility

Most introductions to event-based semantics contain a discussion of reasons why the use of an event variable in the logical representations of sentences is a good idea, cf. for example the discussion in Parsons (1990:chapter 2). I will not discuss these points here, but rather concentrate on whether the representation of adverbial adjectives as predicates of events is a good idea. In the literature, this is sometimes doubted, especially in the case of manner modification, cf. the following quote from Bartsch (1970):

> Dazu kommt noch, daß man nicht alle modalen Adverbien von Ereignissen prädizieren kann. Denn was heißt z.B. 'Das Ereignis, das durch 'Peter läuft' beschreibbar ist, ist schnell'? Tritt das Ereignis schnell ein, oder ist in dem Ereignis ein schneller Bewegungsvorgang enthalten? Es scheint so, als könne man von einem Ereignis gar nicht prädizieren, daß es schnell sei. (Bartsch 1970:29-30)
> [In addition, not all modal adverbs can be predicated of events. What is the meaning of "The event that can be described by 'Peter runs' is quick"? Does this event take place quickly or does it contain a fast movement? It appears that it is impossible to predicate of an event that it is quick.] (my translation)

The point that Bartsch (1970) is trying to make becomes clearer when comparing a sentence like *Peter runs quickly* with the two sentences in (53).

(53)   a.   Peter runs **in Berlin**.
       b.   Peter runs **today**.

For both (53a) and (53b), it is very clear how the adverbial modification can be understood in relation to the event described by the rest of the sentence:

the locative adverbial in (53a) specifies the position in space of the event, the temporal adverbial in (53b) specifies the position in time. This view of the two adverbials is somewhat strengthened by the fact that there is widespread agreement that events have a location in space and time (cf. the introductory remarks in Maienborn 2005).

3.2.   The scope of the event-based approach

The event-based approach is explicitly geared to adverbials which allow for entailment patterns similar to those given in figure 1. Since the approach is extensional, it is limited to those adverbials that do not create opaque contexts. Sentence adverbials do not fall in the scope of this theory, nor do those event-related adverbials that create opaque contexts.

Davidson only assumes an underlying event argument for action sentences, not for statives. The question of whether or not all sentences contain an underlying event argument is the center of some controversy, cf. e.g. Katz (2000).

3.3.   Neo-Davidsonian approaches

Event-based representations where the event variable is given on par with the other arguments of the verbal predicate are often referred to as 'Davidsonian'. This contrasts with Neo-Davidsonian approaches (the label 'Neo-Davidsonian' for this type of notation was introduced in Dowty 1989:83). In Neo-Davidsonian approaches, the verbal predicate is represented as a one-place predicate over events and its arguments are conjunctively added via the thematic relations holding between the event and the respective argument, cf. (54), where the SUBJECT relation in the formula should be understood as a placeholder for those thematic relations typically associated with subjecthood (for this notation, cf. Parsons 1990). Parsons (1990:4) credits the works of the ancient Indian grammarian Panini for the discovery of thematic relations-like structures.

(54) $\exists e \ [RUN(e) \ \& \ SUBJECT(Peter,e)]$

Since the treatment of adverbials is exactly the same in both approaches, I will use the representation format that has been chosen by the authors under discussion. For more on the difference between the two formats, cf. Parsons's discussion of thematic roles in Parsons (1990:chapter 5).

4. Possible combinations: events and the predicate-modifier approach

The predicate-modifier approach as represented so far does not make use of events in the formal representation. In the literature, the relationship between the predicate-modifier approach and events is discussed from two different angles: (a) what happens if the predicate modifier approach is combined with the idea of an event parameter for verbs (cf. Eckardt 1998:12-13), and (b) to what extent can the event-based approach be seen as a refinement of the predicate modifier account (cf. Parsons 1990:56-58)? I will discuss the two points in turn.

4.1.   Adding events

Technically, the predicate-modifier approach can work with as well as without events.[77] That is, a sentence like (55) can be represented either as (56a) or (56b).

(55)   Anna walks quickly.

(56)   a.   QUICKLY(WALK)(anna)
       b.   QUICKLY(WALK)(anna,e)

Quickly in (56a) denotes a function mapping sets of individuals to sets of individuals. In contrast, in (56b) *quickly* denotes a function mapping sets of pairs of individuals and events to sets of pairs of individuals and events.

Eckardt (1998:12) points out that the predicate-modifier approach in conjunction with events does not require that adverbials are applied to the intensions of verbs. Remember that the extensional variant of the predicate-modifier approach proved to be problematic, since it gave rise to patterns like that in (57) (cf. the discussion in section 1.1).

(57)   Suppose: $\{x{:}x$ dances$\} = \{x{:}x$ sings$\}$
       Then: Anna sings. $\leftrightarrow$ Anna dances.

With events added, this pattern will no longer arise, since the extensions of *dance* and *sing* will be different events, cf. the formalizations in (58), where this is shown with the help of indices.

(58)   a. $\exists e_1$ [DANCE(anna,e_1)]
       b. $\exists e_2$ [SING(anna,e_2)]

Eckardt comments on this consequence of the combination of predicate-modifier approch and events that "we find that the event parameter is a means
to create an intermediate level of intensionality which is restricted to the
verb, but not affected by nominal arguments" (Eckardt 1998:12). Although
Eckardt's point is clear, the formulation is perhaps a bit infelicitous in that, as
shown above, the event parameter is a means to get rid of an intuitively unmo-
tivated intensional interpretation (cf. also the arguments by McConnell-Ginet
(1982) and Larson (1998) given in section 1.4.1) in favor of an extensional
account.

4.2.   Event-based semantics as a refinement

Parsons (1990), discussing modifier scope in the predicate-modifier theory,
notes that "The underlying event account may be seen as a refinement of the
operator account." (Parsons 1990:56). Parsons assigns to *x stabbed y violently*
the logical form in (59).

(59) $\exists e$ [STABBING(e) & SUBJECT(e,x) & OBJECT(e,y) &
        VIOLENT(e)]

This form, Parsons argues, can be conceived as the result of inserting *x* and *y*
into the argument places of the two-place predicate in (60).

(60) $\lambda v \; \lambda w \; \exists e$ [STABBING(e) & SUBJECT(e,v) & OBJECT(e,w) &
        VIOLENT(e)]

The predicate in (60), according to Parsons, can be assumed to be derived
from the predicate in (61).

(61) $\lambda v \; \lambda w \; \exists e$ [STABBING(e) & SUBJECT(e,v) & OBJECT(e,w)]

The predicate in (61) can now be viewed as the predicate that the modifier
violently, according to the predicate-modifier theory, operates on, while the
predicate in (60) represents the result of applying the function denoted by
the modifier. Viewed in this way, the event-based account provides a more
fine-grained analysis of the predicate-modifier account.

Whether we can in all cases construct functions that deliver the correct
output predicates from the input predicates depends, according to Parsons,
on what exact theory of meaning is assumed. This leads Parsons to conclude:

In summary, the operator approach may or may not be consistent with the underlying event approach. In its traditional formulation it stands in need of supplementation. It is unclear, for technical reasons, whether the two approaches can be brought into conformity with one another. (Parsons 1990:58)

5.   Conclusion

The aim of this chapter was to provide an overview of the three most influential approaches to the semantics of adverbials, in particular, to the semantics of non-sentence adverbials. It should have become clear that all of the three approaches have their pros and cons. I will refrain from giving a wholesale judgement on these approaches here. Instead I would like to focus on two points, the issue of entailments and the issue of the scope of the three approaches.

An explicit aim of Davidson (1967) was to account for entailment patterns between different action sentences. The elegant mimicking of the entailment diamond as represented in figure 1, which falls out from the formal representations by the simple process of simplification is often mentioned as one of the main advantages of his approach. Because of the prominence of the entailment data in discussion of approaches to adverbial semantics, I have shown ways to handle this data in the other two approaches. While they might not be as elegant, at least they show that it is possible to account for these patterns.

However, the importance of these entailments should not be overestimated, and the decision to represent these entailments in the logical form is quite ad-hoc. Davidson himself seems to have been very much aware of this, as is witnessed by his two statements below, which are also cited in the extensive discussion of this matter by Bennett (1988:165-168):

There is something arbitrary in how much of logic to pin on logical form. But limits are set if our interest is in giving a coherent and constructive account of meaning: we must uncover enough structure to make it possible to state, for an arbitrary sentence, how its meaning depends on that structure, and we must not attribute more structure than such a theory of meaning can accommodate. (Davidson 1967:106)

[...] to determine the logical form of a verbal expression, reduce the number of places of the underlying verbal predicate to the smallest number that will yield, with appropriate singular terms, a complete sentence. But do not think you have a complete sentence until you have uncovered enough structure to validate all inferences you consider due to logical form. If 'There was a breaking' logically implies 'Something broke', give the first sentence the form 'There was a breaking e and an object x such that e was a breaking of x', not 'There was an e such that e was a breaking'. (Davidson 2001:295)

In the end, then, it is a matter of taste, not of necessity, to what extent one wants to cater for these entailments. To close with Cresswell (1985): "There is no more reason why the entailment of *John runs* by *John runs quickly* should be made explicit in the λ-deep structure than should the entailment of *John moves* by *John runs*" (Cresswell 1985:27).

Another aspect that needs to be kept in mind is the scope of the three approaches. The operator approach can be used to formalize sentence as well as non-sentence adverbials. In addition, it can also be used for attributive modification. It is therefore the most general of the three approaches, and this generality must be weighted against the smaller scope of the two other approaches.

If one compares the argument approach with the predicate approach, one can also argue that they might peacefully co-exist. Thus, the argument approach seems a natural account for obligatory adjuncts (cf. the discussion in chapter 1), whereas the predicate-account does not seem very appropriate here (even the entailments would be strange). In addition, the predicate account has the general design disadvantage that its representation for adverbials looks just like its representation for verbs.

This presentation of the three approaches is therefore perhaps most aptly concluded by quoting Kamp (1975):

> It is bad to be left with a semantic phenomenon that is explained by no theory; but it does no harm to have two distinct theories which give equally adequate, albeit different, accounts of those phenomena that fall within the province of both. (Kamp 1975:154)

Except, of course, that Kamp's 'two' should be read as 'three'.

Chapter 7
The semantic analysis of verb-related adverbials

The semantic approaches to adverbials introduced in section 6 distinguished between two classes of adverbials, roughly corresponding to sentence adverbials and non-sentence adverbials. Obviously, this does not match up with the three-way distinction in the descriptive chapters, distinguishing sentence adverbials (chapter 2), verb-related adverbials (chapter 3), and event-related adverbials (chapter 4). But even if we consider only verb-related adverbials, the great variety calls for a formal treatment that allows to capture this variety.

Let's recall the set of example sentences used to introduce manner adverbials, example (4) in chapter 3, repeated here as (1).

(1) a. *Peter hat **laut/leise/schnell/langsam**   gesungen.*
        Peter has loudly/quietly/quickly/slowly sung
        'Peter sang loudly/low/quickly/slowly.'
    b. *Peter hat **elegant/hölzern/wunderbar**   vorgetragen.*
        Peter has **elegantly/woodenly/wonderfully** presented.
        'Peger presented [his talk] elegantly/woodenly/wonderfully.'
    c. *Peter hat sich   **intelligent/geschickt** verteidigt.*
        Peter has himself intelligently/skillfully defended
        'Peter defended himself intelligently/skillfully.'

In a standard Neo-Davidsonian format, all the sentences in (1) can be represented following the pattern in (2), yielding the representations in (3) for the sentences in (1) (illustrated with *laut* 'loud', *wunderbar* 'wonderful', and *intelligent* 'intelligent', respectively).

(2) $\exists$ e [SUBJECT(e, peter) & VERB(e) & ADJECTIVE(e)]

(3) a. $\exists$ e [SUBJECT(e, peter) & SING(e) & LOUD(e)]
    b. $\exists$ e [SUBJECT(e, peter) & PRESENT(e) & ELEGANT(e)]
    c. $\exists$ e [SUBJECT(e, peter) & DEFEND(e) & INTELLIGENT(e)]

Two things are noteworthy here. First of all, none of the distinctions drawn between the different variants of manner adverbials in section 2 of chapter 4 resurface in the formal representation. Secondly, a side effect of a plain Neo-Davidsonian representation is that the verb and the manner adverbial appear to be semantically on par (both providing one-place predicates over events) while intuitively and syntactically, they are not: one element represents the main verb of the sentence, the other element represents an optional modifier.

In this section, I will propose an event-based analysis that allows a much more fine-grained analysis of the adverbials involved. The crucial point in the analysis is the assumption that manners occur as entities in our ontology, an assumption that builds on a long tradition that will be introduced in section 1.1. In the second section, I will introduce the specific formalization that I assume, and finally, in section three, I discuss some of the advantages of this approach and link the derivation of the adverbial reading to the syntactic position of the adverbial.

1.   Manners in the ontology

1.1.   The history of the idea

The idea to use manners as entities in formal representations is certainly not new. Its first, dismissive, discussion can be found in Fodor (1972), where manners served as an illustration of an approach that was considered by Fodor to be just as bad as Davidson's event-based account. In contrast, Dik (1975:117-119) is the first serious attempt to introduce representations based on manners. Schäfer (2003) also proposed to use manner in the formalization. Most recently, manners have been brought back into the discussion by Piñón (2007) and Piñón (2008). I myself returned to the use of manners in Schäfer (2008). The main point made by Dik is simple enough: "in the semantic representation, the predicates corresponding to manner adverbials should be applied directly to the 'manner' of the activity as such" (Dik 1975:117). Issues that immediately arise are then the following: what exactly are manners, do all activities come with manners, and how exactly are the manners linked to the respective activities. While Dik has little to say about the first question except that 'Manner' needs to be a basic element in the semantic representations, he offers some tentative answers to the two other questions. He argues that all situations which involve control on part of the agent or a change, that is, which are dynamic (e.g. processes and activities) do possess an implicit manner in which they are carried out. If a situation fulfills these criteria, manners are introduced with the help of meaning postulates (Dik refers to them as *redundancy rules*), e.g. the one given in (4), cf. Dik's (145), where s is a variable for situations, and M_x stands for *the manner of x*.

(4) $\exists$ s [[+CONTROL](s) $\vee$ [+CHANGE](s)]
        $\Rightarrow \exists$ m [m = M_s]

According to (4), all situations which involve CONTROL or CHANGE (or both) allow the introduction of a manner into the formal representation. This manner does not exist independently, but is linked to the situation that allowed its introduction. Dik then tentatively proposes (5), his (146), as a possible representation for the sentence *Annette dances beautifully*.

(5)   Annette dances beautifully.
        $_{s_1}$ dance(Annette))$_{s_1}$ & beautiful(M_{s_1})

Equating Dik's situations with events in the wide sense of eventualities used here, and rewriting his representation in a Neo-Davidsonian style, we get the representation in (6).

(6) $\exists$ e [SUBJECT(e, annette) & DANCE (e) & $\exists$ m [MANNER(e, m) &
        BEAUTIFUL(m)]]

In order to fully grasp what Dik is proposing here, it is helpful, and here I follow Piñón (2008), to distinguish between two senses of the term *manner*. In one sense, corresponding to the MANNER predicate in (6) and Dik's M predicate in (4) and (5), a manner is a function mapping an eventuality onto its manner. In its second sense, a manner is the specific entity, that is, the m variable in (5) and (6).

On this account, the contribution of the verbal predicate and of the manner adverbial are not treated on par anymore, in that the former provides a predication over the event variable and the latter provides a predication over the manner variable. However, what is still missing is a differentiation between different types of manner modification.

Again, this point was already addressed by Dik, who distinguished between four possibilities. Besides the manner-linked variable for *beautifully*, Dik proposes that an adverb like *quickly* yields a predication over the speed of a situation, not the manner. The respective variable is introduced in a parallel way, only this time with the help of a relation between situations and their speed. In addition, he proposed two further variants to deal with *to write illegibly* and *to answer the question wisely*.

While agreeing with Dik that a modification with *quickly* is closely connected to some speed scale inherent to the event, I also agree here with Piñón (2008) that it is wise to continue to treat these two modifiers as instances of manner modification, at the same time acknowledging the fact that the manner variables targeted by the respective predicates all are connected to the event variable in slightly different ways. Thus, as Piñón writes, "there are potentially many manner functions and not just one [...]" (Piñón 2008:9).

1.2.   The cognitive status of manners

Obvious objections to this approach concern matters of ontology: What exactly are manners supposed to be, and what do we mean when we speak of 'coordinates of events'? Manners, speeds, and sound volumes are all ontologically dependent on the events introduced by the verbs in the respective sentences, that is, they do not and cannot exist by themselves. These ontologically dependent entities can be viewed as coordinates in the conceptual structure of their host events. The exact nature and internal structure of these coordinates is still an unanswered question, but see e.g. Geuder (2006) for some possible solutions.

As Piñón (2007) points out, one argument in favor of assuming manner as an ontological entity is that it can be perceived, as evidenced by expressions such as those in (7), modeled after (5) in Piñón (2007).

(7)   a.   I saw how Henriette danced.
       b.   Peter witnessed Charlotte answer intelligently.
       c.   Martin heard Julia play terribly.

Furthermore, as Piñón (2007) argues, assuming manners also allows us to systematically relate the *in-ADJ-manner*-paraphrase to manner adverbials. What both have in common is that they are used to express predicates of manners. In the case of the *in-ADJ-manner*-paraphrase, it is the head noun of the paraphrasing prepositional phrase that refers to a manner. The attributive adjective adds a predicate of this manner. In the case of the manner adverbial, it is the adverbial adjective that predicates of the manner made available as a conceptual coordinate of the event referred to by the verb.

One final argument for the usage of manners in the ontology is more pragmatic in nature: if we distinguish between event-related and verb-related modification, then we need a more fine-grained distinction below the level of the event-variable. Manners allow such a fine-grained distinction. This view also allows one to address a point raised by Ernst (1984:91), namely that whether the same set of data is analyzed by assuming either predicates of manners or predicates of events seems intuitively equally appropriate. Here, in contrast, predicates of manners and predicates of events are used for different modification structures.

2. Manners in the representation

A representation that allows the differentiation of several manner functions but keeps a uniform general format is given in (9), where each representation corresponds to one sentence of the opening examples for manner adverbials, repeated here for convenience as (8).

(8)   a.   *Peter hat **laut** gesungen.*
            Peter has loudly sung
            'Peter sang loudly.'

        b.   *Peter hat **elegant** vorgetragen.*
            Peter has elegant presented.
            'Peter presented [his talk] elegantly.'

        c.   *Peter hat sich **intelligent** verteidigt.*
            Peter has himself intelligent defended
            'Peter defended himself intelligently.'

(9)   a. $\exists e$ [SUBJECT(e, peter) & SING(e) &
            $\exists m$ [MANNER$_{\text{SOUND\_VOLUME}}$(e, m) & LOUD(m)]]

        b. $\exists e$ [SUBJECT(e, peter) & PRESENT(e) &
            $\exists m$ [MANNER$_{\text{RHETORIC}}$ (e, m) & ELEGANT(m)]]

        c. $\exists e$ [SUBJECT(e, peter) & DEFEND(e) &
            $\exists m$ [MANNER$_{\text{ARGUMENTATION}}$(e, m) &
            INTELLIGENT(m)]]

Note that in these representations, there is a clear difference between the contribution of the verbal predicate, and the contribution of the manner adverbial. The verbal predicate adds a predication over the event variable, whereas the manner modifier predicates over the manner variable which is in turn related to the event variable by the manner function. In addition, the different shades of manner modification are captured by slightly different manner functions. At the same time, the general format of these representations is the same, a specification of the pattern in (10), where R serves as a placeholder for a more specific manner function (This corresponds to one of the versions considered in Fodor 1972).

(10)   ∃e [SUBJECT(e, peter) & SING (e)
         & ∃m [R (e, m) & ADJ(m)]]

The next section will show how these representations can be derived.

2.1. The technical aspects: Getting manners into the representation and specifying them

In deriving the representation, I will use a Neo-Davidsonian format. Correspondingly, the lexical entries for verbs are represented as one-place predicates following the schema in (11), resulting in (12) as a semantic representation for *singen* 'sing'.

(11)   λx [VERB(x)]

(12)   λx [SING(x)]

The argument positions of the verb are introduced with the help of functions like (13) for the subject argument.

(13)   λP λy λx [SUBJECT(x,y) & P(x)]

The lexical entry for all adjectives will look the same, following the simple scheme in (14).

(14)   λx [ADJ(x)]

Accordingly, the lexical entry for the adjective *laut* 'loud' is represented as (15).

(15)   λx [LOUD(x)]

This lexical entry is simplified, since all the adjectives discussed are gradable and therefore need to be able to interact with further degree semantics, cf. for one popular implementation Kennedy (2007).[78]

Finally, we need a template to introduce the manner variable. This template, given in (16), also turns any predicate of type $< e,t >$ that represents an adjective into a modifier of type $<< e,t >, < e,t >>$.

(16)   Template for manner adverbials:
         λQ λP λx [P(x) & ∃m [MANNER (x,m) & Q(m)]]

If this template is applied to the lexical entry of the adjective, we get (17).

(17) Template for manner adverbials applied to the lexical entry of the adjective:

    a. $\lambda Q\, \lambda P\, \lambda x\, [P(x)\, \&\, \exists\, m\, [MANNER\, (x,m)\, \&\, Q(m)]]$
        $(\lambda x\, [LOUD(x)])$

    b. $\lambda P\, \lambda x\, [P(x)\, \&\, \exists m\, [MANNER\, (x,m)\, \&\, LOUD(m)]]$

With this, we have everything in place to derive the introductory examples. I will show this exemplarily for (8a), repeated in (18).

(18)   *Peter hat **laut**   gesungen.*
       Peter has loudly sung
       'Peter sang loudly.'

(19) Derivation

    a.   representation of the manner adverbial (cf. (17)) applied to the lexical entry of the verb (cf. (12))

        (i) $\lambda P\, \lambda x\, [P(x)\, \&\, \exists m\, [MANNER\, (x,m)\, \&\, LOUD(m)]]$
             $(\lambda x\, [SING(x)])$

        (ii) $\lambda x\, [SING(x)\, \&\, \exists m\, [MANNER\, (x,m)\, \&\, LOUD(m)]]$

    b.   Addition of the subject-template (cf. (13))

        (i) $\lambda P\, \lambda y \lambda x\, [SUBJECT(x,y)\, \&\, P(x)]$
             $(\lambda x\, [SING(x)\, \&\, \exists m\, [MANNER(x,m)\, \&\, LOUD(m)]])$

        (ii) $\lambda y \lambda x\, [SUBJECT(x,y)\, \&\, SING(x)\, \&$
             $\exists m\, [MANNER(x,m)\, \&\, LOUD(m)]]$

After the addition of the subject and existential closure over the event variable we then arrive at the representation in (20).

(20) $\exists e\, [SUBJECT(e, Peter)\, \&\, SING(e)\, \&$
       $\exists m\, [MANNER\, (e, m)\, \&\, LOUD(m)]]$

The only step that remains to be done is to specify the parameter MANNER so that it is set to the wanted specific manner function, in this case, to $MANNER_{SOUND\_VOLUME}$. How is this done? I argued in chapter 3 that the ability do combine with specific verb-related adverbials is rooted in the conceptual structure of the event specified by the verbal predicate. Nevertheless, it does not seem feasible to mechanically determine from the modifier and the verb which kind of specific manner function should be selected. The best solution is to leave this specification to pragmatics. This does not mean that all and everything has to be taken into account in order to specify a manner function; in most cases, we will not have to look further than the combination of adverbial and verb. However, working with an underspecified predicate MANNER allows one to assign a manner function even in those cases that clearly require pragmatic support, cf. the examples in (21), the repeated (86b) from chapter 3.

(21)   *Peter singt oberflächlich/intelligent/geschickt.*
       Peter sings cursory/intelligent/skillful
       'Peter sings cursorily/intelligently/skillfully.'

As mentioned previously, it is very difficult to come up with good interpretations for these usages without using contextual information. The usage of a parameter that is specified by pragmatics allows one to make use of this kind of information.

3.   Benefits of the analysis

One obvious benefit of the analysis of manner adverbials given in the last section lies in the close mirroring of cognitively different kinds of modification in the semantic representation. However, the main benefit of the analysis as far as German adverbial adjectives are concerned lies in the possibility to clearly distinguish between verb-related and event-related adverbials, and to link the possibility of the respective readings to specific syntactic positions. In this section, I will first demonstrate how the two readings can be differentiated and how they can be linked to the specific syntactic positions, focusing on single occurrences of adverbials. In a second step, I will extend the approach to cover the more difficult cases of event-related modification.

3.1.   Differentiating the readings and the link to syntax

In chapter 5 I argued that when adjectives can be used as either event-related or verb-related adverbials, these usages are bound to different syntactic positions. Event-related adverbials occur before the direct object, verb-related adverbials occur after the direct object. One minimal pair that allows this differentiation is given in (22), recall also the extensive discussion in chapter 4.

(22)   a.   *Fritz hat **laut** die Einleitung   gesungen.*
            Fritz has loud the introduction sung
            'Fritz has sung the introduction loudly.'

b. *Fritz hat die Einleitung* **forte** *gesungen.*
Fritz has the introduction forte sung
'Fritz sang the introduction forte.'

As argued at length in the previous chapters, *forte* 'forte' can only occur in post-object position and is bound to a manner interpretation, whereas *laut* 'loud' can be used with both readings. However, in pre-object position it is interpreted as an event-related adverbial, as indicated by the availability of the the *wobei*-paraphrase in this position. The representation for the sentence containing the manner adverbial *forte* is, building on the previous section, straightforward, and represented in (23).

(23) $\exists$e [SUBJECT(e, Fritz) & OBJECT(e, the_introduction) & SING(e)
         & $\exists$m [MANNER$_{MUSIC}$ (m,e) & FORTE(m)]]

A preliminary presentation of *laut* in its event-related usage is given in (24). I will refine this representation a bit in the next section.

(24) $\exists$e [SUBJECT(e, Fritz) & OBJECT(e, the_introduction) & SING(e)
         & LOUD(e)]

Note that for (24), we obviously do not need the manner template. But we need to turn the predicate corresponding to the lexical entry of the adjective into a modifier, which can be done with the help of a simple modification template MOD, corresponding to similar operators in Maienborn (2001) and Dölling (2003).

(25)   Modification template MOD:
         λQ λP λx [P(x) & Q(x)]

This template can be applied to predicates of type $< e,t >$, e.g. the lexical entries of adjectives, and yields modifiers of type $<< e,t >, < e,t >>$. These, in turn, can be applied to the verbal predicate, which is also of type $< e,t >$.

3.2.   The syntax-semantics interface

Since event-related adverbials and verb-related adverbials are syntactically tied to different positions, it is straightforward to let the syntax have a say in the derivation of the different readings. For this purpose, I build on the work of Maienborn (2003b) and Dölling (2003). The main idea is the following: an underspecified template is automatically applied in the course of the derivation of the logical form. The syntax determines whether all of the parameters of this template are available or not. For verb-related modification, they are available, for event-related modification, they are not available.

Maienborn (2003b) deals with local modification, a key pair of sentences from her work, cf. her (24), is reproduced in (26).

(26)   a.   *Luise hat auf der Treppe gepfiffen.*
            Luise has on the stairs   whistled
            'Luise whistled on the stairs.'
       b.   *Luise hat auf den Fingern gepfiffen.*
            Luise has on the fingers whistled
            'Luise whistled with her fingers.'

Maienborn takes the prepositional phrase in (26a) to locate the event, whereas she assumes that the locative modifier in (26b) locates some 'integral constituent' of the event.[79] To formally capture the two different readings, Maienborn (2003b) introduces the template MOD*, cf. (27).

(27)   Template MOD*:
       $\lambda Q\, \lambda P\, \lambda x\, [P(x)\ \&\ R(x,v)\ \&\ Q(v)]$

This is structurally very similar to the template for manner adverbials given above, cf. the repeated (16) in (28).

(28) $\lambda Q\, \lambda P\, \lambda x\, [P(x)\ \&\ \exists\, m\, [\text{MANNER}(x,m)\ \&\ P(m)]]$

Instead of the relation MANNER, Maienborn uses the relational parameter R, and she does not existentially bind the variable v. Just as we assume here that the two different uses of manner modifiers are tied to different syntactic positions, Maienborn shows that the different readings of local modifiers are also linked to different syntactic environments, cf. (29), her (24').

(29)   a.   Luise hat [$_{VP}$ [$_{PP}$ auf der Treppe] [$_{VP}$ [$_V$ gepfiffen]]]
       b.   Luise hat [$_{VP}$ [$_V$ [$_{PP}$ auf den Fingern] [$_V$ gepfiffen]]]

Given this, Maienborn postulates the following condition on the realization of the free relational parameter R, cf. (30), her (30b).

(30)   Condition on the application of MOD*: If MOD* is applied in a structural environment of categorial type X, then R = PART-OF, otherwise (i.e. in an XP-environment) R is the identity function.

If we assume the semantic forms in (31) and (32) for the two PPs, and the semantic form in (33) for the verb, then we can derive the representations for the two different verb phrases, cf. (34) and (35), respectively.

(31)   [$_{PP}$ auf der Treppe]: λx [LOC(x, ON(t) & STAIRCASE(t)]

(32)   [$_{PP}$ auf den Fingern]: λx [LOC(x,ON(f) & FINGERS(f)]

(33)   [$_V$ gepfiffen]: λe [WHISTLE(e)]

(34)   [$_{VP}$ [$_{PP}$ auf der Treppe] [$_{VP}$ [$_V$ gepfiffen]]]

        a. λx [WHISTLE(x) & R(x,v) & LOC(v,ON(t)& STAIRCASE(t)]
        b. λx [WHISTLE(x) & =(x,v) & LOC(v,ON(t)& STAIRCASE(t)]
        c. λx [WHISTLE(x) & LOC(x,ON(t) & STAIRCASE(t)]

(35)   [$_{VP}$ [$_{PP}$ auf den Fingern] [$_V$ gepfiffen]]

        a. λx [WHISTLE(x) & R(x,v) & LOC(v,ON(f) & FINGERS(f)]
        b. λx [WHISTLE(x) & PART_OF(x,v) & LOC(v,ON(f) & FINGERS(f)]

For (34), it makes no difference that the operator MOD* is used instead of the operator MOD introduced earlier. Due to the syntactic position of the adverbial,the resulting representation is the same. In (35), however, the parameter R introduced by MOD* is specified as PART_OF. The exact nature of the free variable v and its relationship to the event variable will then be specified with the help of pragmatics.

Dölling (2003) also uses templates in his account of adverbial modification. He separates the templates into templates introducing the free parameters, labeled MET',[80] cf. (36), his (13), and the general modification template MOD, discussed above.

(36)   Operator MET': λP λx [Q y [R(x, y) C P(y)]]

Dölling uses R as a parameter for relations between elements of ontological sorts, and Q and C are paired parameters, which can be realized by either $\exists$& or $\forall \rightarrow$.

By setting the paired parameters Q and C to $\exists$ and &, it can be seen that this operator is the underspecified model for the manner template, cf. (37).

(37)   a.   Partially filled template MET'
           $\lambda P \lambda x. \exists y[[R (y,x) \& P(y)]]$

b.   Template manner variable
$\lambda P \lambda x \exists m [\text{MANNER}\ (x, m)\ \&\ P(m)]$

If we combine the partially filled MET' template of (37a) with the modification template MOD, we get an underspecified operator that can serve as the basis for manner modification as well as Maienborn's event-internal local modification. This operator, MOD+, is given in (38).

(38)   Template MOD+:
$\lambda Q\ \lambda P\ \lambda x\ [P(x)\ \&\ \exists y\ [R(x,y)\ \&\ Q(y)]]$

In addition, we can adopt Maienborn's proposal to make the specific instantiation of the R relation sensitive to the syntactic environment in which the template appears.[81] Maienborn assumes that the event-related modifiers are verb phrase modifiers, and the verb-related modifiers appear within the verb phrase (this conforms to the assumptions made by Frey and Pittner (1998), too).

The condition proposed by Maienborn for MOD*, cf. (30), must then be slightly changed, since the MANNER relation is not a part-of relation.

(39)   Condition on the application of MOD+ :
If MOD+ is applied in a structural environment of categorial type X, then R = PART-OF or MANNER (where MANNER is an underspecified parameter for a manner function), otherwise (i.e. in an XP-environment) R is the identity function.

More needs to be said about possible specifications for R, see in particular Dölling (2003) for an application to secondary predications.

3.3.   Event-related modification: The difficult cases

So far, we have simply assumed that in the case of event-related modification, the adjective predicates over the event variable introduced by the verbal predicate. While this does capture some of the intuitions about event-related adverbials as opposed to verb-related adverbials, most notably the fact that only verb-related adverbials interact with the internal structure of the event introduced by the verbal predicate, it does not say anything about the many other observations. Most importantly, it does not capture at all the intuition that the availability of the *wobei*-paraphrase is connected to the possibility of holistic readings involving objects that themselves consists of several events

(cf. chapter 4 for discussion, especially the Christmas-tree-decoration sce-
nario discussed in section 2.2.1 or the quantified direct objects discussed in
section 2.2.2) or readings where we have to assume additional events that
are linked to the event introduced by the verbal predicate (e.g. the follow-
loudly case discussed in section 3.2.3 of chapter 4). In order to capture all
this, I will adapt the big event-approach by Eckardt (1998:123-126), which
she uses in order to account for the scope facts for sentences with quantified
direct objects, as I argued in chapter 4, likewise instances of event-related
modification. Basically, a big event is a complex event, that is, it consist of
smaller event objects. It is introduced into the semantic representation with
the help of a template for big events, cf. (40).

(40)   Template for big events:
        $\lambda P\, \lambda e^*\, \lambda e\, [PART\_OF(e^*, e)\, \&\, P(e)]$.

This clause is added before the verb phrase level. A further assumption by
Eckardt is that in reaching the verb phrase boundary, all event variables except
the variable of the big event are existentially bound.[82] Everything else is quite
straightforward, and is demonstrated below again for the same sentence, cf.
(41), repeated from (22a).

(41)   *Fritz hat **laut** die Einleitung   gesungen.*
        Fritz has loud the introduction sung
        'Fritz has sung the introduction loudly.'

(42)   *die Einleitung singen* 'to sing the introduction'
        $\lambda e\, [OBJECT(e,\, the\_introduction)\, \&\, SING(e)]$

(43)   Application of the big event template
        a. $\lambda P\, \lambda e^*\, \lambda e[PART\_OF(e^*,e)\, \&\, P(e)]$
              $(\lambda e\, [OBJECT(e,\, the\_introduction)\, \&\, SING(e)])$
        b. $\lambda e^*\, \lambda e\, [PART\_OF(e^*,\, e)\, \&\, OBJECT(e,\, the\_introduction)\, \&$
              $SING(e)]$

(44)   Existential binding of all non-big events at VP
        $\lambda e^*\, \exists e[PART\_OF(e^*,e)\, \&\, OBJECT(e,\, the\_introduction)\, \&\, SING(e)]$

(45)   Semantic form of *laut* after application of the MOD+ template
        a. $\lambda Q\, \lambda P\, \lambda x\, [P(x)\, \&\, \exists y\, [R(y,x)\, \&\, Q(y)]]\, (\lambda x\, [LOUD(x)])$
        b. $\lambda P\, \lambda x[P(x)\, \&\, \exists y\, [R(y,x)\, \&\, LOUD(y)]]$

(46)   Addition of *laut*
  a. $\lambda P \lambda x [P(x) \& \exists y [R(y,x) \& LOUD(y)]]$
        $(\lambda e^* \exists e[PART\_OF(e^*,e) \& OBJECT(e, the\_introduction) \&$
        $SING(e)])$
  b. $\lambda x \exists e[PART\_OF(x,e) \& OBJECT(e, the\_introduction) \&$
        $SING(e) \& \exists y [R(y,x) \& LOUD(y)]]$

(47)   Condition on MOD+ : R is set to the identity function in an XP
        environment
  a. $\lambda x \exists e[PART\_OF(x, e) \& OBJECT(e, the\_introduction) \&$
        $SING(e) \& \exists y [=(y,x) \& LOUD(y)]]$
  b. $\lambda x \exists e[PART\_OF(x, e) \& OBJECT(e, the\_introduction) \&$
        $SING(e) \& LOUD(x)]]$

(48)   Addition of the subject
        $\lambda x [SUBJECT(x, Fritz) \&$
        $\exists e[PART\_OF(x,e) \& OBJECT(e, the\_introduction) \& SING(e) \&$
        $LOUD(x)]]$

(49)   Existentially binding the big event
        $\exists e^* [SUBJECT(e^*, Fritz) \&$
        $\exists e[PART\_OF(e^*,e) \& OBJECT(e, the\_introduction) \& SING(e) \&$
        $LOUD(e^*)]]$

The most important difference between this representation and the previous
representation is that the formal representation now reflects core properties
of event-related modification: what event-related modifiers predicate of is
more than what the event variable introduced by the verbal predicate stands
for. While I refer to Eckardt (2003) for formalizations of sentences involving
quantified direct objects, the general idea should be clear. This approach also
allows one to derive representations for the other instances of event-external
modification, thus, the notorious cases of complex event modification discussed with the help of e.g. (50), repeated from (46) of chapter 4, can be
represented as in (51).[83]

(50)   *Hans hat **geschickt** die Frage   **dumm**   beantwortet.*
        Hans has skillfully the question stupidly answered
        'Hans skillfully answered the question stupidly.'

(51)   ∃e* [SUBJECT(e*, Hans) & ∃e[PART_OF(e*,e) &
OBJECT(e, the_question) & ANSWER(e) &
∃ m [MANNER*ARGUMENTATION*(e, m) & STUPID(m)]
& SKILLFUL(e*)]]

I leave the derivation as an exercise for the reader.

4.   Summary

This chapter proposed an analysis of verb-related adverbials, in particular, of manner adverbials, by resorting to the use of manners as ontological objects. In section one, I gave a short overview over previous approaches that already made use of manners as ontological entities and distinguished between these entities and the manner functions that are used to link these entities to their host events. In addition, some further arguments for the usage of manner were given. Section two introduced semantic representations that allow one to distinguish between different kinds of manner modification. Furthermore, in order to derive the different representations, I introduced a manner template. Finally, in section three I discussed the benefits of the analysis. Besides a better correspondence between formal representation and intuition, this analysis results in distinct formal representations for verb-related adverbials and event-related adverbials. The latter can be represented as predicates of events, while the former now have their distinct manner-based representations. Further, this formal distinction was used to establish a connection between syntactic position and semantic interpretation. In a final step, the representation of event-related adverbials was refined by introducing the notion of 'big events', whose introduction was again linked to their syntactic position, but also closely reflects our intuitions.

Chapter 8
Summary and outlook

The topic of this work has been the syntactic position and the semantic interpretation of German adverbial adjectives. In the introduction, I identified four main questions to be addressed:
(a) What different adverbial usages of adjectives can be distinguished?
(b) Which usages are tied to which syntactic positions?
(c) How can different usages of adverbial adjectives be formally analyzed?
(d) How can the derivation of the formalizations be linked to the different syntactic positions?
In the following, I will first give an overview of the answers to these four questions, and secondly, point to some remaining questions in need of further research.

1. Results

In order to answer the first question, (a), the different adverbial usages were classified into three large groups: sentence adverbials, verb-related adverbials, and event-related adverbials.

Within the class of sentence adverbials, I distinguished between subject-oriented adverbials, speaker-oriented adverbials, and domain adverbials. The class of speaker-oriented adverbials, in turn, was broken down into speech-act adverbials, epistemic adverbials, and evaluative adverbials. The role of adverbial adjectives in these usages is very limited. For one thing, German has a specific class of de-adjectival adverbs, the *weise*-adverbs, that are only used as sentence adverbials. As a consequence, an adjective like *intelligent* 'intelligent' is only employed as a verb-related adverbial, while its *weise*-counterpart *intelligenterweise* 'intelligently' must be used when it serves as a sentence adverbial, resulting in minimal pairs like the one in (52).

(52)   a.   *Julia hat **intelligent** geantwortet.*
              Julia has intelligent answered
              'Julia answered intelligently.'
    b.   *Julia hat **intelligenterweise** geantwortet.*
              Julia has intelligently   answered
              'Intelligently, Julia answered.'

Moreover, adjectives that denote properties of physically perceptible dimensions like sound and speed can in general not be used as sentence adverbials. The only subclass of sentence-adverbials where adjectives are used are the domain adverbials, but again, the class of adjectives used here is mostly lexically limited to de-nominal adjectives.

The situation changes when turning to verb-related adverbials, which are typically realized by adjectives. Chapter three argued that verb-related adverbials are best understood as providing specifications of different conceptual coordinates or dimensions within the conceptual structures of the events denoted by the verbal predicates. Thus, verb-related adverbials can be more or less complex, and more or less direct. Thus, adjectives like *laut* 'loud' and *schnell* 'fast', when used as verb-related modifiers, directly specify the sound and the speed dimension of the respective events, whereas a modifier like *wunderbar* 'wonderful' in e.g. *Peggy tanzt wunderbar* 'Peggy dances wonderfully' describes the culminative effect that a certain way of executing an event evokes, without clarifying in detail which conceptual dimensions of the event are specified.

Besides manner adverbials and their two subgroups, pure and agent-orient-ed manner adverbials, I have described method-oriented and degree adverbials as further subgroups of verb-related adverbials. The rest of the chapter dealt with the differentiation between verb-related adverbials and secondary predications, identifying two areas where the distinction is problematic. Thus, psychological adjectives can be used as manner adverbials or as depictives, but often one reading implies the other reading. And very often when adjectives occur in conjunction with verbs of creation, the resulting readings are blends between manner adverbials and implicit resultatives.

Finally, it was argued that as far as the combinatorics of verbs and manner adverbials are concerned, it is best not to assume a categorial constraint like 'manner adverbials can never co-occur with statives', but to explain the rarity of these cooccurrences with the simpler conceptual structure that comes with statives as compared to the conceptual structure associated with activities.

The chapter closed with a discussion of the relationship between negation and manner modification, arguing that (a) a sentence with a manner adverbial within the scope of sentence negation conversationally implicates the non-negated sentential base and (b) manner adverbials might have scope over negation if the negation of the activity denoted by the main verb can be associated with another specific activity, allowing interpretations of a sentence like *Peter hat geschickt die Frage nicht beantwortet* 'Peter cleverly did not answer the question' as *Peter ist der Frage geschickt ausgewichen* 'Peter dodged the question cleverly'.

The final chapter on the different adverbial usages of adjectives was concerned with event-related adjectives. The feature that connects the subclasses collected under this term is that they semantically clearly relate to events, not to higher entities like facts or propositions. In contrast to verb-related adverbials, they do not access aspects or dimensions internal to the structure of the event characterized by the verbal predicate. I distinguished between mental-attitude adverbials and event-external adverbials. Mental-attitude adverbials and their subgroup, the transparent adverbials, were linked to attitudes towards executing an event or states of mind resulting from the event described by the verbal predicate. The second subclass, event-external adverbials, in turn comprises three distinct subclasses: inchoative readings, holistic readings, and modifiers of complex events. Holistic readings and modifiers of complex events both allowed the usage of the *wobei*-paraphrase, which was discussed in detail in the third section of this chapter. In particular, I argued that the *wobei*-paraphrase is a diagnostic for yet another set of readings, the associated readings. Associated readings occur when adjectives that can traditionally be used as manner adverbials co-occur with verbs that do not by themselves provide attachment points for these adverbials in their conceptual structure. The difference was elucidated with the help of examples like (53).

(53)   a.   *Fritz hat die Marseillaise **laut** gesungen.*
            Fritz has the Marsillaise   loud sung
            'Fritz sang the Marseillaise loudly.'

       b.   *Fritz hat die Marseillaise gesungen, wobei   er laut war.*
            Fritz has the Marsillaise   sung,   in.doing.so he loud was
            (≉ a)

            'Fritz sang the Marseillaise. In doing so, he was loud.'

(54)   a.   *Fritz hat Isolde **laut** verfolgt.*
            Fritz has Isolde loud followed
            'Fritz loudly followed Isolde.'

       b.   *Fritz hat Isolde verfolgt, wobei   er laut war. (≈ a)*
            Fritz has Isolde followed, in.doing.that he loud was
            'Fritz followed Isolde. In doing that, he was loud.'

The *wobei*-paraphrase is not appropriate for (53a), because it is the manner of the singing that is specified as loud. In contrast, in (54a) the paraphrase is appropriate, because the whole event described by the sentence is judged as loud, while the specific contribution of the following to the loudness is left open. That is, Fritz could have been clapping his hands in following Isolde, and it was this that was responsible for the loudness of the composite event.

Figure 3 gives an overview of the classification of adverbials.

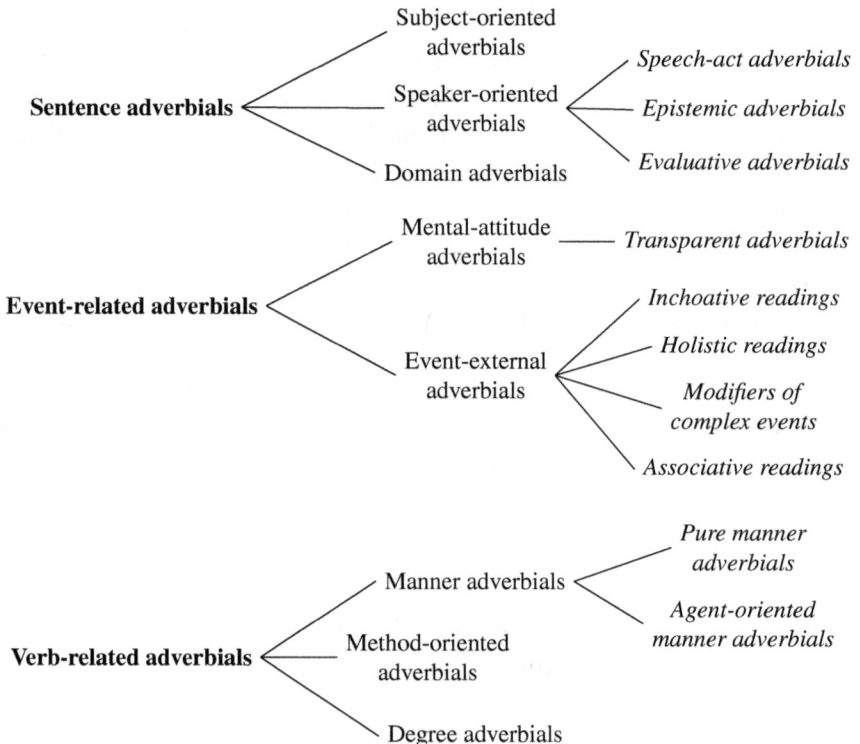

Sentence adverbials
- Subject-oriented adverbials
- Speaker-oriented adverbials
  - *Speech-act adverbials*
  - *Epistemic adverbials*
  - *Evaluative adverbials*
- Domain adverbials

Event-related adverbials
- Mental-attitude adverbials — *Transparent adverbials*
- Event-external adverbials
  - *Inchoative readings*
  - *Holistic readings*
  - *Modifiers of complex events*
  - *Associative readings*

Verb-related adverbials
- Manner adverbials
  - *Pure manner adverbials*
  - *Agent-oriented manner adverbials*
- Method-oriented adverbials
- Degree adverbials

Figure 3. The classification of adverbials

Question (b), the relation between the different usages and the syntactic position of the adverbials, was the topic of chapter 5. Because adverbial adjectives are predominantly used as manner adverbials, I focused on this group. A second reason for choosing this group was the existing controversy in the literature as to whether manner adverbials in German follow or precede the direct object. I argued that while the whole controversy is concerned with the status of the direct object, the semantic contribution of the adverbials in the respective sentences has been neglected. Taking seriously the different readings of the adverbials involved, I have shown that event-related adverbials are positioned before the object, and verb-related adverbials follow the direct object. Thus, the adjective *laut* 'loud' in (55a) occurs as an event-related adverbial with an associated reading, whereas in (55b), it serves as a verb-related pure manner adverbial.

(55)   a.   *Fritz hat **laut** die Einleitung   gesungen.*
               Fritz has loud the introduction sung
               'Fritz loudly sang the introduction.'
      b.   *Fritz hat die Einleitung   **laut** gesungen.*
               Fritz has the introduction loud sung
               'Fritz sang the introduction loudly.'

Clear evidence for this view comes from the fact that only (55a) allows the *wobei*-paraphrase. In addition, only in (55b) can *loud* be replaced by the corresponding musical term for a loud manner of singing, *forte*, whereas this is not possible for (55a), cf. (56).

(56)   a.   **Fritz hat **forte** die Einleitung   gesungen.*
               Fritz has forte the introduction sung
      b.   *Fritz hat die Einleitung   **forte** gesungen.*
               Fritz has the introduction forte sung
               'Fritz sang the introduction forte.'

Furthermore, only for (55a) do we get the impression of Fritz's action being somewhat boisterous, an aspect totally absent from (55b).

While this approach is consistent with the data found in the literature with regard to the topical status of the direct object, it can explain more data than both other approaches, e.g. Eckardt's (2003) approach that makes heavy use of the topical status of direct objects, and Frey and Pittner's (1998) argumentation for object integration.

The formal analysis of some usages of adverbial adjectives, i.e., the answer to question (c), was the topic of chapters 6 and 7.

The aim of chapter 6 was to provide an overview of the three most influential approaches to the semantics of adverbials, in particular, to the semantics of non-sentence adverbials. Besides serving as background for the proposal in the following chapter, the main take-home message here was that there is hardly any empirical reason to totally dismiss any of the three approaches presented, in particular since all of them are compatible with using events as ontological objects, an argument often made in favor of the predicate approach.

In chapter 7, I presented my own proposal. While being based on an Neo-Davidsonian event semantics, verb-related adverbials were analyzed as predicates of manners. After justifying the introduction of manners as ontological objects, I presented the formal implementation and the benefits of this implementation. Besides a better correspondence between formal representation and intuition, this analysis allows one to distinguish between verb-related adverbials and event-related adverbials. The latter can be represented as predicates of events, or, in a further refinement, as predicates of big events, while the former have their distinct manner-based representations.

The last question, (d), was also addressed in this chapter. By using an underspecified template, and linking the setting of parameters within this template to specific syntactic environments, the correct readings are automatically derived.

2.   Outlook

While the main questions this book set out to answer have been addressed, the questions have not been answered completely. In addition, the answers themselves give rise to many new questions. While I cannot possibly address all open questions I would like to use this outlook to point to two such issues, one concerning the lexical semantics of the adjectives involved, the other concerning the analysis of depictives.

Take, for example, the number of lexical items that can serve as modifiers of complex events as discussed in the context of the *to painstakingly write illegibly*-sentences in chapter 4. Judging from the literature, it appears that only very few adjectives can serve as the first, scope taking modifier.[84] For German, *vorsichtig* 'cautious', *geschickt* 'skillful' and *sorgfältig* 'careful' are discussed in this context. For English *ly*-adverbs, *painstakingly* and *carefully* are discussed. What is the reason for this restriction to only such a small number of adjectives? It seems plausible that the answer must lie in some aspect of their lexical semantics. One commonality in the lexical semantics of these items is their unclear status with regard to predications over individuals vs. predications over events. Thus, we can usually classify adjectives into two groups: (a) adjectives that prototypically predicate of individuals and (b) adjectives that prototypically predicate of events. The question of whether a certain adjective is an object- or an event-predicate is by no means trivial, although this issue is seldomly explicitly discussed (exceptions are Geuder 2000:9-10 and Hansson 2007). If we look at the adjectival bases of the word forms serving as scope-taking adverbials from this perspective, it appears at the outset that they all are object predicates, or more specifically, object predicates denoting a certain disposition of an individual (cf. Geuder 2000:9, who uses *careful* and *intelligent* as examples for these types of word meaning). Interestingly, Hansson (2007:123-126) classifies the corresponding German items as 'event-oriented'. Her argumentation is that in many cases only a concrete and perceptible manifestation of a property licenses ascribing that property to an individual. In other words, we can say *Peter is careful* only because we know that he is acting carefully. And this holds both ways. If we are told that *Peter is careful*, we expect him to conduct his actions carefully. Other adjectives, e.g. *elegant*, behave differently: *Peter is elegant* is not related to Peter conducting his affairs in an elegant way. Even *intelligent*, although in Hansson (2007) treated on par with *careful*, is different, in that a statement like *Peter is intelligent* is not necessarily connected to Peter conducting his affairs intelligently.[85] Now, a distinction between *careful* on the one hand and *intelligent* on the other hand, as one being event-oriented, the other object-oriented would go some way towards explaining why *intelligent* cannot be used as a scope-taking modifier, and this sort of explanation could also be extended to account for the general inability of *intelligent* to serve as an event-related modifiers. On the other hand, though, since *intelligent* can be used as a manner modifier, where the target is clearly not a disposition of the agent, but a manner in which an event unfolds, this explanation cannot possibly be the whole story, either.

Another area where the role of lexical semantics is in need of closer examination concerns the analysis of the different readings of event- and verb-related adverbials depending on their syntactic position. While the distinction between the two readings and their link to the pre- and post-object position is a sound finding and the corresponding predictions and derivations are often very straightforward, some cases are not so obvious, as we saw in the discussion of, again, *sorgfältig* 'careful' in different positions.

A second area in need of further investigation is the depictives. This subgroup of secondary predicates has cropped up at several places. First, they were differentiated from manner adverbials in chapter 3, then they were differentiated from transparent adverbials in chapter 4. And finally, in the discussion of the *wobei*-paraphrase, it turned out that this paraphrase works rather well for depictives, leading to the conclusion that there must be more to them than just a shared argument and co-temporality. However, if this is the case, what is then the difference between depictives and associated readings? It is true that the *während*-'while' paraphrase, which was used to introduce depictives, is odd for associated readings, but it might turn out that this is just a matter of degree. Only further research can answer these questions.

Notes

1. The term 'verb' in this usage does not refer to the lexical category. Alternative labels for this function are terms like the German *Prädikat* 'predicate', e.g. in Eisenberg (1999:p. 45), or, for English, 'predicator', cf. e.g. Huddleston and Pullum (2002).
2. For accounts of German topological theory, cf. e.g. Eisenberg (1999:384-399), Grewendorf, Hamm and Sternefeld (1989:213-216), or Höhle (1986).
3. The idea to include a step-by-step discussion that clarifies how to distinguish adverbials from the other clause-level constituents was inspired by Pittner (1999), especially her section 2.1. In that section, she compares non-sentential adverbials against objects, *Prädikative* 'predicatives', and *Verbzusätze* 'verb particles'.
4. This is a slight simplification, since there are also verbs which select for up to four thematic roles, cf. (i).

   i. *Peter fährt ihm das Rad   nach Hause.*
       Peter rides him the bicycle to   home
       'Peter rides the bicycle back home for him.'

   In (i), the prepositional object carries the thematic role 'direction' and the indirect object the thematic role 'beneficiary'. It is not clear whether the indirect object in such sentences has argument status or not. In the following, I will not consider these cases.
5. As will become apparent from the examples, the meaning of the German verb *wohnen* is more specific than the meaning of the English verb *live* that serves as its translation equivalent here. In particular, the German verb cannot be used to mean *to be alive* or related meanings.
6. The sentence *Fritz riecht, und das tut er schlecht/gut* is grammatical if it is interpreted as *Fritz kann gut/schlecht riechen* 'Fritz is good/bad at smelling'.
7. This stands in stark contrast to the situation in English, where the marker *-ly* morphologically differentiates between predicatives and adverbials, cf. e.g. (i).

   i. a. Dogs are stupid.
       b. He answered stupidly.

8. Pittner (1999:98) explicitly states that a syntactic differentiation between free predicatives and adverbials is not possible (for a similar view, cf. the closing remarks in Geuder 2004). Eisenberg (1999:223-224) contains some discussion that hints at a structural difference between what Eisenberg calls *typisch verbbezogene* 'typically verb-related' and *typisch subjektbezogene* 'typically subject-related' adjectives. Eisenberg's argumentation is refuted in Pittner (1999:98).
9. Using the terms of topological theory, these are the positions between the *Vorfeld* 'prefield', the position preceding the finite verb, and the *linke Klammer* 'left bracket', and the position after the *rechte Klammer* 'right bracket', which is usually constituted by the infinite verb.
10. The appeal to prototypical occurrences is necessary, because a limited number of particles can be used in the prefield, cf. e.g. (i).

i.   a.   ***Auch** hat Peter das Lied gesungen.*
          also   has Peter the song sung
          'In addition, Peter sang the song.'
     b.   ***Nur** hat Peter das Lied gesungen.*
          only has Peter the song sung
          'But it is the case that Peter sang the song.'
     c.   ***Jedoch** hat Peter das Lied gesungen.*
          however has Peter the song sung
          'However, Peter sang the song.'

11. This definition is very minimal and is tailored to the word class of adjectives in German. It was mostly inspired by the longer definition given in Heidolph, Flämig and Motsch (1981:601). The usage of the word 'canonical' in the definition is due to newer attempts to define the word class of adjectives that reflect on the difficulties of providing necessary and even sufficient characteristics for this class, cf. e.g. the extensive discussion of the word class 'adjective' in English in Huddleston and Pullum (2002:527-542).

12. It is demonstrated with the help of three minimal pairs, because morphological marking in German is heavily underspecified. A single inflectional suffix out of a very limited repertoire of suffixes is used to mark case, number and gender. Note also that the glosses only give the grammatical information relevant for the discussion, but not full specifications (as in e.g. runner.NOM.SG.MASC).

10. Schmöe, following Müller (1997), regards idiomatic pairings, e.g. *samt und sonders* 'completely', also as mono-lexematic.

11. Apparent counterexamples to this condition are given in (i).

i.   a.   ***Hier** ist rechts.*
          here is right
          'This is right.'
     b.   ***Vorne**   ist noch frei.*
          in.front is still   free
          'Up front are still empty places.'
     c.   ***Heute** ist geschlossen.*
          today is closed
          'Today we are closed.'

All adverbs in (i) fail one important criterion for subjecthood, because they do not answer the question *What/Who?* but rather the question *Where/When?* Interestingly, in all cases the adverbs are also deictic.

15. All of the adverbs in (56) and (57) have derived adjectival cognates that can be used in this position, cf. (i).

i.   a.   *Der **hiesige/dortige** Kampf*
          the here/there   fight
          'the fight here/there'
     b.   *der **jetztige/baldige/morgige** Kampf*
          the now/soon/tomorrow   fight
          'The fight now/The speedy fight/The fight tomorrow'

16. The adjectival short form does allow the formation of comparison forms, cf. (i) for the predicative use and (ii) for the adverbial use.

   i.   *Fritz ist **schneller/am schnellsten**.*
      Fritz is faster/the fastest
      'Fritz is faster/the fastest.'

  ii.   *Fritz denkt **schneller/am schnellsten**.*
      Fritz thinks faster/the fastest
      'Fritz thinks faster/the fastest.'

    Heidolph, Flämig and Motsch (1981:622) argue that the formation of superlative forms with help of the prepositional dative case (cf. *am schnellsten* 'the fastest' in (i)), can be taken as another indicator of the adjectival status of the word forms under discussion, but I do not find this very convincing, since the prepositional dative is not possible in the attributive usage of adjectives and the differentiation between predicative and adverbial usage, which both allow this form, is in itself difficult, cf. the discussion in section 2.1.3.

17. It is not clear whether the term 'derivation' is appropriate for the relation between the adjectives and the adverbs in these cases. Haspelmath (1996), for example, argues that the English suffix *-ly* is an inflectional suffix. For Haspelmath (1996), the criteria to decide whether a given formation is inflectional or derivational are whether they are regular, general and productive or irregular, defective and unproductive. If the first three criteria are fulfilled, the formation results from inflection, if the latter three are fulfilled, the formation is a derivation. According to these criteria, *-ly* is an inflectional suffix, albeit one with the special characteristic of being a word-class changing or *transpositional* suffix. For transpositional inflection, so Haspelmath argues, it is useful to distinguish between what he calls *lexeme word-class* and *word-form word-class*. The lexeme word-class of *quickly*, for example, is adjective, the word-form word-class is adverb.

18. A similar account can be found in Kamp and Partee (1995).

19. If in the following examples specific contexts are assumed, they should therefore be taken as possibilities for context specifications.

20. For the distinction between these two usages, cf. Bellert (1977:349); the term 'speech-act adverbial' corresponds to her term 'pragmatic adverb'.

21. Bartsch (1972) refers to them as *die Prädikation limitierende Adverbiale*. Bartsch (1987) likewise calls them 'predicate limiting adverbials'.

22. In German, it is sometimes also possible to use the preposition *in* 'in' instead of *auf* 'on', but its usage is restricted and often seems somewhat unnatural.

23. The usage of this terminology is inspired by the use of the attribute 'pure' for a subclass of manner adverbs in Ernst (1984:94) and Ernst (1987).

24. The first example is taken from a popular car magazine, cf. `http://www.autobild.de/artikel/hamann-san-diego-express_40613.html` (2010-09-13, 10:27). The second example is taken from the newspaper *Neue Kronen-Zeitung*, 22.08.1995, p. 22.

25. I thank Irene Rapp for these example sentences.

26. For the distinction between the two readings, cf. Dölling (2003), Eckardt (1998, 2003), Geuder (2000).

27. Geuder (2000:chapter 3) uses the term 'resultative adverbs' for the usages which I call implicit resultatives. Geuder's terminology reflects the fact that in English, word forms

interpreted as implicit resultative are often morphologically adverbs, while the word forms used for resultatives are adjectives. This allows him to contrast *resultative adjectives* with resultative adverbs. This terminology does not make sense in German, as the word forms used for resultatives and implicit resultative are in both cases adjectives, not adverbs.

28. Quirk et al. (1985:560) introduce this term in their discussion of the following examples:

   i. a. She fixed it perfectly. [in such a way that it was perfect - manner and result]
       b. He grows chrysanthemums marvellously. [in such a way that the results are good - manner and result]
       c. The soldiers wounded him badly. [in such a way and to such an extent that it resulted in his being in a bad condition - manner, intensifier and result]
       (their comments)

29. Positionals corresponds to dynamic states in the classification of Bach (1986) and to the position subgroup of D(avidsonian)-statives in Maienborn (2003a).

30. Importantly, the conception of manner adverbials in Maienborn (2003a) differs from the one used in this work. For her, all modifiers that relate to the internal functional structure of a situation fall into a more general group of manner adverbials. This group comprises instrumentals and comitatives, for example. In the discussion here, I will use my narrower conception of manner adverbials.

31. This argumentation is also compatible with the views expressed in Rothstein (2005), where she uses the somewhat unfortunate term 'pragmatic constraints'. Similarly, Ernst (1984:90) comments on the rarity of manner adverbs in combination with state-denoting verbs by saying that "[s]tates [...] simply have less content to 'latch onto' and modify".

32. Similar argumentation can also be found in Huang (1988:285) and Maienborn (2005:310). Huang discusses Chinese data parallel to the German data presented here, that is, where sentence negation is incompatible with manner modification. Maienborn argues that "[t]he result of negating *The train arrived* does not express an event anymore. Thus, the addition of [...] a manner adverbial is excluded".

33. Jacobs (1991:586): "Replaziv ist eine Negation genau dann, wenn sie notwendig mit der Ersetzung mindestens eines Teiles des negierten Inhalts verknüpft ist."

34. This example is taken from the weekly newspaper *Die Zeit*, 16.09.2004, p. 39.

35. The term 'mental-attitude adverbial' is again taken from Ernst (1984:75-88), cf. also Ernst (2002:62-69). The German term used in Pittner (1999) is *Adverbiale der Subjektshaltung* 'adverbial of the attitude of the subject'. Bartsch (1972:30) classifies adverbials like *irrtümlich(erweise), absichtlich, versehentlich, willentlich* 'erroneously, intentionally, accidentally, deliberately' as 'sentence adverbials (K'_2)'.

36. Ernst (1984:87) introduces the term 'volitional' for these kinds of mental attitude adverbials.

37. Their example, which uses the adverb *volontairement* 'intentionally' and is judged be them to present an invalid inference, is reproduced in (i), their (36a).

   i. a. *Jean a **volontairement** insulté Marie.*
           Jean has intentionally   insulted Marie
       b. *Marie est la femme du pésident.*
           Marie is the wife of the   president

      c.   *Jean a* **volontairement** *insulté Jean.*
           Jean has intentionally   insulted the   wife of the president

38. This does not come as a surprise, since even a verb like *seek* can be given a first-order treatment as long as only specific readings are taken into account, cf. Zimmermann (1993).

39. In the whole discussion of transparent adverbials, I draw very heavily on Geuder (2000) and Geuder (2004). This includes example sentences constructed to mirror his example sentences.

40. Maienborn (2003a:93-94) speaks of the difference between *externer Modifikator* 'external modifier' and *interner Modifikator* 'internal modifier'.

41. In Pittner's (1999) terminology, *ereignis-bezogene Adverbiale* 'event-related adverbials'.

42. This example appears first as (7) in Lakoff (1972) and is also discussed in Thomason and Stalnaker (1973:204 and fn.13), Bartsch (1972:168-172), and McConnell-Ginet (1982:152-154). Lakoff argues that *carefully* in (30) must be formalized as a sentence operator for both (30a) and (30b). Otherwise, according to Lakoff, the scope effects cannot be captured. Thomason and Stalnaker (1973:204) argue that the scope effects do not show that *carefully* is a sentence adverbial. The interpretational difference can also be captured by treating *carefully* as a predicate operator in both instances. I will come back to Bartsch's and McConnell-Ginet's comments below.

43. This seems to be the interpretational difference that is also made by McConnell-Ginet, who writes that (30) "entails something like Sam's having taken care not to miss any of the bagels in his slicing operation (possibly doing a quite sloppy job on each individual bagel), whereas 23b [(30b)] says nothing about how it came about that he ended up doing them all, but instead asserts that he took care with respect to the individual slicing events" (McConnell-Ginet 1982:153).

44. Note that *sorgfältigerweise* 'carefully' is very rare in written German (0 hits on 20.04.2004 in the DeReKo via cosmas II, all corpora of written language selected, 0 hits on 20.04.2004 in http://www.wortschatz.uni-leipzig.de). It seems to have a specialized usage in law, though, compare (i).

    i.   *Sie werden in den Saal gebeten. Dann kann es sein, dass das Gericht Sie* **sorgfältigerweise** *noch einmal ganz persönlich über Ihre Pflichten als Zeuge belehrt.* 'You will be asked to come into the courtroom. It might happen that the court will **carefully** once again explain to you your duties as a witness.' [20.04.04 in 2008, ZeugenvorGericht.pdf, page 5, accessed via http://www.hmdj. justiz.hessen.de]

The correct interpretation of *sorgfältigerweise* in this context seems to be something like *In executing the care towards witnesses that is required by the law, ...*

45. Eckardt (1998:116) gives a similar example, except that Alma is now named Clara and a is b.

46. I asked two native speakers of English, of whom one could at least follow Eckardt's argumentation; the other dismissed it.

47. The opening example of Clark (1989), given in (i), bears some similarities to (46) and the context given in (47).

i. James Bond, freshly captured, cleverly stammered stupidly to his interrogators. Later on, exhausted from the interrogation, he stupidly incisively said clever things to them.

However, this similarity is only superficial, as the contrasts in (56) arise not from differences in the semantic scope of manner adverbials, but from the co-occurrence of subject-oriented adverbials and manner adverbials.

48. Bartsch's original example, cf. Bartsch (1972:151), also gives the paraphrases in (i.a) and (i.b).

    i. Petra kocht **sorgfältig**. ($\approx$ a,b)
       'Petra is cooking carefully.'
       a. Petra kocht, wobei sie sich sorgfältig verhält.
          'Petra is cooking; in doing so she acts carefully.'
       b. Petra kocht, wobei sie sorgfältig handelt.
          'Petra is cooking; in doing so she acts carefully.'

The availability of these kinds of paraphrases can be taken as further indication that the constructions allowing these paraphrases do not target the internal structure of the event introduced by the verbal predicate. Here, though, I will not discuss these paraphrases further.

49. The papers differ in parts. For the topics discussed here, the most notable differences are between Frey and Pittner (1998) and Frey (2003): the latter (a) only uses three tests (existentially interpreted w-phrases, scope, and principle C effects) and (b) provides a separate definitions for mental-attitude adjuncts, treating them as a special case of event-internal adjuncts.

50. I follow Eckardt (2003:292) in the view that it is not helpful to simply substitute the adverbial adjectives with paraphrases containing quantifiers, as done for example in Frey and Pittner (1998), cf. their (32).

51. Höhle (1982) speaks of 'elements' and not of 'constituents', because he assumes that elements in the focus must not form a constituent, cf. the discussion of his (50d) in Höhle (1982:92).

52. Höhle's conception of focus is given in (i), a translation of his (32).

    i. Focus (informal definition)
       If a sentence S_i is uttered, that part of S_i is the focus $Fc(S_i)$, whose function in S_i is not known on the basis of the relevant context. (The other parts of S_i form the topic $Tc(S_i)$)

53. Frey and Pittner (1998) credit Höhle with the observation that in order for focus projection to occur with accentuation of a non-verbal element, it must be the non-verbal element closest to the verb that is accented. Apparently, they allude to the hypothesis in Höhle (1982:108, hypothesis 103), reproduced here in translation as (i).

    i. For some three-place predicates and the word order
       subject > object > object,
       the last object constitutes the focus exponent of S, whenever the objects are definite non-pronominal NPs.

For the link of this observation to syntactic base positions, they credit Cinque (1993) and Haider (1993), who adopts the decisive part of Cinque's argumentation. Cinque (1993) argues that his null theory of phrasal and compound stress assignment predicts that for German VPs, "the primary stress falls on the XP to the immediate left of the verb, or verbal group [...]"(Cinque 1993:250-251). Cinque's theory generates the correct stress assignment from the syntactic structure of the sentence in question.

54. Lenerz makes use of a similar notion of in-group reading when he discusses an example with an acceptable indefinite indirect object, for which according to Lenerz (1977) 'there seems to exist' a constraint which only allows a reading 'of several possible gifts: the book', cf. (i), his (18).

i.   Hier sind mehrere mögliche Geschenke zur Auswahl; was würdest du einem Schüler schenken? 'Here are several possible gifts to choose from; what would you give to a student?'

    a.   *Ich würde einem Schüler das Buch schenken.*
       I   would a   student the book give
       'I would give the book to a student.'
    b.   *Ich würde einem Schüler ein Buch schenken.*
       I   would a   student a   book give
       'I would give a book to a student.'

55. Frey and Pittner (1998:501) point out that this departs from Jacobs view of integration, as he does not assume that the integration relations are structurally reflected in the syntactic representation.

56. For me, [b] sentence is OK if interpreted holistically, cf. footnote 57. One reviewer states that it is ungrammatical only on a specific reading.

57. Frey and Pittner argue that quantized noun phrases can be integrated if they are interpreted holistically. To force a holistic interpretation, they use the quantifier *alle* 'all' instead of *jeder* 'every'. For a direct object containing the quantifier *alle* 'all', the word order manner adverbial > direct object is acceptable, cf. (i), their (38).

i.   *weil   Hans **sorgfältig** alle Hemden bügelte.*
    because Hans careful   all shirts   ironed
    'because Hans ironed all shirts carefully.'

As evidence for the different status of the direct object depending on whether they contain the quantifier *alle* or *jede*, they use data involving fronting of the verb without the direct object, cf. (ii), their (39).

ii. a.   **Gebügelt hat Hans **sorgfältig** alle Hemden.*
       ironed   has Hans careful   all shirts
    b.   *Gebügelt hat Hans jedes Hemd **sorgfältig**.*
       ironed   has Hans every shirt careful
       'Hans carefully ironed every shirt.'

I myself do not notice a difference in acceptability in these sentences depending on the usage of *alle* 'all' or *jedes* 'every'.

58. Eckardt (2003:296) argues that this is impossible because the resultative adverbial and the verb do not form a common focus domain. However, I do not think that this is a convincing argument.

59. Note that this view of integration stands in conflict with the view expressed in Jacobs (1993), which explicitly states that, above the word level, only arguments can integrate, cf. (35bi).

60. Yet another possibility to explain this data follows from a comment by a reviewer: if we assume that resultatives always have to be c-commanded by the constituent over whose denotation they predicate, then the word order **resultative > direct object** would also be ruled out.

61. Cf. also Eckardt (1996),

62. Cf. e.g. Höhle (1982:92), Eckardt (2003:294). For a general critique of the usage of questions to model out-of-the-blue contexts, cf. Weskott (2003:12-13). Höhle (1982:91) already contains the caveat that the function of these and similar questions should be understood as assistance for the reader to see what is supposed to be new information and what is supposed to be in the relevant context.

63. A reviewer of the manuscript used the example in (i) to argue that manner adverbials can occur in out of the blue contexts.

    i. Was ist denn los? Warum wird der Dirigent ausgepfiffen?
       'What is happening? Why is everybody booing the conductor?'

        Das Orchester hat etliche   Arien viel   zu laut begleitet.
        the orchestra has quite.a.few arias much too loud accompanied
        'The orchestra accompanied quite a few of the arias way too loud.'

Firstly, I don't see in how far this works as an out-of-the-blue context, given the obvious link between the given conductor and the orchestra. Secondly, the direct object receives a partitive interpretation. At least in Eckardt's system, this itself already leads to scrambling.

64. A reviewer pointed out that for him a sentence like (i) and question-answer pairs like (ii) are acceptable.

    i. *Er hat piano ein Schubert-Lied gesungen.*
       he has piano a   Schubert-song sung
       'He sang a Schubert-song piano.'

    ii. a. Was ist passiert? 'What happened?'
         b. *Ein Mann hat forte ein Lied gesungen.*
            a   man   has forte a   song sung
            'A man sang a song forte.'

For me, both sentences are unacceptable.

65. Eckardt (1998:133-135) contains a similar example.

66. German w-phrase also have usages that correspond to the usages of English wh-phrases, to which they are historically related. That is, they can be used as true interrogative in questions.

67. The original example contains an additional optional *nicht* 'not'.

68. As an approximation of what a prototypical theta-role is, cf. the list taken from Dowty (1991):

    i.   Contributing properties for the Patient Proto-Role:
        a.   undergoes a change of state
        b.   incremental theme
        c.   causally affected by another participant
        d.   stationary relative to movement of another participant
        e.   (does not exist independently of the event, or not at all)
        = (28) in Dowty (1991)

69. This is in accordance with Jäger (1996:117), who says that specific indefinites are interpreted partitively (though this does not exhaustively characterize their special characteristics). Eckardt (2003) does not hold this position herself. Instead, she writes that "..., an indefinite can have an *in-group* reading although the speaker is not acquainted with the referent, and an indefinite can receive a specific interpretation ('a certain') without necessarily being one of a known group." Eckardt (2003:301, footnote 11).

70. According to Haider (1993:209,footnote 9), it is in a way a special case of the focus projection principle. For a critical view of this test, cf. Höhle (1982).

71. For a definition of the term 'satzglied', cf. (10) in chapter 1.

72. A reviewer gave (i), using an indefinite plural direct object instead of a definite singular object, as an example where according to him a manner reading is available.

    i.   Wie hat heute Otto Lieder vorgetragen?
        How did Otto today recite songs?
        Otto hat heute laut Lieder vorgetragen.
        Otto has today loud songs recited
        'Today, Otto loudly recited songs.'

For me, a manner reading is not available here, *laut* 'loud' is used as an event-related adverbial, allowing the *wobei*-paraphrase. But see the remarks in section 7.2 on the event- and verb-related readings of *laut/leise* 'loud/quiet'.

73. Lenerz (1977:85-87) also uses his test in order to determine the word order of some adverbials relative to the DO and the indirect object, but he does not use it for manner adverbials.

74. Such metaphoric usages seem to be possible in English, cf. (i).

    i.   The Marquis..looked thoroughly worn out and as **piano** as a beaten dog.
        1900 E. GLYN Visits of Elizabeth 188 (OED online, second edition)

It is also possible in colloquial German, in phrases such as (ii).

    ii.   *Nun mach mal* **piano!**
        now make PART piano
        'Take it easy!'

75. This principle is introduced by Landman to account for the patterns of attributive ad-

jectives (his example is the entailment from *blond blue-eyed forty year old American* to *blond forty year old American*). For adverbials, Landman (2000:7-11) argues that the case is not parallel because monotonicity is not given. He demonstrates this with the help of a comparison of (i) with (ii).

(i) a.   Every Yankee is an American.
      b.   John is a forty year old Yankee.
      c.   Hence John is a forty year old American.

(ii) a.   If you talk to a crowd, you move your thorax.
      b.   John talks to the crowd through a megaphone.
      c.   Hence, John moves his thorax through a megaphone.

According to Landman (2000), the fact that (ic) follows from (ia) and (ib) but (iic) does not follow from (iia) and (iib) shows that monotonicity as defined in (37) holds for attributive adjectives but not for adverbials.

In my view, this is a simple data problem. We can easily find examples where the opposite holds, e.g. the entailment involving attributive adjectives fails but the entailment holds for adverbials, cf. (iii) vs. (iv).

(iii) a.   Every car is an object.
      b.   This car is a good car.
      c.   Hence, this car is a good object.

(iv) a.   If you stab someone, you injure him.
      b.   Brutus stabbed Caesar with a knife.
      c.   Brutus injured Caesar with a knife.

Even though *car* semantically entails *object*, (iiia) and (iiib) do not entail (iiic). In contrast, the entailment from (iva) and (ivb) to (ivc) goes through without problems.

These problems can be avoided if we require that the head of the constructions in which we apply the monotonicity condition is kept constant. That is, in cases of adverbial modification, the verb will be the same, in the case of attributive modification, the head noun will be the same.

76. In the original paper, the very last formula is $S \subset \Re \times \text{Den}(\xi) \neq \emptyset$. I changed $\subset$ to $\cap$. McConnell-Ginet's original formulation does not make much sense: it can only be interpreted as a shorthand for the two separate statements $S \subset \Re \times \text{Den}(\xi)$ and $\Re \times \text{Den}(\xi) \neq \emptyset$. The first statement does not make any sense: why should it be a requirement on S to be a proper subset of the Cartesian product of $\Re$ and Den ξ? What if the Cartesian product contains just one element? The second statement will always be true, except when both sets, $\Re$ and $\text{Den}(\xi)$ are the empty set.

77. This is not a trivial point. The event-based approach, for example, requires events, since the event variables are responsible for the link between the separate conjuncts.

78. In Kennedy's framework, a degree phrase is used to turn the adjective from a function mapping entities into degrees into a function from entities into truth and, in addition, to provide the appropriate further semantics, here those of the positive form, so that [DegP [Deg pos] [AP loud]]]] is analyzed as (i), where "s is a context-sensitive function that

chooses a standard of comparison in such a way as to ensure that the objects that the positive form is true of 'stand out' in the context of utterance, relative to the kind of measurement that the adjective encodes" (Kennedy 2007:17) .

i. $\lambda x \, [LOUD(x) \succeq s(LOUD)]$

These considerations play no role for the problems at hand.

79. In Maienborn's (2003b) terminology, the former serves as an event-external modifier, the latter as an event-internal modifier.

80. Dölling (2003) also discusses a more complex version of this parameter, labeled MET".
However, for our purposes, MET' suffices.

81. This step is already suggested in Shaer (2003:233).

82. Note that Eckardt assumes that the subjects are generated inside the verb phrase, while I do not assume this. As a consequence, in my account the subject is related to the big event, and the object to the small event. I do not think that this is problematic.

83. In Schäfer (2005), I present an alternative account for these sentences. In short, I argue that the key for the analysis of these kind of sentences lies in the resolution of the context parameter for the two adjectives involved. In particular, I argue that an adjective like *geschickt* 'skillful' needs to be adjusted to its context in two steps. In a first step, the material in the syntactic scope of the adverbial is used to establish the main scale of comparison (in this particular case, it would be *events of answering stupidly*). In a second step, the contextually relevant subscale is chosen. See there for details of this idea.

84. This is also noted in Parsons (1990:289, fn. 17).

85. In fact, it is often save to expect to the contrary.

References

Alexiadou, Artemis (ed.)
  2004   *Taking up the gauntlet- Adverbs across frameworks.* (Lingua 114).
Austin, Jennifer R., Stefan Engelbert and Gisa Rauh (eds.)
  2004   *Adverbials. The Interplay of Meaning, Context, and Syntactic Structure.* Amsterdam: Benjamins.
Bach, Emmon
  1986   The algebra of events. *Linguistics and Philosophy* 9: 5–16.
Bartsch, Renate
  1970   Die logische Analyse von Modaladverbien. *Linguistische Berichte* (10): 27–34.

  1972   *Adverbialsemantik. Die Konstitution logisch-semantischer Repräsentationen von Adverbialkonstruktionen.* Frankfurt (Main): Athenäum.

  1976   *The grammar of adverbials.* (North Holland Linguistic Series 16) Amsterdam, New York, Oxford: North-Holland.

  1987   The construction of properties under perspectives. *Journal of Semantics* 5: 293–320.
Bellert, Irena
  1977   On semantic and distributional properties of Sentential Adverbs. *Linguistic Inquiry* 8 (2): 337–351.
Bennett, Jonathan
  1988   *Events and Their Names.* Oxford: Oxford University Press.
Bolinger, Dwight
  1972   *Degree Words.* The Hague: Mouton.
Bonami, Olivier, Daniéle Godard and Brigitte Kampers-Manhe
  2004   Adverb classification. In *Handbook of French Semantics*, F. Corblin and H. de Swart (eds.), 143–184. Stanford: CSLI.
Brentano, Franz Clemens
  1874   *Psychologie vom empirischen Standpunkte. Von der Klassifikation psychischer Phänomene.* Duncker & Humblot. New German edition in one volume edited by T. Binder and A. Chrudzimski, Ontos Verlag, Frankfurt 2008; engl. transl. Psychology from an Empirical Standpoint, 2nd revised edition, Routledge, London 1995.
Chierchia, Gennaro and Sally McConnell-Ginet
  2000   *Meaning and Grammar. An introduction to semantics.* Cambridge, Massachusetts: The MIT Press, 2nd ed.
Cinque, Guglielmo
  1993   A null theory of phrase and compound stress. *Linguistic Inquiry* 24 (2): 239–297.

1999   *Adverbs and Functional Heads. A Cross-Linguistic Perspective.* Ox-
         ford: Oxford University Press.

Clark, Romane
   1970   Concerning the Logic of Predicate Modifiers. *Nous* 4: 311–335.
   1989   Deeds, Doings and What is Done: the Non-extensionality of Modi-
          fiers. *Noûs* 23: 199–210.

Cresswell, Max J.
   1985   *Adverbial Modification. Interval Semantics and Its Rivals.* (Studies in
          linguistics and philosophy 28) Dordrecht: D. Reidel.

Davidson, Donald
   1967   The logical form of action sentences. In *The logic of Decision and
          action*, N. Rescher (ed.). Pittsburgh: Pittsburgh University Press.
   2001   Adverbs of Action. In *Essays on Actions and Events*, Donald Davidson
          (ed.), 293–304. Oxford: Oxford University Press, 2nd ed. Originally
          published in Vermazen, Bruce and Hintikka, Merrill (eds.), Essays on
          Davidson: Actions and Events, Oxford University Press 1985.

Dench, Alan Charles
   1995   *Martuthunira: A Language of the Pilbara Region of Western Australia.*
          (Series C-125) Canberra: Pacific Linguistics.

Dik, Simon C.
   1975   The Semantic Representation of Manner Adverbials. In *Linguistics
          in the netherlands 1972-1973*, A. Kraak (ed.), 96–121. Assen: Van
          Gorcum.

Dölling, Johannes
   2003   Flexibility in adverbal modification: Reinterpretation as contextual en-
          richment. In Lang, Fabricius-Hansen and Maienborn (2003), 511–
          552.

Dowty, David
   1989   On the semantic content of the notion of thematic role. In *Proper-
          ties, Types and Meaning II*, Gennara Chierchia, Barabara H. Partee
          and Raymond Turner (eds.), 69–129. (Studies in Linguistics and Phi-
          losophy 39) Dordrecht: Kluwer.
   1991   Thematic Proto-roles and argument selection. *Language* 67 (3): 547–
          619.

Dryer, Matthew S.
   2007   Clause types. In *Language Typology and syntactic description. Volume
          I: Clause structure*, Timothy Shopen (ed.). Cambridge: Cambridge
          University Press, 2nd ed.

Eckardt, Regine
   1996   *Intonation and Predication. Arbeitspapiere des SFB 340, Bericht Nr.
          77.* Frankfurt (Main).

1998   *Events, Adverbs, and Other Things. Issues in the Semantics of Manner Adverbs.* Tübingen: Niemeyer.

2003   Manner Adverbs and Information Structure. Evidence from the adverbial modification of verbs of creation. In Lang, Fabricius-Hansen and Maienborn (2003), 261–305.

Eisenberg, Peter
1999   *Grundriß der deutschen Grammatik. Der Satz.* Stuttgart: J. B. Metzler.

Engel, Ulrich
1996   *Deutsche Grammatik.* Heidelberg: Julius Groos Verlag, third corrected ed.

Engelberg, Stefan
2000   *Verben, Ereignisse und das Lexikon.* Tübingen: Niemeyer.

Ernst, Thomas
1984   *Towards an Integrated theory of adverb position in English.* Ph.D. thesis, Indiana University, Bloomington, Indiana.

1987   Why Epistemic and Manner Modifications are Exceptional. In *Proceedings of the 13th Annual Meeting of the Berkeley Linguistics Society*, J. Aske, B. Beery, L Michaelis and H. Filip (eds.). 1987: BLS.

2002   *The Syntax of Adjuncts.* Cambridge: Cambridge University Press.

2004   Principles of adverbial distribution in the lower clause. *Lingua* 114 (6): 755–777.

2007   On the role of semantics in a theory of adverb syntax. *Lingua* 117: 1008–1033.

2009   Speaker-oriented adverbs. *Natural Language and Linguistic Theory* 27: 497–544.

Fodor, J. A.
1972   Troubles about actions. In *Semantics of Natural language*, Donald Davidson and Gilbert Harman (eds.), 48–69. (Synthese Library) Dordrecht: D. Reidel.

Frey, Werner
2001   About the whereabouts of indefinites. *Theoretical linguistics* 27 (2-3): 137–161.

2003   Syntactic conditions on adjunct classes. In Lang, Fabricius-Hansen and Maienborn (2003), 163–209.

Frey, Werner and Karin Pittner
1998   Zur Positionierung der Adverbiale im Deutschen Mittelfeld. *Linguistische Berichte* (176): 489–534.

1999   Adverbialpositionen im deutsch-englischen Vergleich. In *Sprachspezifische Aspekte der Informationsverarbeitung*, Monika Doherty (ed.), 14–40. (Studia Grammatica 48) Berlin: Akademie Verlag.

Geuder, Wilhelm
    2000   Oriented Adverbs. Issues in the Lexical Semantics of Event Adverbs. Dissertation, Universität Tübingen.

    2004   Depictives and transparent Adverbs. In Austin, Engelbert and Rauh (2004), 131–166.

    2006   Manner Modification of States. In *Proceedings of Sinn und Bedeutung 10*, Christian Ebert and Cornelia Endriss (eds.), 111–124. (ZAS Papers in Linguistics), ZAS.

Giannakidou, Anastasia
    1999   Affective Dependencies. *Linguistics and Philosophy* 22: 367–421.

Goldberg, Adele E. and Farrel Ackerman
    2001   The pragmatics of obligatory adjuncts. *Language* 77 (4): 798–814.

Grewendorf, Günther, Fritz Hamm and Wolfgang Sternefeld
    1989   *Sprachliches Wissen*. Frankfurt (Main): Suhrkamp, 3rd ed.

Grice, Herbert Paul
    1975   Logic and Conversation. In *Syntax and Semantics*, P. Cole and Jerry L. Morgan (eds.), vol. 3. New York: Academic Press. Reprinted in: The philosophy of Language (1990), A. P. Martinich (ed.), second edition, Oxford University Press, Oxford: 149-160.

Haider, Hubert
    1993   *Deutsche Syntax Generativ. Vorstudien zur Theorie einer projektiven Grammatik*. Tübingen: Narr.

Hansson, Kerstin
    2007   *Adverbiale der Art und Weise im Deutschen. Eine semantische und konzeptuelle Studie*. (Acta universitatis Gothoburgensis) Göteborgs Universitet.

Haspelmath, Martin
    1996   Word-class-changing inflection and morphological theory. In *Yearbook of Morphology 1995*, Geert Booij and Jaap van Marle (eds.), 43–66. Kluwer.

Heidolph, Karl E., Walter Flämig and Wolfgang Motsch (eds.)
    1981   *Grundzüge einer deutschen Grammatik*. Berlin: Akademie.

Heim, Irene and Angelika Kratzer
    1998   *Semantics in generative grammar*. (Blackwell textbooks in linguistics 13) Oxford: Blackwell.

Helbig, Gerhard and Joachim Buscha
    2001   *Deutsche Grammatik*. Berlin: Langenscheidt.

Hentschel, Elke and Harald Weydt
    1994   *Handbuch der deutschen Grammatik*. Berlin: de Gruyter, 2nd ed.

Himmelmann, Nikolaus P. and Eva Schultze-Berndt

2005   Issues in the syntax and semantics of participant-oriented adjuncts: an introduction. In *Secondary Predication and Adverbial Modification. The typology of depictives*, Nikolaus P. Himmelmann and Eva Schultze-Berndt (eds.), 1–67. Oxford: Oxford University Press.

Huang, C.-T. James

1988   Wŏ pǎo de kuài and Chinese Phrase Structure. *Language* 64 (2): 274–311.

Huddleston, Rodney and Geoffrey Pullum

2002   *The Cambridge Grammar of the English Language*. Cambridge: Cambridge University Press.

Höhle, Tilman N.

1982   Explikation für 'normale Betonung' und 'normale Wortstellung'. In *Satzglieder im Deutschen*, Werner Abraham (ed.), 75–153. Tübingen: Narr.

1986   Der Begriff 'Mittelfeld'. Anmerkungen über die Theorie der topologischen Felder. In *Akten des VII. Kongresses der Internationalen Vereinigung für germanische Sprach- und Literaturwissenschaft*, Walter Weiss, Herbert Ernst Wiegand and Marga Reis (eds.), vol. III, 329–340. Tübingen: Niemeyer.

Jackendoff, Ray

1972   *Semantic Interpretation in Generative Grammar*. Cambridge, Massachusetts: The MIT Press.

Jacobs, Joachim

1982   *Syntax und Semantik der Negation im Deutschen*. (Studien zur theoretischen Linguistik 1) München: Wilhelm Fink Verlag.

1991   Negation. In *Semantik. Ein internationales Handbuch der zeitgenössischen Forschung*, Arnim von Stechow and Dieter Wunderlich (eds.), 560–596. Berlin: de Gruyter.

1993   Integration. In *Wortstellung und Informationsstruktur*, Marga Reis (ed.), 63–116. Tübingen: Niemeyer.

1994   Das lexikalische Fundament der Unterscheidung von obligatorischen und fakultativen Ergänzungen. *Zeitschrift für germanistische Linguistik* 22 (3): 284–319.

Jäger, Gerhard

1996   *Topics in Dynamic Semantics*. Ph.D. thesis, Humboldt Universität, Berlin.

Kamp, Hans

1975   Two theories about adjectives. In *Formal Semantics for natural languages*, E. L. Keenan (ed.), 123–155. Cambridge: Cambridge University Press.

Kamp, Hans and Barbara Partee
  1995   Prototype theory and compositionality. *Cognition* 57: 129–191.
Katz, Graham
  2000   Anti Neo-Davidsonianism: Against a Davidsonian semantics for state
               sentences. In Tenny and Pustejovsky (2000), 393–416.
  2003   Event arguments, adverb selection, and the Stative Adverb Gap. In
               Lang, Fabricius-Hansen and Maienborn (2003), 455–474.
  2008   Manner modification of state verbs. In *Adjectives and adverbs. Syntax,
               semantics, and discourse*, Louise McNally and Christopher Kennedy
               (eds.), 220–248. Oxford: Oxford University Press.
Kennedy, Christopher
  2007   Vagueness and Grammar: The semantics of Relative and Absolute
               Gradable adjectives. *Linguistics and Philosophy* 30: 1–45.
Kuroda, S.-Y.
  1972   The categorical and the thetic judgment. *Foundations of Language* 9:
               153–185.
Ladusaw, William A.
  1984   Thetic and categorical, stage and individual, weak and strong. In
               *Proceedings of the conference on Semantics and Linguistic Theory
               4*, Mandy Harvey and Lynn Santelmann (eds.), 220–229. Ithaca, NY:
               Cornell University, Dept. of Modern Languages and Linguistics.
Lakoff, George
  1972   Linguistics and Natural Logic. In *Semantics of Natural language*,
               Donald Davidson and Gilbert Harman (eds.), 545–665. (Synthese Li-
               brary) Dordrecht: D. Reidel. First published as Lakoff, G. Linguistics
               and Natural Logic, Synthese 22, 151-271, 1970.
Landman, Fred
  2000   *Events and Plurality. The Jerusalem Lectures.* (Studies in Linguistics
               and Philosophy 76) Dordrecht: Kluwer.
Lang, Ewald, Cathrine Fabricius-Hansen and Claudia Maienborn (eds.)
  2003   *Modifying Adjuncts.* Berlin: Mouton de Gruyter.
Larson, Richard K.
  1998   Events and Modification in Nominals. In *Proceedings from Semantics
               and Linguistic Theory 8*, D. Strolovitch and A. Lawson (eds.). Ithaca,
               NY: Cornell University.
Lenerz, Jürgen
  1977   *Zur Abfolge nominaler Satzglieder im Deutschen.* (Studien zur
               deutschen Grammatik 5) Tübingen: Narr.
Löbner, Sebastian and Harald Stamm
  2005   On the Semantics of the Gradation of Verbs: The Case of German
               Emotion Verbs. Handout for the conference Sinn und Bedeutung 10,
               Berlin.

Lüdeling, Anke
2001   *On Particle Verbs and Similar Constructions in German.* Stanford, California: CSLI.

Lyons, John
1977   *Semantics 2.* Cambridge: Cambridge University Press.

Maienborn, Claudia
1996   *Situation und Lokation. Die Bedeutung lokaler Adjunkte von Verbalprojektionen.* Tübingen: Stauffenburg Verlag.

2001   On the Position and interpretation of locative modifiers. *Natural Language Semantics* 9 (2): 191–240.

2003a   *Die logische Form von Kopula-Sätzen.* (studia grammatica 56) Berlin: Akademie.

2003b   Semantic Underspecification and conceptual interpretation. In Lang, Fabricius-Hansen and Maienborn (2003), 475–509.

2005   On the limits of the Davidsonian approach: The case of copula sentences. *Theoretical Linguistics* 31 (3): 275–316.

2007   On Davidsonian and Kimian states. In *Existence: Semantics and Syntax*, Ileana Comorovski and Klaus von Heusinger (eds.), 107–130. (Studies in Linguistics and Philosophy 84) Dordrecht: Springer.

Maienborn, Claudia and Martin Schäfer
2011   Adverbials and Adverbs. In *Semantics. An international handbook of natural language meaning.*, vol. 2, 1390–1420. Berlin: Mouton de Gruyter.

Marty, Anton
1940   *Psyche und Sprachstruktur.* Bern: A. Francke. Edited and annotated by Otto Funke.

McConnell-Ginet, Sally
1982   Adverbs and Logical Form. A Linguistically Realistic Theory. *Language* 58 (1): 144–184.

Mittwoch, Anita
1977   How to refer to one's own words: speech-act modifying adverbials and the performative analysis. *Journal of Linguistics* 13 (2): 177–189.

Montague, Richard
1970   English as a Formal Language. In *Linguaggi nella Societa e nella Tecnica*, Bruno Visentini (ed.). Edizioni di Comunita. Reprinted as chapter 6 of Formal Philosophy. Selected Papers of Richard Montague. Thomason, R. H. (ed.), Yale University Press, pp. 188-221.

Müller, Gereon
1996   A constraint on remnant movement. *Natural Language and Linguistic Theory* 14 (2): 355–407.

1997   Beschränkungen für Binomialbildung im Deutschen. Ein Beitrag zur Interaktion von Phraseologie und Grammatik. *Zeitschrift für Sprachwissenschaft* 16: 5–51.

Nilsen, Øystein
2004   Domains for adverbs. *Lingua* 114: 809–847.

Parsons, Terence
1972   Some problems concerning the logic of grammatical modifiers. In *Semantics of Natural language*, Donald Davidson and Gilbert Harman (eds.), 127–141. (Synthese Library) Dordrecht: D. Reidel.

1990   *Events in the Semantics of English. A Study in Subatomic Semantics.* (Current Studies in Linguisitcs 19) Cambrigde, Massachusetts: The MIT Press.

Partee, Barbara
1995   Lexical Semantics and Compositionality. In *An invitation to Cognitive Science: Language*, Lila Gleitman and Mark Liberman (eds.), vol. 1, chap. 11, 311–360. Cambridge, Massachusetts: The MIT Press, 2nd ed.

2010   Privative Adjective: Subsective plus Coercion. In *Presuppositions and Discourse*, Rainer Bäuerle, Uwe Reyle and Ede Zimmermann (eds.), 273–285. Bingley: Emerald Group.

Peterson, Philip L.
1997   *Facts Propositions Events*. Dordrecht: Kluwer.

Piñón, Christopher
2007   Manner adverbs and manners.   Handout, 7. Ereignissemantik-Konferenz, Tübingen.

2008   From properties to manners: a historical line of thought about manner adverbs. *Studies van de Belgische Kring voor Linguïstiek – Travaux du Cercle Belge de Linguistique – Papers of the Linguistic Society of Belgium* 3.

Pittner, Karin
1999   *Adverbiale im Deutschen. Untersuchungen zu ihrer Stellung und Interpretation.* (Studien zur deutschen Grammatik 60) Tübingen: Stauffenburg.

2004   Where syntax and semantics meet: adverbial positions in the German middle field. In Austin, Engelbert and Rauh (2004), 253–287.

Platt, John T. and Heidi K. Platt
1972   Orientation of Manner Adverbials. In *Papers in linguistics*, 227–249. Carbondale, Ill.

Quirk, Randolph, Sidney Greenbaum, Geoffrey Leech and Jan Swartvik
1985   *A comprehensive grammar of the English Language.* Harlow: Longman.

Reichenbach, Hans
  1966   *Symbolic logic.* New York: Free Press. First paperback edition, pub-
           lished originally 1947 with The Macmillan Company.

Rothstein, Susan
  2003   Secondary predication and aspectual structure. In Lang, Fabricius-
           Hansen and Maienborn (2003), 553–590.

  2005   States and Modification: A reply to Maienborn. *Theoretical Linguis-
           tics* 31 (3): 375–381.

Sasse, Hans-Jürgen
  1987   The thetic/categorical distinction revisited. *Linguistics* 25: 511–580.

Schmöe, Friederike
  2002   'Folglich trat Hubert barfuß und dennoch ungemein heftig gegen
           die zue Tür' Über einige Eigenschaften der deutschen Adverbien.
           In *Akten des X. Internationalen Germanistenkongresses Wien 2000
           "Zeitenwende- Die Germanistik auf dem Weg vom 20. ins 21. Jahrhun-
           dert"*, Peter Wiesinger (ed.), vol. 2, 157–164. Bern: Peter Lang.

Schäfer, Martin
  2003   Before or after the the direct object: German adjectival adverbs and the
           syntax-semantics interface. In *Proceedings of 'sub7 – Sinn und Bedeu-
           tung'*, Matthias Weisgerber (ed.), 272–281. (Konstanzer Arbeitspa-
           piere Linguistik), Konstanz.

  2005   German Adverbial Adjectives: Syntactic Position and Semantic Inter-
           pretation. Dissertation, Universität Leipzig.

  2008   Resolving scope in manner modification. In *Empirical issues in syntax
           and semantics 7*, Oliver Bonami and Patricia Cabredo Hofherr (eds.),
           351–372. Paris: CSSP.

Shaer, Benjamin
  2003   "Manner" adverbs and the "association" theory: Some problems and
           solutions. In Lang, Fabricius-Hansen and Maienborn (2003).

Stechow, Arnim von
  2001   Temporally opaque arguments. In *Semantic interfaces: studies of-
           fered to Andrea Bonomi on the occasion of his sixtieth birthday*, Carlo
           Cechetto, Gennaro Chierchia and Maria Teresa Guasti (eds.), 278–
           319. Stanford: CSLI Publications.

Steinberger, Ralf Günter Wilhelm
  1994   *A study of word order variation in German, with special reference to
           modifier placement.* Ph.D. thesis, University of Manchester, Faculty
           of Technology.

Tenny, Carol and James Pustejovsky (eds.)
  2000   *Events as Grammatical Objects. The Converging Perspectives of lexi-
           cal semantics and syntax.* Stanford: CSLI.

Tenny, Carol L.
    2000   Core events and adverbial modification. In Tenny and Pustejovsky
             (2000), 285–334.
Thomason, Richmond H. and Robert C. Stalnaker
    1973   A semantic theory of adverbs. *Linguistic Inquiry* 4 (2): 195–220.
Wahrig, Gerhard
    1986   *Deutsches Wörterbuch*. München: Mosaik Verlag, new ed.
Weskott, Thomas
    2003   Information Structure as a processing guide. Dissertation, Universität
             Leipzig.
Wyner, Adam Zachary
    1994   *Boolean Event Lattices and Thematic Roles in the Syntax and Seman-
             tics of Adverbial Modification*. Ph.D. thesis, Cornell University.
Zimmermann, Ede
    1993   On the proper treatment of opacity in certain verbs. *Natural Language
             Semantics* 1: 149–179.

Index

adjectives
    adverbial adjectives, 17
    definition, 17
    domain adverbials, 46–47
    intersective, 25
    lexical semantics, 163
    non-intersective, 26
    object vs. event predicate, 209
    participle-based, 62
    psychological, 77
    restricted readings, 150
    secondary predicates, table 3, 95
    sentence adverbials, table 1, 48
    set-theoretic classification, 25–28
    speech-act adverbials, 38–39
    subject-oriented adverbials, 36–37
    subsective, 26
    verb-related adverbials, table 2, 95
adverbials
    adverbial adjectives, 17
    classification, figure 1, 206
    definition, 5
    free, 6–8
    functional, 25
    participant, 25
    predicational, 25
    semantic analyses, 167–186
    subcategorized, 8–11
adverbs
    definition, 19

    degree of perfection, 73
    intentional, 102
ambiguities
    degree-manner, 66–67
    manner-result, 71, 101
argument approach, 176–178
associated readings
    'associative sense', 114
    general characteristics, 124
    positionals, 80
    quantified direct objects, 114
    scrambling, 165

blends, 73

conceptual dimensions, 51
    animacy, 58
    one- vs. multidimensional modification, 55–56
    pure manner adverbials, 56–57
conversational implicatures, 87–89

degree adverbials, 63–67
    conceptual structure, 65
    verb classes, 65–66
depictives
    free predicatives, 14
    general characteristics, 75
    mental-attitude adverbials, 100–101
    transparent adverbials, 103
domain adverbials, 45

entailments

argument approach, 178
   entailment diamond, 179
   operator approach, 175
   predicate approach, 179
epistemic adverbials, 39
evaluative adverbials, 42
event nominalizations, 61
event semantics, *see* predicate approach
event-external adverbials, 104
event-related adverbials, 97
   formal analysis, 198–201
   syntax-semantics interface, 195
   wobei-paraphrase, 117
events
   conceptual structure, 50–51, 190
existentially interpreted w-phrases, 152–153
experiencer-oriented adverbials, 62

focus projection, 131
free predicatives, *see* depictives

holistic usages, 106
   complex events, 115–117
   internal event structure, 106–110
   quantified direct objects, 110–115

in-group readings, 138–140
inchoative readings, 105
indefinites and topicality, 138
information structure, 130–135
integration, 142
   direct objects, 141
   resultatives, 144–145
   w-phrases, 153–154

manner adverbials, 51–63
   agent-oriented, 58–59
   animate agents, 57
   conceptual structure of verbs, 82
   depictives, 75–77
   eliciting, 52
   minimal pairs, 160
   paraphrases, 53
   pure manner, 56–58
   semantic template, 193
   stative verbs, 79–84
   verbs of creation, 141
manners
   event- and verb-related readings, 194–195
   formal representation, 191–192
   function vs. ontological object, 189
   ontological objects, 188–190
mental-attitude adverbials
   general characteristics, 97–98
   transparent adverbials, 101–104
method-oriented adverbials, 67–69
modal adverbials, 40

negation
   entailment vs. implicature, 87
   mental-attitude adverbials, 98
   replacive, 86
   sentence, 85
   transparent adverbials, 103
   verb-related adverbials, 85–93
Neo-Davidsonian semantics, 182
normal word order, 134

opacity, 29
   epistemic adverbials, 40–41

evaluative adverbials, 44–45
mental-attitude adverbials, 99–100
operator approach, 169–170
subject-oriented adverbials, 35
operator approach, 167–169
cognitive plausibility, 173–175
events, 183–185
generality, 172–173
opacity, 169–170
scope, 170–172

paraphrases and tests
auf ADJ Art und Weise-paraphrase, 53–56
degree adverbials, 65
depictives, 75
mental-attitude adverbials, 98
Wie-das-ist-paraphrase, 53
degree adverbials, 64
depictives, 75
mental-attitude adverbials, 98
quantified direct objects, 113
word order, 149
Wie? 'How?'-question, 52
mental-attitude adverbials, 99
wobei-paraphrase
associated readings, 123
event-external modification, 121–123
mental-attitude adverbials, 120–121
vs. *während*, 118–120
word order, 149
Zustandspassiv-entailment, 73–74, 101
particles, 14–16
predicate approach

cognitive plausibility, 181
entailment diamond, 179
predicatives, 12–14

resultatives
general characteristics, 69
implicit, 72, 101
verbs of creation, 136–137
vs. adverbial modification, 70–71

Satzglied, 5
scope
operator approach, 170–172
speaker-oriented adverbials, 38
subject-oriented adverbials, 34
syntactic position, 128
verb-related adverbials, 89–93
scrambling, 135, 164–165
sentence adverbials
general characteristics, 28, 33
semantic constraints, 47
speaker-oriented adverbials
general characteristics, 37
speech-act adverbials, 38–39
strong reading of indefinites, 140–141
subject-oriented adverbials, 34
syntactic positions
overview of diagnostics, 129–130
relative vs. fixed, 128

theme-rheme condition, 157
thetic sentences, 148
transparent adverbials, 101–104

verb-related adverbials
conceptual structure, 50–51

general characteristics, 49
syntax-semantics interface, 195
verbs
    conceptual structure, 82–84
    double-movement, 108
    of creation, 136–137
    positionals, 79

statives, 79–84
veridicality, 30
    domain adverbials, 46
    epistemic adverbials, 42
    evaluative adverbials, 44
    verb-related adverbials, 86